Knowing others is to be c
Knowing yourself is to be enli
Overcoming others requires
Overcoming yourself requires s

To know that you have enough is to be rich.
Push through and you may get your way,
but return home and you will endure.
Live out your days and you have had a long life.

From Tao Te Ching by Lao Tze, verse 33

LightPerspective

Business Coaching

An integrated dialogue methodology in four steps
Daring to be clear is an art

Business Coaching
An integrated dialogue methodology in four steps
Daring to be clear is an art

This new edition was first published by LightPerspective AB in 2008.
Reprinted, revised and published 2011 by LightPerspective BPC AB, Våxtorp, Sweden.

Illustrations:
Bergman Malin: 151
Creative Common Share Alike: 1, 5a, 5b, 8, 17, 31, 65, 69, 74, 85, 91, 93, 95, 97, 103, 121, 127, 145, 162, 165a, 167, 171, 175, 176, 177, 178, 183, 185, 187, 192, 199
Dahlgren Sofia: 26, 128, 156, 179a
Gnu Free Documentation Licence: 5c, 83, 113, 124, 154
Public Domain: 9, 43, 76, 77, 104, 106, 110, 111, 114, 115, 117a, 117b, 126, 135, 136a, 136b, 137a, 137b, 155, 166b, 179b, 181, 188
Öunpuu Eleonor: 48, 54, 57
Öunpuu/Dahlgren: front, 5d, 6, 7, 12, 13, 21, 23, 24, 27, 29, 32, 34, 35, 47, 49, 51, 55, 60, 62, 63, 67, 68, 80, 81, 100, 119, 138, 147, 150, 159, 165b, 166a, 170, 172, 173, 184, 186, 191, 195, 197, 200, 206

Printed by:
Hofors Digitaltryck/StjärnDistribution AB 2012

Translated by:
Nigel Tooke (nigel.tooke@telia.com)

Published by:
LightPerspective BPC AB

ISBN: 978-91-979917-0-4

LightPerspective Training Campus
Business through People

Dear Business Coach!

Business Coaching always puts "business" first. If there is no business, profitability or efficiency then there will eventually be no work. But no business deal can be achieved without people. The mutual starting point must be "Business through people".

Business Coaching is about making decisions

Without decisions, nothing happens. Or things happen very slowly, which is far from what can be called effective leadership. The manager is appointed to make decisions, whether they are easy or difficult. Business coaching never, or rarely, involves taking decisions by consensus. However, it does involve culturing a democratic atmosphere, where employees have the opportunity to discuss, comment, suggest and influence. And this is done before the decision is made. Once the decision has been made, everyone must accept it and adapt accordingly. It is totally unacceptable to allow "decisions to serve as the basis for new discussions".

The Conductor and the Instrument = Talent Management

The manager who makes the decisions is the guide and "conductor" for his or her team. This means that they indicate the direction and objectives, manage and distribute work and set up the necessary framework. The framework can involve a position, a goal, a management decision, or a management decision taken on the basis of information from the Working Group. The framework states clearly what is involved and what the limits are. Within these boundaries the group can act creatively - that is to say freedom within set limits. When the employee is experienced and confident then the boundaries of the framework can be broad and allow for greater freedom than for the inexperienced employee, or the employee who has previously strayed outside the limits of the framework, who will be given much less freedom. It is also within the framework that business coaching becomes a tool that gives support to employees in their creative work. Here, the business coaching manager acts both as a 'conductor' (ensuring that the job is done within the framework) and as an 'instrument' (listens, outwardly to others, inwardly to themselves, chooses methods for dialogue, and secures the whole - the big picture - and ensures the fulfilment of objectives).

Framework and creativity

Organizations that, for example, decide to work with the Balanced Scorecard can easily integrate an approach based on a framework and freedom within set limits. The management team decides which components each scorecard should contain. These can include the company's vision, mission, goals, strategies, values, market strategy, and so on. This decision, based on the Balanced Scorecard, is not something that any employee can have views on – it will simply be put into effect. This is the framework within which to work.

However, everyone who is given a scorecard will be invited to discuss the content of the scorecards and their personal goals. These conversations thus provide the creative freedom for each staff member, within the set framework. The business coaching manager will eventually ask questions like "What do you think you need to do to achieve your goal?" The response from the employee gives them the opportunity to weigh up the various options, and compare their pros and cons. The manager acts as the active support and sounding board, but does not really have views on *how* goals are to be achieved - just *that* they reached. And the manager monitors the compliance rate at given times during the fiscal year. The level of effectiveness becomes apparent in the pay check.

We wish you luck with leadership through business coaching.

Our very best regards,

Bodil and Hindrik

(authors)

List of content

FOREWORD

FORMING GROUPS, COUPLES AND FRIENDSHIPS is mostly a source of great joy, fellowship and inspiration, and gives business and private life extra meaning. This is described with great affection in many stories, poems, and lyrics.

When people meet, what they want most is to be both popular and positively affirmed. They believe themselves to be, and wish to be perceived as, good people. When these good people come together in groups, tremendous forces develop in interpersonal relationships at all levels.

The manager may, in his or her interactive management, control these forces so that the group achieves great things for both the business and the working environment. If the forces are allowed to operate freely, however, with neither direction nor control, then there is a risk that they destroy the company's efficiency, profitability, working atmosphere, and the sense of job satisfaction. This may be perceived as "plain bullshit", malice, adult bullying, exclusion, or pure evil. By accepting that this is a real possibility in all groups, it is possible to fully appreciate when the positive forces prevail.

Something that can be seen as harmful in some group processes may, at a later stage in life, seem like an important lesson. Usually, it is difficult to find the energy to go through difficult processes alone. The authors therefore appeal to anyone who has such problems to seek help and professional partners in dialogue, in order to rediscover the good processes in life.

THE ART OF BEING VAGUE

Ad Agency
I want you to look at my proposed lay-out of this brochure. Can we continue?

Manager
Well, it looks good. It will be good if you can just remove two thirds of the illustrations so it fits into what we usually do.

Ad Agency (after 2 days)
A little boring, I think, but I did what you said. Can we hand it over to the printers now?

Manager
It's better. But it would be good if you could look over the headings and fonts as well ...
... after four months, eight revisions and no decision the advertising agency feels uncertain. How should they interpret this client? Is the brochure bad or good? Will it ever go to print? Is there any point in the agency making an effort? How much more time, and therefore money, will this brochure cost both parties?

THE ART OF BEING CLEAR

Ad Agency
I want you to look at my proposal. Can we go to press now?

Manager
I see that you put a lot of time into this. Hmm ... I feel both frustrated and irritated. I feel that this is too different, and not at all compatible with our style manual for printed material, which is a requirement! Customers must recognize our style when they see our material. How can you fix this?

Ad Agency
Response alternative 1: We believe that we stayed within the limits but we've allowed an interpretation that we think will suit the modern customer better. But if you say that the style manual applies 100% then we will change accordingly. You will have new proposals on your desk tomorrow morning.
Response alternative 2: We have done what we think is best and we cannot back down. In that case we will lose the creative credibility we have with other customers. For now, we'll just have to say thanks and hope that you renew your trust in us in the future.

A good manager

What does it take to be a "good manager" today? It isn't just a role at work. There are many roles. Of course, life would be easier if becoming a good manager simply meant acting as "the authoritarian boss who points with his whole hand", or simply learning "coaching leadership." An approach that is more complex, but also more exciting and challenging, is to become aware of the manager's versatility. Having the ability to select the role and management style required by the moment enables a creative leadership for those who dare to be more flexible. Public victories achieved together with others are important for managers - often more important than their own, personal victories.

Life is a theatre

Put simply, it can be said that the manager must be able to make decisions, while a dedicated coach almost never takes decisions for someone else, but only for himself or herself.

Examples of roles that a manager often has to adopt in parallel include coordinator (such as project manager), pedagogue and trainer (e.g. for new employees), decision-maker (when all the information has been collected), artist (such as when presentations have to be made for management or customers), coach (on a daily basis to affirm and encourage employees), and strategist (to enable involvement in high-level issues).

This material concentrates on increasing the reader's professionalism and awareness in acting as the coaching manager, with all the accompanying strengths and weaknesses. Other roles are equally important but are described in other literature.

INTEGRATED DIALOGUE METHODOLOGY

Four steps

- Pre-contact
- Full Contact
- After Contact
- Reflection

Four perspectives, at the same time

- Externally (the person / the others)
- Inwards (the person himself)
- Choice of strategic intervention
- Holistic overview and new perspectives

A theoretical platform with immediate practical applicability

'Curling parents', comrade or coach

The old type of manager was often a man, trained in the old military school. The company could be lead with clear orders and clear management. In true authoritarian spirit, the great leader would decide the path and direction, and did not expect to be challenged or that others could present a better proposal than his. This was often the way Swedish industry was built up - it was the spirit of the times.

A milder form of authoritarian leadership exists in the modern manager who acts with "dictatorial care". This is the "curling parent" who brings their experiences from home and acts in a similar way at work. This manager is happy to listen to their employees, and gives answers to any question, big or small. The manager seeks to be affirmed as the one who knows everything. And this manager often has problems finding the time to manage everything. He or she has good intentions and wants to decide what he or she believes is best for the employee, for the group, and for the company. The employee is automatically considered incompetent and is seldom allowed to make their own decisions or take initiative. There are also coaches who act according to a principle of care-taking in which they forget both the company's profitability requirements and the right of the individual to make their own choices based on the company's decisions. The coach means well, diagnoses and suggests "medicines", but individuals rarely develop based on such "treatment".

The comrade wants to be friends with everyone and may therefore have difficulty in making controversial decisions. The Comrade Manager does not want conflict. He will find it difficult to remain loyal to the leadership in front of his staff. It'll be easier to put the blame on upper management in order to maintain the role of comrade. On the other hand, the person who is aware of how he or she moves in and out of various invisible roles at work has no problems going out and having a beer with the group, and can also afford to be personal, without being private.

A sustainable management... for the company with the person

The coaching manager wants to create an interactive leadership with their employees. Work becomes much easier once the operational platform has been clearly established, with purpose and measurable objectives in place. The same applies when the employees have a clear picture of their role, responsibilities and 'delivery obligations' for the company, team, manager and themselves.

This approach is not more time consuming. The same amount of time is now spent in a different way and with new focus, based on what everyone already knows.

Fast or reflective

This book can be read as a whole, but each part can also be read separately and still make sense. We also aim to inspire the reader who wishes to first skim through the headlines, look at the pictures, and read the fact boxes. Mark the pages, where necessary, underline or put in paper clips - the material is there to be used! The wide margins should encourage the reader to write down or sketch their own thoughts.

The author's ambition has been to write according to the pedagogical principle of 'experimentation', reflection and, finally, theoretical discussion.

- The 'experiment' in this book is presented as a story, a short story, or excerpt from an essay - that is, something more reminiscent of the fiction genre.
- Reflections and thoughts that the reader may have after reading the initial story are viewed with new perspective in the introduction to the chapter.
- The discussion covers the theory and the platform of business coaching. Facts and other people's research and literature are considered in relation to the author's experiences and reflections after several years of working with business coaching by managers.

There are several schools and theories surrounding the form and methodology of the dialogue. The authors have chosen to focus on three main theoretical paths, in addition to the methodology of the dialogue itself. The theories of dialogue's four phases and four perspectives are integrated. The selected theories are: perceptual research, field theory and philosophy of individual choices, consequences, and responsibility. This material is therefore divided into these main sections:

DEFINITIONS IN THE BOOK

Manager
A person in a decision-making position, with or without direct reporting staff (e.g. project manager)

Business Coach
A supervisor with expertise in special interviewing technique for the person(s) in the workplace

Employee
A person regardless of hierarchical level in the workplace

Coachee
A person who is coached or tutored by another person

Chapter 1: The integrated method of dialogue. A short introductory element on the scientific basis of the dialogue methodology leads the reader through to the four basic steps in business coaching. In the companies that, for years, have slimmed down their organizations, there is an increasing realization that the future is largely a question of having skilled managers who make clear decisions that fulfil set goals for efficiency and profitability. And it's about getting employees with them in a humane manner. Sometimes the company wants to get help from an external business coach. At other times, managers must take a course in business coaching and clear coaching leadership.

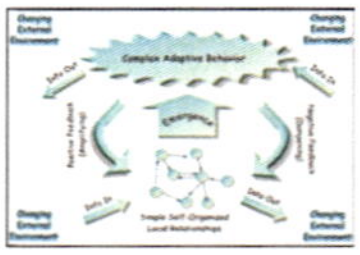

Chapter 2: Field Theory. The scientific basis of chaos- and field theory is considered in detail, and is related to practical examples from working life.

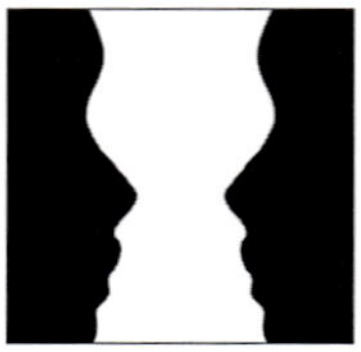

Chapter 3: Perception. The scientific basis of perception, i.e. how everyone sees, experiences, and creates an understanding of "the world", is studied in detail. This is related to examples from different workplaces.

Chapter 4: Existential philosophy. The scientific basis of the philosophy that all managers and coaches face each day, often unconsciously, is studied in detail. The philosophy is based, inter alia, on choice, the analysis of consequences, and responsibility.

The concepts of manager/coach and co-worker/coachee are mixed in the text to illustrate the two possibilities. The concepts are also completely gender neutral. "He" and "she" are used randomly, or replaced by the singular 'they'. The same applies to the choice of names in the examples. An "Emma" could equally well have been a "Stephen". The names are selected as typical of a generation, but can never be related to someone at a company, or an acquaintance. The examples included are a mix of real and fictional events. Everyone can, in some way, recognize themselves since the examples are universally human, but any similarity with real life is pure coincidence.

The reader's choice and responsibility

The reader chooses what is meaningful or not. The reader can ponder over what is to be accepted or rejected, or needs to be reflected upon further. "Truth" has many faces. The authors' experiences show us some of these "faces". There are more!

Anyone who is interested in developing a creative, diverse, business coaching leadership will hopefully find a lot of very useful information here. This form of leadership requires activity and involvement of both the manager/coach and co-worker/coachee. No one knows in advance what is best for the other, or can give a diagnosis of right or wrong. It is a case of having the courage to act consciously, without having full control.

About the Authors

The authors are based in Sweden and have worked for several years with leadership development and business coaching for companies and other goal-oriented organizations. As part of their masters program they developed the course IHM Coaching for IHM Business School. Both became certified coaches after two years at a Norwegian university. They are both members of the European Mentoring & Coaching Council, EMCC.

Bodil Dahlgren

She has studied economics, marketing, behavioural science, medicine and journalism. She has worked in sales, animal husbandry, marketing and project management, primarily in the food, pharmaceutical, and biotechnology industry with direct or indirect reporting staff.

Bodil has, for some years, studied and reflected on the philosophy of life and existence, and has, over the years, formulated theories about "a belief without authority". What does the person really dare to believe in, or rely on, when she really is all alone? Bodil is currently working as a consultant with business coaching for the development of individuals and groups.

Hindrik Öunpuu

He has studied computer science and electronics, logistics, economics and behavioural science. He has worked as a programmer, systems analyst, intelligence analyst with 'business intelligence' as well as engineer, confectioner, dockworker, and with analytical strategy. He has mainly worked in procurement, logistics, supply 'audits', project management and future scenarios for the telecommunications and biotechnology industries. He reflects on how chaos theory can be translated into organizational theory.

Hindrik has spent a number of years studying different political persuasions. He reflects on what lies behind the word and image. And he often wonders who it could be who benefits from a statement or positioning of the facts. What is really new? And who decided it? Hindrik currently works as a consultant with business coaching for the development of individuals and groups.

MEANING OF "GESTALT"
German word for "whole" or the essence or shape of an entity's complete form. The operational principle of Gestalt is that the brain is holistic, parallel, and analogue, with self-organizing tendencies. The Gestalt effect is the form-generating capability of our senses, particularly with respect to the visual recognition of figures and whole forms instead of just a collection of simple lines and curves. In psychology, gestaltism is often opposed to structuralism. The phrase "The whole is greater than the sum of the parts" is often used when explaining Gestalt theory.

Source: Wikipedia

Thanks!

The authors would like to thank Kristin Austheim in Norway for her inspiration and generosity in allowing the writers to use part of her article on the development of coaching in the four stages of consciousness. Kristin Austheim is an engineer, producer and teacher in the two-year university course of coaching in Norway. She is also a psychotherapist and administration manager at the University of Norwegian Gestalt Institute AS, Oslo.

Warm thanks also go to the people who used a large part of a summer vacation to read the rough manuscript and then submit their comments, their own scripts, reviews, clever ideas for improvements, attractive photographs and examples.

Wisdom

"By three methods we may learn wisdom:
- First by reflection; which is the noblest.
- Second by imitation; which is the easiest.
- And third by experience; which is the bitterest."

Confucius

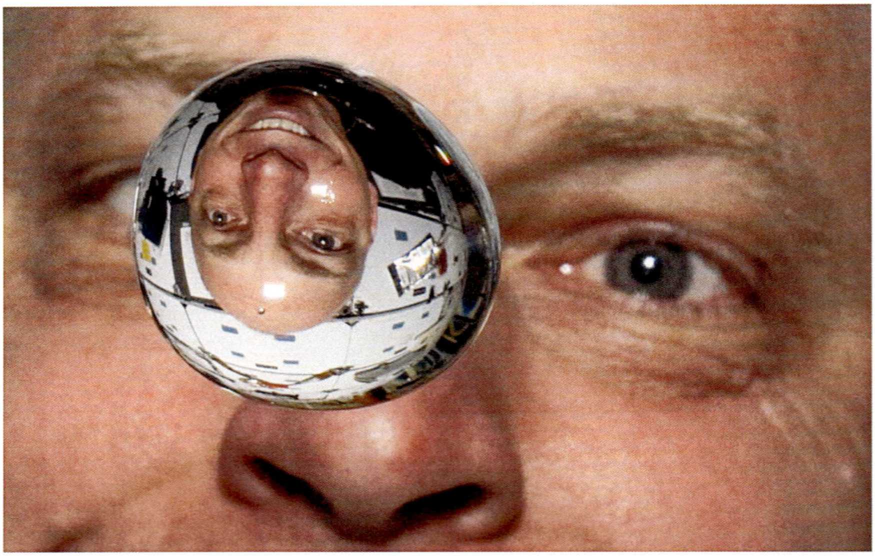

INTEGRATED DIALOGUE METHODOLOGY

The constructive dialogue

Extract from a university essay from 2005

A COACHING RELATIONSHIP that included three meeting is described by an extract from an essay. These are descriptions of how a coaching, reflective dialogue might look and how interviewing has been built up, from the coach's point of view. The basis for the dialogue is a mission statement set up by the coachee together with her managers. Thus, the "business hat" is worn during the talks, while at the same time the individual / employee herself is in focus.

KEYWORDS CHAPTER 1.
Business Coaching from request to "delivery"
Work in relation to the interactive development cycle dialogue method

I will describe one coaching that involved three separate meetings in the autumn of 2004/spring 2005 between myself and a person called Anna.

Purpose and background

Anna is a salesperson. I had previously had a long coaching relationship with Anna's manager, Maria. Maria felt that Anna had "lost the sting". That is to say, this "extremely intelligent" woman with so much potential didn't "give her all". And Maria felt that she did not get any contact with Anna. Therefore, Anna was offered coaching with me as external consultant to discuss her future within the company. What was it she wanted with her future?

Coach - coachee

Despite the fact that this coaching period was relatively short, it has a clear beginning and end and has followed a clear interactive development cycle. My reflections on the coaching are recorded in personal notes and emails, and I have tested different methods. There is also a written contract.

In addition to this rational way of selecting my "case" for the essay there is also an emotional aspect. I as a coach become depressed when I encounter many young people today. They work hard, they are so "talented", they earn a lot of money ... And yet they say words like Sad, Frustrated, Stuck, I do not know what I want, What is the meaning of everything really ... I ask them what they need. And they usually respond that "I need someone who has time to listen and someone I dare to talk to!"

And many, especially Anna, talk, talk and talk. She does, does and does. But when I ask what she feels, there are almost no words. I wonder if this is me being overbearing. The next moment I think: ... but if I don't help them right now, then no one will. I do the best I can.

The structure of the coaching

1. The coaching has been discussed with Anna's head (Maria). Her goal with the coaching has been revealed. I have gone through the conditions and methods of work and then put together a contract she has had to approve before start.
2. I have met Anna along with her boss, before the start. Everyone agrees on the same goal.
3. Coaching Opportunity 1: October 2004
4. Coaching Opportunity 2: November 2004
5. Coaching Opportunity 3: January 2005.

DEFINITIONS USED IN THE ESSAY
The terminology and definitions mentioned in the essay are described in detail in this book.

Theoretical Platform

- In preparation for every conversation and meeting, it was important to identify which fields had become available there and then.
- One could also say that we conducted a survey every time, partly to examine in which 'now' the coachee finds herself, and partly which phase of the interactive development cycle she is in.
- In coaching, I have worked with the phenomenological research methodology, pointing out the obvious, and I have highlighted what appeared to be the figure and let other things remain in the background.
- Query methodology has been based on open questions such as What and How questions. I have had the ambition to ask around the outer, inner and middle zones and pause where polarizing situations arise.
- In every case, we have had some form of "exercise" which the coachee had to reflect on and which has since been discussed - that is to try to get the coachee to experience things herself and not just 'talk about'.

The offer to Anna to report after every contact is in the field for each new meeting, but Anna has never completed this task and submitted a report. It is the case, however, that this "non-task" still works as a task since Anna always touches on the subject at our meeting - a paradox in itself.

This is Anna

The Anna who meets me for the first time is a very talkative person. She is short and round and has clothes that look expensive. Shawl hangs over her shoulders. Her lips are made up pink and marked with pencil. Those lips are, initially, tucked into a faint smile the whole time. Sometimes she laughs, clucking while she talks. She has freshly-varnished nails which look well-manicured. She has a firm handshake, with a hand that is warm without being sweaty. She moves with gentle movements and talks all the time, in a special dialect. Her eyes are a bit half-closed and I think she is looking at me. When she sits down, she leans backwards and we have a table between us. Anna talks about her background.

Coaching Opportunity 1 – Initial presentation

After the initial presentation, I wanted Anna to survey the fields that she believes are important right now. She sketches her "family", based on the "family" when she is 9 years old and her mother has recently divorced. She expresses a lot of "we" concerning her mother and she claims to feel responsible for her. I tested by asking more about this and try to mobilize energy to see if this can be a figure to work with. But I feel no 'energy' and therefore no contact.

One possible figure I pick up is not what Anna says but how she talks. It concerns "all the words" flowing out of Anna's mouth. They flow almost without interruption, with the same tone and with no real emphasis. How can I interrupt Anna? I feel frustrated.

Something starts to grow...

I try to make contact by asking Anna to do an exercise with the polarities in a "polarity wheel". I ask her therefore to take up the characteristics that she herself primarily perceives that she has and shows. Then I ask what these words have as opposites. She rattles off words and antonyms - until we end up with the word "verbal". I think she should say that "silence" is the opposite word when I ask about it. But she finds instead no words at all. Rather, the pen in her hand breaks as she tries to find the opposite word – at the same time, the words flow from her mouth.

I meet Anna with my own silence to see if she reacts to the fact that I am acting out the word she cannot find. (She does not). I make a conscious decision not to follow up on the breaking of the pen.

Coaching Opportunity 1 - My reflections

Exploration around Anna's field was for me a very tiring experience. All of these words from Anna made me I feel frustrated, irritable and very thoughtful. I also wondered how on earth anything is going to come out of this when we have only three meetings allocated. I felt inadequate and dejected.

- I was aware that the field between me and Anna was mainly an intermediate zone. The Inner Zone appeared to be completely absent (apart from my own "silent" feelings) - up to the moment when Anna was to go home and she then expressed a lot of emotion in connection with my dogs. She remembered her now dead dog. "He had such a bad heart condition but was still happy and alert. His expressive face with those eyes ... he looked so sad and pitiful, all the time. I loved that dog so much".
- Figures are worked out using questions and exercises, particularly the polarity wheel. I do not feel that we are in contact when it comes to the

figure "words". But there are "words" that generate mostly frustration and energy in me and we therefore stop at this point and the field organizes itself.

- I feel that we do not reach full contact; we do not get through the interactive development cycle - it is as if the sea and the beach never meet. The beach (contact boundary) moves constantly away, making space for the sea. We must mobilize energy more or less (mostly in the exercise with polarity wheel) but do not reach all the way to contact. Is it perhaps my "resistance" to contact that is the problem, including my frustration and irritation?
- I feel that the contact style needed to reach the figure was retroflection in particular, with an element of projection in the exercises.
- My role, my feelings and thus my chosen strategy can make it appear that my main impulse at this meeting is dissatisfaction. Then I become frustrated. And I want to "do" things, experiment and test. I therefore become action-driven. One challenge may be to instead do nothing but wait and see ...

To talk to or to talk with...

Coaching Opportunity 2 - Contact

During the initial contact, which is a kind of approach, Anna says, "Not much happened last time ". I refer to the figure I still feel is current - that is, all the words that Anna uses even now when she describes the previous coaching session- and her experiences right now. I feel both annoyed and confused and feel a strong need to get Anna to be quiet. My suggestion is to do an exercise together with a focus on "project work" in the hope that she now must be quiet, reflect, and only then discuss the situation. In silence, this exercise develops to include many more fields than just the working-life field.

It feels like the air thickens when I start asking her about the drawing which she has eventually drawn concerning her life - she is, in fact, completely quiet! She has drawn a large tree with strong green foliage. I ask if the wind blows ... I ask if there are any sounds ... If there are birds ... Anna responds that it is totally quiet around the tree and that there is complete silence. I wonder who or what is the tree? Anna reacts strongly. *"This is certainly not me! I want to find this silence in others. I'm not like that! I don't want to be like that".* I wonder if the tree might illustrate the opposite word to all the "words"?. I get no answer.

The dialogue continues: *"What do the words do for you, do you think?" "I do not know, I have always talked a lot." "What happens if you are silent?" "I do not know, I do not want to know. The words are like protection for me. Nobody has the right to get behind. It is probably so that if I talk a lot then no one has a chance to get at me. This tree cannot, must not, be me. It's something I seek in other people and other things!"*

Coaching Opportunity 2 - My reflections

- Through this exercise, I got the tools to capture new angles and thus new fields. In parallel with Anna's and my work, I have questions for myself, about Anna, and concerning some existential issues. The field I-I appears to be more or less unnoticed in Anna while the field I-you/I-others is over-developed. She talks a lot about her responsibility for her mother and how she wants to meet her mother's needs. She even says *"I don't know if time spent on my hobby is something I really want myself - I think most of this has to do with making my mother happy and proud. And then, of course, I'm happy too. "*
- She seems to have contact with the field I-nature because she had previously told me about her dog and also talks about her summerhouse and the nature surrounding it. The field around I-spiritualism/existence affects her more and more during our work together, when she talks about the baby she is expecting and reflections on the meaning of life.
- Thanks to the exercises, I feel that our work has included all zones: outer zone, intermediate zone, and inner zone.
- The Word was the figure in the beginning of the dialogue, but then became more and more background. The new figure that developed was the tree and all that this tree symbolizes.
- I feel that this time we reached full contact. This happened when Anna drew her tree, was quiet and then got such a clear response. She expressed the reaction with words, she also became quite red in the face, eyes wide open, and she looked straight at me. Beach and ocean met and were together for a good while.
- We worked actively with the contact style of projection, when Anna projected on the tree. She drew quickly and chose colours easily after closing her eyes and listening to music for a few minutes.
- My main impulse during this meeting was expectation. Then I pay attention and sharpen senses.

Coaching Opportunity 3 - After Contact

Anna had just returned from a couple of weeks of vacation. Phenomenologically, Anna was different from before. She had somewhat "looser" mother-to-be clothes on, and she sat leaning forward. The words were many, but with long breaks in between. I sat and waited and felt calm. I was quiet after the initial greeting.

Anna said: *"It was so wonderful on holiday and I thought ... Why does everyone at home talk - and me as well - about what I should do next. It's a matter of living every day! To pause. And the baby has come so much closer. "*

The conversation revolves around what we mentioned earlier, such as the polarities verbal - quiet, do - be. I myself have to fight against my own motivation to become confluent with Anna. I recognize myself in her polarities. The meeting ended with two phenomenological observations: *"I see that you sit holding your chin and I notice that you often are silent."* Anna responds, *"I am satisfied and calm inside. It is strange, because really it's still the same chaos around me, but I feel I can live in it. I know, in some way, more about myself ... "*

Coaching Opportunity 3 - My reflections

- The field 'vacation' was in the room, as well as the fields 'Anna's husband' and 'Anna's baby'. These fields served as background during the dialogue. The field concerning existential questions about life itself was definitely present.
- Contact Zones: Unlike the first time when we met, when the conversation was mostly in the intermediate zone, Anna now easily expressed words in the inner zone.
- The figures came up by themselves this time. I did not have to ask; Anna talked spontaneously and she herself took up the figures we had been through at the previous sessions. Together 'we looked at them' and closed the gestalts one by one.
- I myself experienced joy when she talked without resistance. I felt that this time we quickly came into contact, with a form of contact that was partly quiet and open retroflection - long silences for both, where thoughts were expressed within the room. I also experienced conscious confluence many times. She repeated what I had previously asked about, and I repeated her words. At the same time, she was she and I was me.

Afterword

I have described one coaching conducted from an introductory session to a clear completion. The goals of the contract with Anna's managers were met, both for Anna and according to Maria (Anna's manager). If I had the opportunity to continue working with Anna, I would have focused on the polarity of words - silence with more exercises, reflections and discussions. I would also have wanted to work with the polarities do – good, or activity - stillness.

> *Through this exercise, I got the tools to capture new angles and thus new fields. In parallel with Anna's and my work, I have questions for myself, about Anna, and concerning some existential issues.*

Contract: The client and the Company

After talking with Eric, Maria and Anna the approach to coaching/mentoring appears to be as follows:

- Anna / Barbara meet three times, with email follow-up one week after each meeting (meeting number one took place in the middle of October).

- Each meeting is for 2.5 to 3 hours and has its own agenda depending on what is current at the time. The overall objective is to reflect on how Anna's work could be in the future.

- Anna is the driving force in planning the meetings. Cancellation or rebooking must be done no later than three working days before the scheduled meeting so as not to "freeze in". "No show" to meetings or cancellation / re-booking too late will be charged (except in the case of illness). All three sessions must be completed before February 2005.

- Confidentiality is agreed between Anna / Barbara, which means that it is Anna who decides what may be reported to Eric / Maria / the company.

- This, the last time we also came through the interactive development cycle for the entire coaching period. I now had Anna's manager's objectives for coaching in my mind - that is what was set as a target and what would be "delivered". And I therefore raised questions about Anna's work in relation to her maternity leave.

- The impulse for this last coaching was melancholy. I was humbled by life itself. What do I do? I remain in the room, alone and simply 'was'.

Sustainable leadership

THE APPROACH TO LEADERSHIP that is described here presupposes that a business needs to be very efficient. This means that the manager or coach always puts the business first. The client and management must feel that the time and money put into leadership coaching can be financially justified, preferably in terms of Euros and cents.

This means that the business coach must take into account the company's needs for profit, profitability, customer satisfaction, competitive position, etc. As a consequence of this the coachee will, apart from anything else, reflect on how much they are willing to, or to able to adapt to meet the needs of the company in different situations.

...together with the individual

Business coaching puts the company in focus while the individual is given a lot of freedom within certain limits. The employees are the company and there is no business without them. The starting point is that if the company is efficient and profitable then the employees have the opportunity to enjoy work, develop and feel good, and vice versa. If the employees enjoy work, the company has more opportunities to become effective. It is a question of chicken and egg: which comes first?

Business Coaching is clear, without being mean. It requires interaction. It asks questions, sometimes tough and always clear, to which the coachee must take a stance. A business coach knows that the individual can best help herself and always has her own answers to questions.

The business coach does not feel sorry for a coachee but offers support. The business coach is just like a partner who helps her coachee to grow. The business coach who has succeeded is told "now I understand", "I think that I actually knew this already." More rarely the business coach may get confirmation that she is good. The business coach, and the manager acting with a coaching leadership, may obtain affirmation in a different way. Public victories, where others also succeed, become important.

Leadership and change

Developments in business have, over time, increasingly lead to the conclusion that the personnel are its most important resource and the most important creator of value. The concept of human capital is no longer new. All employees are expected to be independent and have a mission to add value to the company. The Leader Concept develops in order to be able to follow and/or create new trends. The added value lies in what individual employees can bring, and how one, as manager, can get the best from ones employees.

The employee is expected to bring skills to their role and is 'bought' and paid for these. How these skills are managed, traded and used depends on the educational, emotional and social skills of the individual and her surroundings. Business coaching offers an opportunity for both the commercial and the public sector to remain efficient during dynamic change. It involves being able to develop and learn more in terms of emotional and social skills in a climate which focuses on profitability and efficiency.

WHAT IS A COACH?

A business coach is a coach who works towards defined goals. The person can either be a professional coach or an employee. This may be one of the manager's roles.

The person rarely gives answers but instead works more frequently with questions. The goal may include

- to make clear decisions or company guidelines
- to ascertain the employee's reaction to the decision and if she chooses to adapt or not
- to highlight the consequences of choice and that everyone takes responsibility for their own choices
- to be able to and dare to be clear in a difficult communication situation without being "nasty"
- to contribute to others' personal development, taking advantage of potential, while developing oneself
- to act strategically in daily operational chaos

Risks and possibilities

Is there a danger that the actors in the organization can be harmed by being reduced to the status of an object or commercial tool by a unilateral economic approach? Yes, there is certainly such a danger if this is the primary focus.

Business coaching combines a humanistic with a financial perspective to achieve a comprehensive result. What at first glance may seem to be based on hard facts (i.e. operations, profitability and quantifiable targets) often depends on 'soft' questions.

Making plans is one thing. To live the plans and realize them is something else. In any case, the communication between people is crucial. The successful person will not see herself as outstanding, but rather sees herself in relation to other employees. She does not simply like others but recognizes her role and her sense of responsibility in the correct functioning of the whole.

The company secrets

Leadership and coaching that works and is profitable exists. Even back in the 1980's Edvinsson and Malone declared in their book "The intellectual capital" how important it is to find the company's true value by finding the "brain power" that lies hidden in the company.

Toyota has also developed a management model – the LEAN model, which has become popular, especially in production-focused industries. This shows how employees can work in lean organizations without becoming objectified. The art is once again to move from words to action.

AN INTEGRATED DIALOGUE METHODOLOGY
... builds on each person's previous experience with focus on four aspects in parallel:

- Own processes (I)
- Listen to others (you)
- Consciously choose the best communications method in each situation (choices)
- The whole and perspectives

This integrated perspective-shift always follows four distinct stages in the dialogue. Practice makes perfect in all disciplines - to dare to be clear is a great art!

A QUERY METHOD
... is quick to learn and usually focuses only on "the other".

Deliver results

Companies require leaders with ability, the will to act, and who dare to tackle various leadership roles with creativity. The business world demands profitability. Management always wants to know what they can expect to get in return when they send someone for training or when they bring in consultants. Can they justify the investment in the same way that they can justify maintenance costs for machinery? The satisfied employee does not always mean that the management is satisfied. Management may have expected something other than what is actually delivered. The probability of positive outcome for all can be increased by setting reasonable goals on expected deliveries, whether in business deals or with respect to human resources. This material is written with emphasis on the development of awareness in four clear steps:

1. **Outside and In**
2. **Inside and Out**
3. **Choice of strategic intervention/focus**
4. **Holistic overview and new perspectives**

To write about insight is, of course, not the same as experimenting and training oneself, and thus achieving personal insight. The authors can only encourage the reader to train at home or attend courses in which pedagogy is based on experimentation, reflection and discussion to reach support in theory.

What is business coaching - really ...

Coaching is an active driving force to learn about and develop resources for the individual and the company's best.

Kvalsund, 2005

Coaching is a specific meeting where the goal above all else is the development of people working on the commercial and private plane. The relationship is one on one (or a few) and consists of equal partners.

Gjerden, 2004

Business Coaching is a method that helps the healthy person in employment to perform better for herself and her company. It is a clarification of values, experiences and sensations. Business coaching facilitates development of knowledge, skills, attitudes and the power to act, which will benefit the organization.

Business Coaching is a personal development of the manager as well as the employee through the discovery of their own abilities. Business Coaching involves supporting an employee to dare to test ideas and new behaviour in reality and everyday life.

Business Coaching is based on a phenomenological approach, i.e. to observe the facts, "the phenomenon", and await personal interpretations. This type of business coaching also draws on existential philosophy, humanistic psychology from different "schools", and experience-based learning.

In business coaching the company always has an interest in coaching. On one hand, the coaching discussion is unbiased since there is no agenda. On the other hand, the coaching manager or the external coach knows that the company expects a return on investment.

The person who is offered coaching rarely receives "a personal gift just for fun" but is instead expected to contribute to the company's profitability in an even clearer or more efficient way. It can in turn mean that the coachee quickly becomes aware that this work does not offer him anything in terms of personal development and that he therefore resigns and moves on elsewhere to achieve his goals. But ultimately, this is also profitable for the company. The process just goes faster.

Re-organization is more common than redundancy. The result could be that the employee does not get the job that he or she expected. Or they experience a period of living in "limbo" - in a vacuum, without knowing which way their career will take. The Business Coach's job is to enable the coachee to make the best choices based on the actual situation. It will therefore often be a matter of the type or degree of adjustment that the coachee can, or is willing to make. Again, in a way, these talks are unbiased since the dialogue can only relate to the coachee's personal view. But on another level, the company's decision is in the background all the time. The company expects alert, loyal and productive co-workers who are quickly back on track after a re-organization.

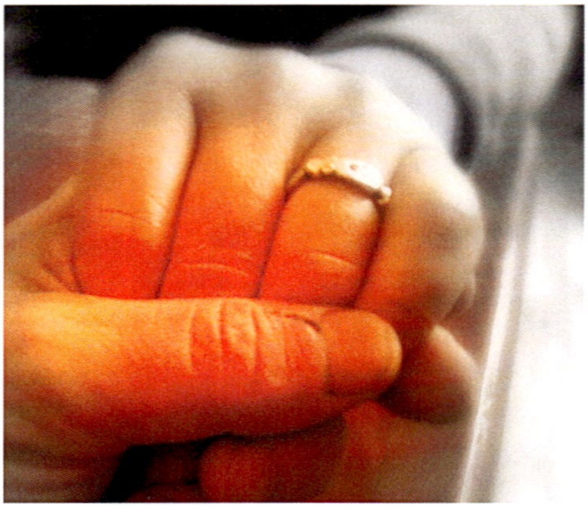

Business Coaching for the healthy

Business Coaching takes up what the employee considers to be relevent here and now. The discussion will focus on the person's working life, even if the whole person's life just as often comes into the discussion. A person is not just a worker, or just a wife, or only the child of an alcoholic. They are everything together, and more. The roles that appear depend on the situation, context, what has just happened etc. The coachee always decides what might be useful to include in the discussion.

As the whole person's life can come into the dialogue, it will be important for the coach or manager to distinguish between a healthy person and a person who is ill. Sometimes this can be difficult. Working when one should take sick leave is a phenomenon at work, as well as people who show symptoms of fatigue without having been on sick leave.

Business Coaching is about the healthy and is a dialogue with a person who considers them self to be healthy. The manager should be sensitive to "Warning signs" to the contrary. They have the responsibility to ask questions about health and illness so that the coaching dialogue does not risk becoming psychotherapy or medical care.

Employees must be offered choices such as referral to a therapist, termination or suspension of the coaching discussions, or re-focusing the coaching to "healthy" or perhaps difficult aspects.

In psychotherapy the therapist meets a person who is feeling bad, is in crisis or feels sick. Often the person fidgets, has difficulty in focusing and has difficulty in formulating the actual problem. Business Coaching differs from therapy in the definition of what is to be discussed and the result to be obtained. In contrast to the psychotherapy of a therapist, business coaching focuses on topics such as:

COACHING OF THE WHOLE PERSON

Sofia has to go to a coach because her manager is worried that she is too stressed at work. Where does her stress go - she looks so calm on the surface?

During the first discussion Sofia talks about herself. After an hour, she begins to talk about how her afternoons and evenings are. She must first pick up her dog from the kennel, then a child at the day-care centre and another child in kindergarten. After dinner, the children are driven to soccer and dance - two times per week. Sofia asks "can I bring up this here? It's all about my personal life and not my job!".

Business Coaching is about the person at work - but where the whole person and her "field" are included. What affects one part of life often influences other parts. So, yes! Sofia can talk about her children with her coach. It then becomes the joint responsibility of the coach and coachee to see how and in what way this relates to her efficiency and work.

- Orientation towards economy and earnings;
- Orientation towards values;
- Expectations from the leadership and managers in relation to personal values and career;
- Understanding that coaching is expected to result in action;
- Employee or coachee's career with expectations of self-development;
- Themes taken from daily work but also private life can be used as a mirror.

The method works in all types of dialogue: in everyday life in the meeting between the manager and employees, between project managers and project members, between the dedicated business coach and the coachee, and between the mentor and the adept. And it can also be a good communication method between husband and wife, parents and children. The roles and situations are different, but communication methodology can be used in many contexts.

No predictable results

The goal of coaching is to enable the coachee to be independent of others. The starting point is to get the coachee to realize from the first moment that he can do so much more than what he believes is possible. The realisation that the individual has infinite possibilities and that development is ongoing.

In human psychology, and even in business coaching, there is a belief in man's innate ability to live in a way that feels fulfilling. By developing awareness, which is based on creating a meaningful "wholes", the coachee will exploit more and more aspects of himself.

The role of the manager or business coach is to act as an instrument in this process of change and to influence with a humanistic, existential approach and to intervene phenomenologically, i.e. to point out facts without being judgmental (read more about phenomenology later in this chapter).

Dialogue and reflection

Business Coaching is based on dialogue. By dialogue we mean that the manager is present, physically and mentally, for their employees in a "one-to-one" meeting. You and I meet and the moment is very real. Both affirm the other as a unique human being. The contact is usually both informative and insightful. These moments occur in genuine dialogue.

Dialogue is to make contact with the other person. The core of the interactive coaching dialogue is to bring about a dialogue that feels focused and without external disturbances. In this close contact it is important that the coaching manager resist the temptation to step in and steer, "judge" or give advice. To steer is to influence the employee towards a development in a particular direction. This direction is perhaps not the employee's own wishes, unless he or she is given a chance to reflect.

Time for reflection through dialogue in a calm environment

Dialogue is also an existential dialogue. It presupposes that the business coach is able to perceive the other person with their differences and similarities to the business coach himself. And that it is possible to accept the other in their existential situation without losing the experience of oneself.

The similarity and empathy that is sought after in a normal dialogue, to ensure comfort, is not relevent in the coaching dialogue. Seldom will the word "we" be used in the coaching dialogue.

It may take a while before the dialogue flows well because it is the employee who determines the direction and development. It can be quiet. And the manager can feel a sudden desire not to fail in the dialogue, a responsibility for achieving results and that something must be done! Here it is important to have control over the situation and a confidence that the process must take its course. Something always happens. To rely on process is crucial to success in business coaching.

Awareness in the workplace?

What is awareness and insight?

In English "awareness" can be defined as presence, attention, "wide-awakeness", sharpness. Awareness is a process in which emotions, thoughts and life energy join forces in a newly discovered contact with the circumstances surrounding an event. If this process can continue without disruption, it will be rounded off with a flash of sudden awareness that in itself is an insightful and immediate understanding; in other words it is a synthesis of what is happening between the individual and their environment. A new meaning and understanding is created.

Consciousness is thus based on information that is retrieved from the environment, through that which can be seen or heard, through attention to perceptions, and from thoughts from the past, present or concerning the future.

In business coaching the employee learns to use their senses to explore the world and find their own solutions to their challenges. The manager or coach teaches the process of being aware of how the employee does instead of talking about how he should be, why he is who he is, or why he did what he did. The manager gives co-workers a tool. In a sense you could say that the manager teaches the co-worker to cook instead of serving them a finished meal.

But does everyone want it like this? Isn't it good to get food served directly onto the plate and not have to think? Isn't it nice to be affirmed as manager and always have answers to questions? These are issues that are relevent and do not have unequivocal answers. There are issues that are important to senior management when they consider how managers and employees work at the company now and will do in the future. What will make this company successful globally? What degree of authoritarian or authoritative environment works best for both the business and the personnel who will support it?

AUTHORITARIAN - AUTHORITATIVE

Authoritarian: domineering, absolute, authoritative, autocratic, despotic, dictatorial, disciplinarian, doctrinaire, dogmatic, harsh, imperious, magisterial, rigid, severe, strict, totalitarian, tyrannical, unyielding

Authoritative: accurate, attested, authentic, authenticated, circumstantiated, confirmed, definitive, dependable, documented, factual, faithful, learned, legit, proven, reliable, righteous, scholarly, sound, straight from horse's mouth, supported, trustworthy, truthful, validated, verified, veritable

Source: www.thesaurus.com

Awareness in the workplace

In business coaching, people are expected to adapt in meaningful ways. This adaptation is a function of two processes: physical sensations and use of strength and energy. Physical sensations and feelings provide information from "the inner life" while the energy is the driving force for action. The company's performance depends on the employees' power to act.

To sustain life, even in a working environment, energy is created together with the surroundings. You can take in that which gives sustenance, and avoid that which tastes bad. The awareness process starts with a form of physical sensation (such as the joy of seeing a co-worker succeed). To act on this perception (for example, giving a compliment) needs energy.

The company's performance depends on the employees' power to act.

Business Coaching is to work with these external and internal sensations, to discover how to create, to find new meaningful entities, and to translate the lessons into practice.

Negative to positive force

It is not always true that a person wishes to probe deeper into himself. He may signal "resistance". In business coaching, resistance is considered as something healthy and sound.

Resistance is a source of energy (directional counteractive force) and acts as a regulator. "I resist what is offered to me right now." Resistance might seem like coming to a sudden stop right now but cannot be seen as an isolated phenomenon. Resistance is seen instead as a manifestation of a person's integrity but shows that he deviates from what is expected. At the time this is often seen as negative. But a creative manager can help to reverse this into

something positive; it will become an asset to the person, the group and the company as a whole.

In every field there are forces that want change and there are forces that want to maintain the status quo. It is therefore possible to analyze together when and how a person experiences or demonstrates resistance at work and how he reacts. Resistance looks different in different phases of the dialogue. Each phase poses an individual challenge.

The Body talks

Many wonder what certain physical sensations have to do with business coaching.

All unmet needs, or past events that have not been resolved, will make themselves felt through signals from the body. This includes needs that can be directly related to work. In perceptual research gestalt psychologists referred to these unresolved events or situations as "unfinished business" and later as the "Zeigarnik effect". Unfinished Gestalts often surface at the most unexpected occasions and then block the free flow of momentum and energy. The incomplete Gestalt can be completed when the need can be met and the situation goes from awareness to understanding.

The coaching dialogue can be used as a tool to understand and resolve unresolved Gestalts.

Anna in the example (see the box, right) does not dare to say no. She obviously felt that she was hot and it was heavy, but did not act on her needs. She felt sure that it was inconvenient, but could not see that it was possible to do something about it. Anna had learned to be kind and decent, easy to deal with. This spun around in her subconscious, without protest! She would not protest in everyday life or together with her manager in an experiment.

In this way, Anna always adapted to the situation at work. Anna was hardly aware of what her body was signalling and certainly did not associate physical sensations with thoughts. She definitely did not realize that, by simply saying 'no', she could stop her manager overloading her with cushions.

To train the mind is to learn from experience.

THE BODY SHOWS THE WAY

Anna was completely worn out when she was to have her coaching dialogue with her manager. She took on more work than she could handle. During the dialogue, she realized that she always has difficulty in saying no.

The coach suggested that together they could do an experiment with this perceived shortcoming.

He put her on a chair and began to pile onto her files, pillows – everything he had at the office. And Anna politely received everything she got. And there she sat. It was hot, heavy and uncomfortable. But she didn't say a word. She just accepted the situation without reflection.

Learning includes the sensory system of feelings, thoughts and energy. Awareness is effective when it is based on, and gains energy from, a real need.

Awareness always happens here and now and working actively with reflection, invites employees to watch what they do here, now, in this situation. Anna, in the example, repeats her behaviour in the dialogue. Anna's awareness of her situation is not complete until she sees the reality and comprehends how she handles the situation. There is a big difference between actually sitting with a coach, overloaded with things, and just sitting and talking about it! This is one of the major differences between reflective business coaching and other types of coaching. Experimentation increases the level of insight.

The next time Anna recognizes the physical sensation "overloaded" and a feeling of hopelessness, she can maybe do something active and positive about it. In this way awareness of an "impossible" situation develops towards real action.

Subjective experience

Phenomena are therefore something that the manager becomes aware of during meetings with co-workers. One might ask why it is interesting to raise an employee's subjective experiences and not "get straight to the point".

The reason is that it is better to focus on current behaviour, since this behaviour can prevent the co-worker from seeing any alternative courses of action. To arrive at new solutions the co-worker must have the opportunity to discover and experience that he or she has their own innate resources at hand.

One way to gain access to these resources is to focus on what actually "is" - the phenomenon - and explore it further. For example, someone who has a fidgeting foot may be irritated by a colleague, may be nervous, or simply have eczema between their toes. The exploration involves giving the co-worker the opportunity to talk about what is wrong. If it is irritation with a colleague then there is the opportunity to stop talking "about" the colleague and instead start talking "with" him or her.

Reflection over time

The key to success in business coaching is the realization that everyone influences each other, though in different ways. Active concentration here-and-now creates contact with the other person and at the same time enables focus on oneself. Reflection and discussion are encouraged instead of the "quick and dirty" approach.

A short coaching dialogue at work sets up a framework and asks questions but rarely answers them straight away. The dialogue may seem to waste time but it is, in fact, just a different approach that saves time in the long run. As we know, everyone must first learn to crawl before they can walk. The same applies to becoming a professional business coach.

RETURN ON INVESTMENT?
What does it cost the company when the highly-salaried manager chases all the balls, without thinking?

The penny drops at the most unexpected moments. This process cannot be rushed; breaking new ground can be both tiring and time-consuming.

The goals set with an external business coach are often more long-term. A working period of six months is common, with a three-hour meeting once a month. There is also the chance to go back to work and test what was practiced. The penny drops at the most unexpected moments. This process cannot be rushed; breaking new ground can be both tiring and time-consuming.

In this context it may be noted that the "good soldier" who is "always ready" and immediately executes an order without personal reflection will feel resistance during the coaching dialogue. The same applies to the person who accepts everything the managing director, priest, prime minister or the media utters. These sources may be right, but they can also be wrong, at least in relation to the individual's own values. What counts here is to take time to reflect and get to know yourself.

Perception and observations

Perception is a broad term. To be brief, perception for the business coach means realising through which "glasses" she sees in every meeting and dialogue. At the same time, she will try to highlight the "glasses" that the coachee sees through, to give insight, and for her own sake.

Phenomenology

The phenomenological research approach has become recognized in research methodology. Phenomenology aims to study the "phenomenon" without trying to understand or interpret it.

Interpret facts, data and... phenomena

The manager who wants to work interactively and allow their employees to keep their truths to themselves must rely on his capability for phenomenological observation.

This means that, while conversing with employees, the business coach must observe and mentally note other things. It could be a facial colour, picking with the fingers, how the person is sitting, or the pace she keeps.

Another part of the brain also checks how the business coach handles the situation himself during the dialogue. Does he suddenly get goose bumps or becomes sweaty? The dialogue becomes secondary, and the business coach listens with one ear. The dialogue and questions can therefore be based more on phenomena – either the business coach's or coachee's – than on the dialogue itself. What is true or false is in a way unimportant. The phenomenon can be explored to give new information for the business coach and new insights for the employee.

The phenomenological method is used in business coaching to get close to the employee's experience without judging or assessing the situation. It is a way to observe, hear or feel phenomena that emerge in the employee's subjective world and to examine them.

Figure and background

The phenomena that occur during the dialogue will be defined by the business coach or coachee: the manager or co-worker. Phenomena occur all the time and all can be said to be "figurative" and to form patterns during the dialogue. During the dialogue the business coach and coachee must agree on which phenomenon to focus on. The business coach tests one phenomenon after another. The coachee may choose or reject each in turn.

Examples of phenomena that can form figures are:

- the co-worker constantly comes back to the manager's lack of leadership;
- the employee fidgets and cannot sit still;
- the employee talks all the time "about" other people and things;
- the employee arrives late, as always;

- the employee looks away or down;
- the employee has many opinions about others.

A phenomenon at a time can form figures. Everything else automatically forms background.

Polarities

Polarities are words, reactions, postures, and more that are each other's opposite. In Buddhism, they are yin and yang. The philosopher Friedrich Hegel called them thesis and antithesis, which produce synthesis.

Business Coaching listens for opposites or asks actively for them. The idea is that one word is linked with the other. If there is one, then there is the other. The question is how conscious the words are and how much the coachee dares to consciously explore the extremes of each "new" word.

If the person perceives himself as a "good" employee in a conflict-filled team then the business coach can ask for the polarity word. It could be the word "evil" ... What happens then? Can one be "a little evil" and when can this show itself? Or does the coachee know someone who they regard as being a little evil, very evil or in between? And what does it mean to be "good"? The goal again is to create awareness gradually, and finally understanding.

THESIS, ANTITHESIS, SYNTHESIS
The triad, thesis, antithesis, synthesis is usually described in the following way:

The thesis is an intellectual proposition. The antithesis is simply the negation of the thesis, a reaction to the proposition.

The synthesis solves the conflict between the thesis and antithesis by reconciling their common truths, and forming a new proposition.

The Field concept

All events are a function of multiple, creational forces. These forces transform into a field. In this field every single force has effects on the whole, and the whole affects the parts. No event occurs by itself and can be isolated.

Anna and her manager create the field together (see box) where Anna experiments with being overloaded. Neither the response to the manager nor that to Anna can be seen in isolation. Together they help Anna to learn.

In business coaching, what is happening in the field is described as being

MULTI CO-EXISTING POWERS
It is often obvious that what is happening in one place in the company also occurs in another. In other words, a poor conduct in the board room is often obvious in other departments as well. It can be called reflections or interacting fields where the patterns suddenly become visible.

The coachee can in the coaching situation be made aware of the patterns and the co-existing fields and can make relevant choices, for the work situation, accordingly.

phenomenological. Manager/coach, team/coachee, the surroundings and that which the coachee takes up for discussion creates the field and determines what will be important in the meeting. This "important" is "the figure". In the example of Anna the figure was "not to speak up."

It was the psychologist Kurt Lewin who first described the field theory (see more details in Chapter 2). He saw before him a field with both strength and direction to explain behaviour and social influences. Kurt Lewin's work laid the foundation for what is today called systems theory and social psychology.

Dare to choose to be yourself

Existential philosophy

Anna can tell how she experiences being overloaded. Anna's description is subjective and she conveys what it's like to be Anna. She describes her existence. In the reflective business coaching dialogue, the manager listens to the employee's subjective description as it is. And it is accepted as an expression of the employee's experience. The level of truth or realism in the description is not prompted for. Anna's narrative is her reality.

Responsibility and freedom are key terms in existential philosophy. The concept of freedom is also understood as "freedom to choose". Anna can choose how she wants to act in those relationships that are relevent to her. To do nothing is also a choice.

The word "responsibility" stands for "ability to respond". Anna responds and acts spontaneously during coaching to adapt, as she usually does. Gradually, she will respond in other ways and make more informed choices. And she will make new choices.

All choices have consequences, both positive and negative. The coaching manager will help employees to identify more alternative courses of action, more choices. The manager can also discuss the pros and cons with the co-worker and be on hand for these consequence analyses. Finally, it is time for the employee to make her own choices. She also realizes what the consequences might be, and takes responsibility for these.

To make choices visible, see the consequences and accept responsibility provides a clarity that would otherwise often be barely perceived. It is something that can be discussed. Some may initially experience clarity as unpleasant but most people appreciate it. To take responsibility minimizes the risk of putting blame on others and pointing out scapegoats. Anyone can begin to feel they can influence their lives.

> *A business coach must be cautious and seldom or never take their coaching leadership further than what he has lived through - and survived.*

The meaning of "everything" may be brought up in the coaching dialogue, providing the business coach has sufficient practical experience, including handling existential issues such as fear and loneliness. Sooner or later these issues come up even in the working environment. A business coach must be cautious and seldom or never take their coaching leadership further than what he has lived through - and survived. Otherwise there is a danger that such cases end up in a situation that is painful for everyone involved and hinders more than helps. In these cases the business coach can gain strength from his own discussion partner, or coach, to discover his own reactions in private before it is time to manage those of others.

Who is the survivor at work?

It is often said that it is the strongest who survive. Perhaps this is true, sometimes. In the workplace it is often enough so that anyone who survives the longest in an organization is the one who is good at quickly adapting to new circumstances.

It is about adapting to new managers, new organizations, new targets, capricious owners, and so on. Adaptation is made after careful consideration, and done in relation to one's own personal values, may be a price worth paying. Up to a certain point.

This differs from person to person. And many, too many, never think about it. But, as good soldiers, they obey orders, lie low and hope to survive by not standing out. The price could be high. Perhaps the day the person gets fired. Or the day when their own values have unwittingly taken so many blows that the individual has "lost himself". But he does not realize what happened.

CONTACT STYLES – MEMORY HOOKS
Projection: To imagine
Introjection: To learn
Confluence: To join
Deflection: To keep at a distance
Retroflection: To keep within

Contact styles as coping strategies

The human self matures in meetings and confrontations with others. For man to survive, she learned early how she should relate to her fellow human beings. This is true in times of prosperity, but especially in adversity. The manner of connecting and relating to her fellow citizens will be critical for how life will turn out.

These contact styles have often been crucial to survival; in the sibling group, or as a single child, or in relationships with parents and teachers. All people have a large set of contact styles. Quite naturally a person becomes better at certain contact styles and worse on others, since even in this "practice makes perfect".

All contact styles have positive and negative sides. But no contact styles are wrong or unhealthy, or should be rendered "harmless", or destroyed. However,

> *To make choices visible, see the consequences and accept responsibility provides a clarity that would otherwise often be barely perceived.*

it is illuminating to become aware of those that are used and those that could be used, the positive aspects and the more negative. More strings to the bow give more creative leeway.

For the business coach, it is important to be aware of the contact styles that she or he chooses intuitively. In discussions, the business coach must be aware of their own contact styles and those of the coachee, and make the coachee conscious of what is happening, both with the coachee herself and in the meeting with the business coach. The business coach is active in challenging, testing, questioning and experimenting with the various contact styles.

The coachee has the opportunity to choose when and how different styles can be used at work or at home. They can determine which are sustaining and reinforcing, and which are debilitating and weakening. This can be practiced together with the business coach, and tested at home and at work. The results can be discussed with the business coach.

Listed below are descriptions of contact styles as they can be expressed in the workplace by both managers and employees. Chapter 4 develops and describes each contact style further. In the literature there are suggestions for more than the five styles described here, but these five offer the business-oriented coach a sufficiently comprehensive toolkit to use:

The five Contact styles:

1. Projection - *"to judge"*

The manager feels that the employee "judges" others more than he thinks about his own role in meetings and discussions.

The employee is often irritated by what the manager perceives as trivial. Instead of looking at the facts, he re-interprets again and again and again. He talks often about all the misery that will happen in the project, the forthcoming congresses, the next customer seminar and so on. It never ends.

On the other hand, the manager considers the co-worker to be very creative in their projects. In addition, the co-worker has no difficulty in talking with foreign guests, where he is an asset because he always finds pleasant topics for conversation and makes contact.

2. Introjection - *"to learn"*

The coachee describes her job situation for the business coach. It is stressful.

She must be at work already at seven o'clock in the morning to cope with all her tasks. She understands that she should be fully prepared for all the meetings, or at least the Monday meetings. And just because the meetings are on Monday mornings, preparations must be made on Sunday evening. And when she is there on Sunday she may as well go through the mailbox too. She understands that everyone in the department does. That is just the way it is! When did the coachee learn this behaviour of "must" and "should"?

Introject means to learn, accept or reject

3. Confluence - *"coming together"*

"Peter and I have worked together for 10 years. We know each other inside and out. It has been good in tough situations. I have always felt supported by Peter. It has in turn meant that Peter has often called the weekends when he had problems in his marriage or when he has drunk too much. But it has been worth it because he's always been so loyal at work. But now I have become Peter's manager and the situation does not feel right. It is as if we have bonded together. I do not know what I have to do to break away. "

4. Deflection - *"to keep at a distance"*

The manager sits and thinks about one of her employees. She feels that this employee is a really strong person. She has just gone through a divorce and has met a new man at work. But her private life never influences her work. They are kept entirely separate. Perhaps she was never particularly concerned by the divorce? Maybe it's true: the manager hasn't noticed anything.

Deflection means an ability to not take notice

The situation with the new man at work would have been tricky, but, again, can she really keep work and private life apart? They sit in the same project, but both are totally into the role of co-workers and colleagues. The manager cannot understand how they do it! Shouldn't it be obvious if one is in love? She herself would not have succeeded, but she will try to ignore that for now. The company needs both of them badly.

5. Retroflection - *"to hold within oneself"*

When the manager comes into the meeting it will always become a little quiet. A feeling of uncertainty creeps into the room. Some participants may get a bit of stomach ache while others may doodle. There will be an abrupt transition from chatting and telling funny stories to utter silence, before starting the meeting. The manager comes in, sits down and then sits perfectly still during the meeting. No one can say that he seems unpleasant. But it is just that it takes him a long time to get going. But when he does he is straight to the point. Although he has not shown it, he seems to have taken in everything. He asks some questions perhaps, but then he almost always goes directly to the decision.

Integrated dialogue methodology

Business Coaching is logically structured. By practicing the basic structure everyone has a common thread, or foundation, which can always be related to. Creativity grows along with the knowledge that the foundation always works.

A business coach or an employee may wish to discuss a particular case and this "case" immediately becomes the "figure" of the dialogue. The figure is seldom ready when the meeting begins between coach and coachee, but will gradually appear. Apart from that the dialogue progresses in the same way.

The dialogue is followed up at various levels and in a conscious way by the business coach and taken up with the coachee.

The parts can include the following:

- To distinguish what is content and the story itself, what are the facts or guesses and interpretations;
- How what is said affects intellect and thoughts, feelings and senses, physical sensations, etc.;
- Observations of both managers and staff regarding body language, patterns of dialogue, pace;
- Proposals for intervention in the form of exercises and experiments that the coachee may select or reject.

Interactive development cycle in steps

Business Coaching is thus not an agenda for the dialogue, but rather follows a development cycle from start to finish. This interactive development cycle is a development from what is, in the literature, sometimes called the experience cycle, or cycle of experience. It shows how one coaching dialogue can be structured to create, explore and clarify what forms the figure and ends with a follow-up reflection.

The interactive development cycle is general and applies to all situations: dialogues, meetings, periods of life, stages in business development, etc. You can look at one development cycle at a time, for example the development of a working group.

The situation becomes progressively more complex as more and more development cycles begin to interact with each other (for example, several working groups that jointly form a function). Smaller development cycles are built in a major development cycle. This forms, therefore, the basis for Chapter 2 where it is presented as field theory with quantum physics' complex systems. Chapter 4 develops further ideas about the relationship and the meeting and what is seen as healthy and unhealthy in meetings and organizations.

THE INTERACTIVE DEVELOPMENT CYCLE
A summary

Pre-contact: Mobilize energy and make contact

Full Contact: Contact is established

After Contact: Clarification and the contact ends

Reflection: Thoughts that come up after the event. It is perhaps here that most learning will take place...

A new interactive development cycle can start.

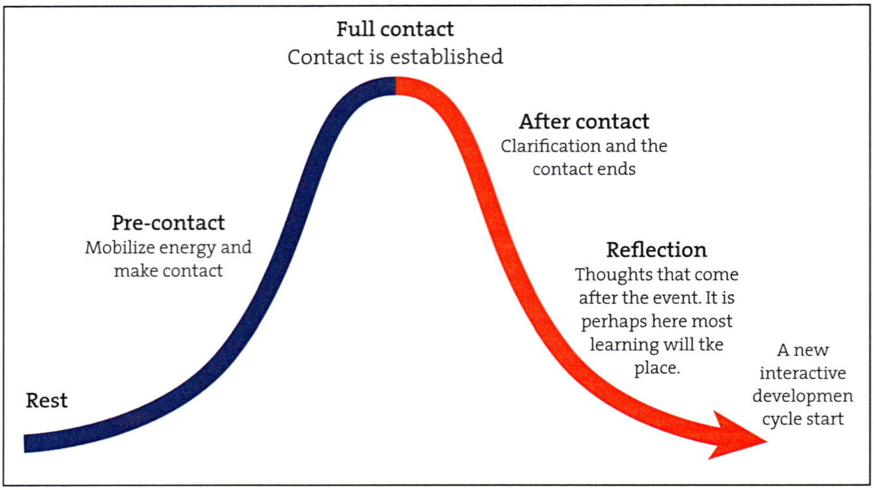

An interactive development cycle

Dialogue and change

1 **Rest:** *The employee Sue comes to the manager Brian. They talk about the weather and how the weekend has been. The conversation centres on family, friends, and work. Sue and Brian "land" slowly and are both mentally and physically in the same room.*

2 **Mobilizing Energy:** *But Brian starts to think about what Sue really wants. Sue begins to squirm a bit. She fidgets with her hands. There are a few silent moments. Brian waits.*

3 **Contact:** *Brian repeats verbatim some things that Sue has said about the weekend. He reflects on what he sees (he notes that Sue is fidgeting). Sue looks down at the floor. Yes, there is something she must say that makes her feel a bit nervous. The fact is that she just found out that she is pregnant. It is good news but it came a bit sooner than planned. There is a lot to do at work - even in the autumn. Brian asks - to find out what the "figure" actually is. Is it that Sue is pregnant? That it will be sooner than ideal? That she feels nervous? The figure which emerges is "nervousness".*

4 **Full Contact:** *The choice to have children is one that Sue has made. The choice may have several consequences. Sue mentions a few spontaneously. Brian encourages her to see more. One of the consequences is nervousness. Brian asks about this and what might lay behind it. Sue talks about her feelings and thoughts*

for the job, career, her CV. Brian asks and listens. Together they make an analysis and they see the positive consequences and how these can be maximized.

5 Clarification: *Sue finally says that she now feels better and relieved. She realizes that this pregnancy is not just something inconvenient for her surroundings but that there are actually really good aspects to it - for everyone. Sue promises to write down what Brian and she agreed upon.*

6 Conclusion: *The meeting finishes. Sue returns to her room. The figure "nervous" withdraws and it is time to tackle the next figure.*

7 Reflection: *Brian thinks it is good that what he had guessed has now been confirmed. He feels that Sue can now, in peace and quiet, focus and prioritize, which is good for the team and for the company. Sue feels a great relief. It cannot be worse. She feels comfortable with having Brian with her, and calm, having together with him sorted out what should be done.*

Flow

Professor Mihály Csikszentmihályi describes "flow" as that feeling when everything works as it should, when everything goes well and when we face challenges that can be met. "Flow" is, in the context of coaching, a development cycle without interruption. In the step "Clarification" there is the opportunity to experience a revelation! There is a feeling that things fall into place.

A development cycle in another cycle

Once an interactive development cycle stops then another takes over. It can be difficult to know exactly when it happens. Usually it does not matter. It is in the encounter with another person that it might be useful to be clear about when this is happening. If not then there is a risk that two people quickly end up out of step with each other, resulting in misunderstanding. They talk past each other, or they both believe that they fully understand the other when they are really talking about two different things.

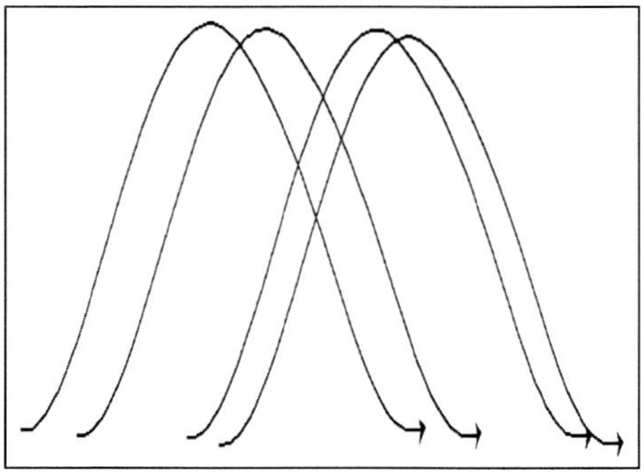

A cycle in the cycle - one finishes and a new one starts...

Interactive development cycles are interwoven

In a working group everyone works and lives in different, interactive development cycles. At the same time, the group as a whole also has a development cycle, as do other groups, and the company at large.

In this way working life is really exciting. The challenge is therefore that most of the company must "march in time" to take the company forward.

This is a complex situation and is called "complex adaptive systems" (Chapter 2).

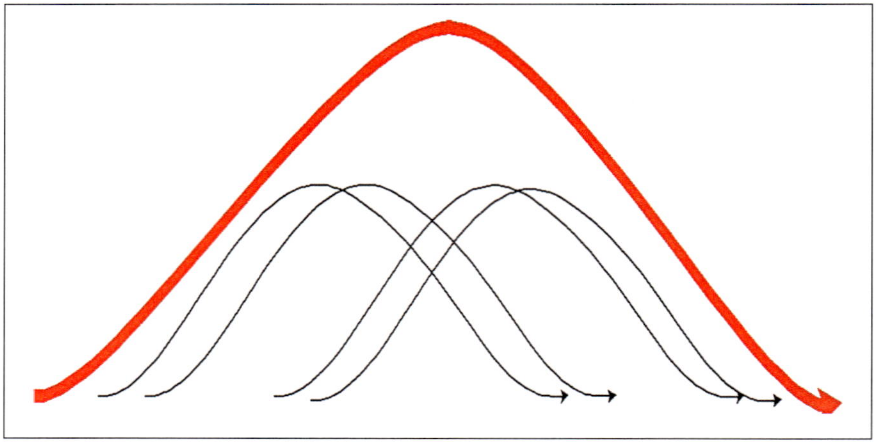

Complex adaptive systems

Change of focus in the dialogue

Several researchers and authors have described research into the development of awareness to deeper understanding. This book builds on this research. Theoretical research forms the basis for an effective communication methodology. It is clear and immediately useful in an operational, often chaotic daily life.

In addition to the four steps of prior contact, full contact, after contact, and reflection there will be a gradual change in focus. After initially judging and thinking about other people and what they do the focus shifts to personal responsibility in relationships with others. Sometimes, but not always, thoughts continue about the self in relation to groups and finally the individual sees themselves as part of a whole which also includes society and private life. Each shift in focus has its own full interactive development cycle. It is only when the contact-reflection phase is reached that a new cycle can start.

The gradual shift in focus goes, in turn, through the four steps of the interactive development cycle.

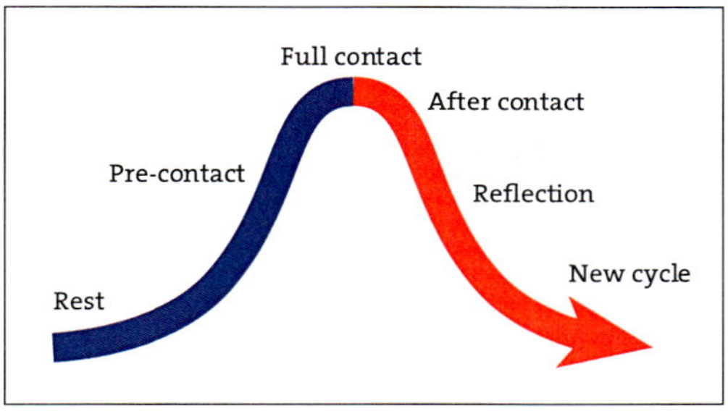

It should be said that description and instruction is one thing but to become comfortable with the methodology demands more than understanding. It requires hard work, training and more training. Each meeting for the rest of one's life is a training camp. The methodology emerges and with it a personal development with an understanding of the self in relation to others.

Each step is in itself an interactive development cycle. The communication method can go through all the stages or cycles. It occurs mainly in a long coach-coachee relationship that extends over several months.

In everyday dialogue between manager and employee, it is sufficient perhaps to raise the awareness of the difference between focusing on others (the others are wrong) and seeing the employees own role and responsibility (I) in a situation or event.

What are the ideal results of coaching?

It is important to consider what the goals are for the dialogue, before a coaching relationship starts, either for the manager at work or for a business coach with his clients.

What is really "delivered"?

This mapping is a prerequisite for becoming clear about what should be supervised or coached, and how the outcome will be measured. Results can be both business-oriented and relationship-oriented. The objectives of the talks certainly do not have to be reached at the first meeting, but rather underpin the entire series of dialogue as background information.

During the survey the business coach substantiates issues and the process-oriented questions to the people who may be of interest. Fields are mapped and both parties agree on goals, direction and what this effort will cost in time or money. Decisions are also made on how the reporting should be done and by whom, to whom.

A business coach observes confidentiality up to a limit that is perfectly clear to all parties. This limit cannot be exceeded without the business coach losing credibility. It is an ethical approach that every coach must be fully aware of.

The Dialogue Method Phase 1 – From outside and in
To expand understanding with thoughts

Employees talk about problems and challenges in a coaching dialogue. They have not realised that they themselves are part of the process, both privately and in their work environment, and often relate "to others", i.e. a "You"-focus. It is, in other words, "others" who make the person feel in one particular way or another. The person often thinks about what he can do to "understand others" better and what he should do to get "others" to change.

The employee in this position does not understand the concept of "consciousness" and that it could apply to him. Few, if any, thoughts have been given to the fact that the employee always has a relationship with, and affects, his surroundings. This is true even during the dialogue with his manager.
The Coaching Process is about the inner life – what happens to "me" when I meet "you."

Phase 1 is characterized by the actual dialogue. The dialogue generates reflections on the employee's daily life. This is a job for the brain. Together, there is a sorting, prioritising, and opportunities are explored and valued. Logical reasoning is pursued, centring on possible solutions.

TALK 'ABOUT'
"It was a man who got the job and I didn't even get an offer. Though I am qualified and have extensive experience. I think of course that this is a typical trap for women.

I have just returned from maternity leave. This is about gender inequality and that's what I would like to talk about today. There are structures in society that makes it like this. You just have to open the newspaper and see for yourself ... "

Talking ABOUT

Coaching is often described as a dialogue in which you talk about this and that and not much else happens. 'To talk ABOUT' gives, in due course, no improvements in efficiency for either organization or person. The employee only gets results and develops when he can, wants, and dares to take in new knowledge during the dialogue.

Many understand intellectually what "dialogue" stands for, but few really master the art of dialogue. It is very easy for the dialogue to be reduced to an interesting discussion and one party in the discussion often has the intention of winning by driving home a particular viewpoint. In the discussion we talk ABOUT. To talk ABOUT provides fertile ground for conflict. In business coaching, the employee is rather encouraged to talk WITH.

Should - moralism

"I must," "I ought" or "I shall" ... Who or what is it that says that? Is it really something that the person himself wants and feels any enthusiasm for? Or is it a case of trying to live up to an image of a person who isn't actually oneself? As human beings we are influenced by socialization, demands, expectations, ideals, impressions, and models from the moment of birth (introject). The human being can resist, consider, or accept these influences outright. By accepting something outright, an expectation from the surroundings is taken in without thought or reflection on what it means. This is a "shall" and "should" and tells us how we shall or should behave. The concepts of "shall" and "should" are often something strange and swallowed as a whole - rigid guidelines that are neither flexible nor engaging.

In business coaching "the coachee is held onto." By focusing and getting the coachee to analyze, to taste his words, and consider his "shall-" and "ought-" statements he is given the chance to accept or reject what is really true, or not, for himself.

I SHOULD...

I should have time for all the appraisals before the month is out!

The customer should always be in focus!

It is essential that everyone always has their cell phone turned on. We must have high availability at all times, both with telephone calls and emails.

I should not take more than two weeks of vacation consecutively.

I must be available during the Christmas break!

Mentoring

In private and public sectors, mentoring is an important contribution to training and sharing of knowledge, and often acts as a map to orientate new recruits. Often the mentor is a senior person within the company or a senior person from the outside.

Unlike the manager, who is trained in a business coaching dialogue method, the mentor falls back on extensive experience within a specific area of work. It is important that the mentee to a mentor also sees his own responsibilities in running the meetings so they are meaningful. The mentee will have an advantage if he or she can articulate the goals to be achieved in the relationship, and what it takes for the mentor to be perceived as "right". Facing a mentor can be a challenge in terms of relating to should/shall/must.

- How aware is the mentor of a mentee's resistance, considerations, or unthinking acceptance?
- How aware is the mentor of the risk that she, with the best of intentions, merely creates a copy of herself and her own successes in her work with the mentee?
- How aware is the mentor of the mentee's attitude towards authority and how the mentee has learned to behave and react to them?

When the mentor presents a possible solution it is offered as a finished concept. The coachee is not given the possibility of developing his own skills to solve problems. The possibility of finding a common solution is often severely reduced.

Sweep the track clean for the employee

Curling manager

Like some mentors, a curling manager (like a curling parent) 'knows' what is best for the employee.

Using the analogy of curling, the curling manager sweeps the track clean for the employee, who, in turn, glides without reflecting on what is happening. Hard work according to orders will be best for everyone.

The curling manager has answers to every question, and discusses how things should be done and what is best for the employee's work and self-development.

To break the behaviour of both the curling manager as well as the "curled" employee demands willingness on both sides to change

The curling manager feels affirmed, as manager and human, as being capable and always ready with an answer. How will the manager be able to change his behaviour? Are there other types of acknowledgment that will do just as well?

For employees, it can be comfortable having a curling manager. The employee will always appear to do the right thing by handing over the answers and decisions to the curling manager. And if it leads to a "wrong" decision then the employee can always cast the blame on the manager and make him a scapegoat. The employee just follows orders - however weird, silly, or strange those orders might be.

A curling manager often feels tired and overloaded with work. To delegate anything other than the simplest of activities is impossible. One must also always be available otherwise work will come to a grinding halt.

To break the behaviour of both the curling manager as well as the "curled" employee demands willingness on both sides to change. The manager teaches himself to gain insight through self-coaching. The employee must, first under protest as the seemingly comfortable life passes, slowly but surely be faced with new choices in his approach and working relationships. To deliver according to goals becomes more important than performing a variety of activities.

THE EXAMPLE OF EMMA,
thoughts and analysis

Emma has received a request from her boss to consider another job in the department, which means more business travel. She has been waiting for this offer for a long time but when it finally arrives, she feels ambivalent. Is this really what she wants? How will it work with her husband and children?

Together with her manager, Emma has worked her way through the ambivalence and analyzed the situation properly. "Project New Job" is divided into smaller parts and together they focus on details, the surroundings (husband and children), and they talk about the new job's functions and values, the purpose of changing jobs, etc. All her concerns are written down, including Emma's analysis of their lives. Emma is then ready to choose.

The coaching characterized by reflection and analysis of the actual situation. Emma got a much broader perspective that could serve as the basis for how she would choose. Emma was very happy with this and satisfied with the situation for the time being.

The dialogue method in Phase 1

In the process leading up to making choices, Emma focuses on what is important to her. It is Emma and her needs that steer; she lands on the ground and feels contact. She gains insight into her needs and acts accordingly. Emma feels that she has clarified her choices, and the company profits from the fact that she knows where she stands. The effect is maybe a new manager, or at least a more dedicated Emma.

In situations similar to Emma's, but with a coach or coaching manager, Emma would have gone many rounds with herself and been through all phases of the interactive development cycle. She needs someone to sit with to sort her thoughts, and someone who dares to ask the uncomfortable questions.

Consciousness can be defined as the state of being aware of, and responsive to, one's surroundings. Business coaching supports the natural process of change with a focus on the coachee's degree of awareness. A natural consequence of this is resolution whereby the coachee is encouraged to check out any confusion with colleagues and start talking to them, rather than talking 'about'. The coaching manager supports the coachee in focusing on the realities of working life, and the coachee's own needs, feelings and values. By putting all this together a "solution" can be found that suits the coachee.

From Phase 1 to Phase 2

In Phase 2 the coachee will be clear about her feelings, her thoughts and is willing to respond directly in various situations. The transition to Phase 2 is characterized by the coachee starting to talk about colleagues, talking about what she should do, and the expectations associated with her position at work. Awareness is always about "something". Awareness is about "lifting oneself out of oneself" to look at this "something" from an external viewpoint. A Business Coach tries to get to Phase 2 by posing phenomenological questions: "I see that your leg is restless and I have a fantasy that there is a lot going on in your head right now." "What do you become aware of when Helen looks at you that way?"

The coach may also conduct research on the emotions and bodily sensations: *"What is it like for you to ...?"* Or by reflection: *"What do you think about this ...?"*

TRANSITION FROM PHASE 1 TO PHASE 2 – changing focus from YOU to ME

"Helen is completely hopeless," says the coachee and looks at her coach.

They are in the initial phase of their dialogue and the coachee is talking about Helen. The coach asks more about the situation with Helen and the coachee explains that every time Helen says something, especially during lunch, she thinks that Helen is stupid.

Coach: *"What happens to you when you meet Helen?"*

Coachee: *"Pooh, Helen says odd things as soon as she opens her mouth. I'm starting to seriously think she is unintelligent. Do you want to know what popped out of her mouth today? "*

Coach (thinking): How do I get the coachee to become clear about herself so that she can see what is going on inside herself in the meeting with Helen? (i.e. transition to phase 2).

Coach repeats: *"What happens to you when you meet Helen?"*

Coachee: *"In me?"*

Coach: *"Well, what do* **YOU** *feel when you see Helen?"*

The process halts

If the process does not proceed to Phase 2 then this could be due to one of the following:

- The coachee is not ready for further research into her emotional life in relation to her job.
- The coachee sees no point in working with herself and her working relationships.
- The coachee is fully satisfied with talking "about".
- The coachee is pleased to get a clear picture of how she will choose.

The Dialogue Method Phase 2 - Inside and out
Expanding awareness with thoughts and feelings

As mentioned earlier, the development of awareness is a process that includes the system, emotions, thoughts, momentum, and energy. The coach and coachee work together and collect information from these areas. There are perceptions, feelings, what one sees, hears, tastes, and smells, together with values, rationalizations and reflection with focus on relationships with both daily work and to colleagues and managers. A coachee is encouraged to explore herself through relationships within her network, her own values.

In Phase 1, the coachee has begun to understand the importance of awareness. Phase 2 builds on Phase 1. Awareness is now used to acquire information from all the senses and combine this with expertise. In the coaching dialogue this is done with focus on "what is happening with me in meeting you", that is to say more a "me-focus ". The work is performed in relation to employees, managers, colleagues, the coachee's expectations of managers, the organization's strategy, and the organization's corporate culture. The conversation still takes the form of a dialogue, including the phenomenological issues, and with an existential approach. It is at this level that business coaching stands out among many other methods.

Business coaching strives to lay the foundations for learning that lead to a real eye-opener, to something new, or the rediscovery of something old. It is important that something new is produced but it should be remembered that the new builds on what already existed - the old. Instead of dwelling on things, the coachee is encouraged to describe how an event is perceived in the present. The ambition is to achieve a learning process based on self-understanding - in other words, to learn through personal experience. This is in contrast to the learning process that is based on a teacher's (mentor's or manager's) explanations, which the recipient must then study or practice.

Understanding becomes fully integrated after a period of conscious or unconscious thought. It is "just" a case of giving the process time. There are several working methods in Phase 2, including the so-called projection chair and "psychodrama".

Projection chair - projections

To project is to form images of things and other people, and believe that this is the only truth. In various exercises, such as the "projection chair", projections are exposed for what they are and the coachee can adjust their images and think about what is true and what is untrue. A projection is more about the one who "regards" than the one who is "being regarded".

Chris is the CEO and John is the chairman of the board, and they have a hard time working together. The relationship does not work. Chris is looking around for a coach in order to work on his relationship with John.

Many may well ask whether it would have been better if Chris and John had met and together talked with a coach. That would have been an option. Another option is, however, the use of the projection chair. It is an empty chair where Chris can imagine John sitting. Chris talks with the chair as if he was talking to John:

Chris to the chair: "You make big decisions for the company without giving me the chance to voice my opinion."

When Chris sits in the projection seat himself and sounds like John, Chris works with his own image - his own projection - of John, and he responds based on how he believes that John would have answered.

John (i.e. Chris) sits uneasily in his chair and looks away as he says: *"And you doubt my competence?"*

Chris - back in his own chair - slumping - looks dejectedly at me: *"This is how we are."*

Coach: *"I see you are slumping?"*

Chris: *"Yes, I'm slumping."* Chris sighs.

Coach: *"I heard a sigh."*

Chris: *"I give up."*

Coach: *"OK, so you give up. What happens if you say that to John?"*

Chris: *"Can I say that to John?"*

Coach: *"Can you tell John that you give up?"*

Chris smiles: *"Yes, I can."* Turning to the projection chair he says: *"I give up when it comes to you."*

Coach: *"Do you give up John?"*
Chris: *"No, I do not give up on John I just give up trying to influence him."*
Chris becomes aware that he feels dejected, which he shows by slumping in the chair.
Coach: *"Dejected?"*
Chris: *"Yes, dejected."*

To ensure that Chris really is able to feel the sensation of feeling dejected, the coach doesn't go further, but keeps Chris in contact with this feeling.

If Chris and John do not resolve their relational problems and remain caught in prestige or power issues then there will be dire consequences for the company. Poor communication in top management tends to spread to many levels. A previously good working climate can, in a moment, switch to the opposite, with the risk of being costly for not only the company, but also society.

Difficult to relate to legs and feet

The relationship with the coaching person

Peter was finance manager at a pharmaceutical company. His "goal" with coaching was to improve at getting people with him. He worked a long time around the theme of language and how he could improve his language (a Phase 1 job).

Peter and the coach had had a few productive hours together and the coach felt that the time had come to point out a phenomenon that often occurred between the two of them.
Peter had the habit of sliding down in his chair, with his legs straight out and arms behind his head. This position made the coach feel that he was being assessed and that there was an immediate mental distance between them. The coach considered that this could also affect Peter's subordinates if he sat in the same way at work. The coach asked if that was the case. Indeed, Peter confirmed it.

Coach: *"When you sit in that way, I don't know if I reach you. It's as if I just reach your feet. "*

Peter: *"Really?"*
Coach: *"It's as if your legs prevent me from getting through to you. I would really like to have contact with more than just your legs. "*

Following this intervention the coach waits and says no more.

Peter sits more upright in the chair and looks at the coach - not a word. The coach immediately perceives that the relationship alters, doesn't feel the same distance, and the coach remarks on this. The coach asks if it is okay to explore additional ways to sit. This stimulated Peter to experiment with different ways to sit in relation to his employees. He noticed immediately that it was easier to get people with him when he sat more upright in his chair.

The coach choose not to say anything about the feeling of being sized up by Peter. There is a risk that being sized up is taken into the field, then it leads to the coachee feeling that he is also being sized up - by the coach. The coach is clearly making an assessment when he points out the way the coachee sits. The situation is somewhat less serious when reference is made to the feet and legs instead of the way of sitting.

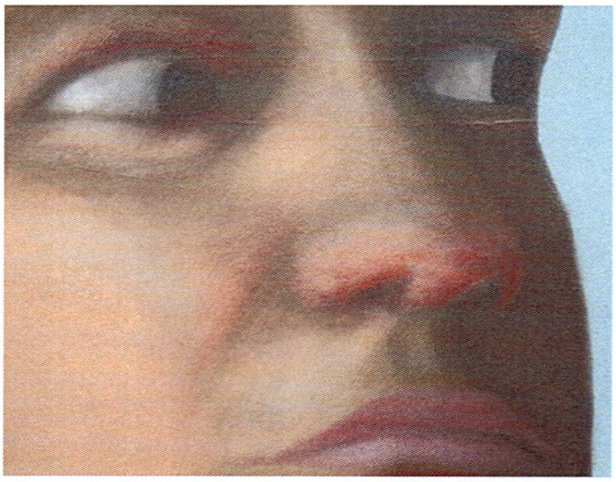
"You are stabbing me in the back"

"Psychodrama"

Jenny works in a large organization. She has been coached for a long period under the theme "to give a lot of myself." But then the circumstances surrounding an employee come up. Jenny was very skilled and had been offered a major job higher up the Organization. The job involved a re-organization and several employees are now disillusioned, including Paul, the head of a large group.

Paul used unfair methods to make life unpleasant for Jenny. He would like to have Jenny's job.

During the coaching Jenny become clear that she is afraid that Paul will "knife her in her back", by spreading lies about her and malign her. With this as a background, the coach and coachee set up a mini-psychodrama. Jenny stands with her back to the coach and the coach, playing the role of Peter, stands with his hand on Jenny's back. The "drama" begins.

The coach pushes his hand lightly into her back. Jenny goes a few steps away from the coach without saying anything. She doesn't look at the coach, and has an expressionless face. The coach is surprised that Jenny doesn't turn towards her, and says so.

Jenny: *"Turn?"*
Coach: *"Who is dangerous. You can get a "knife" in the back. And you can't see me and you don't care about me. You just walk! "*
It now looks as if Jenny cringes. It's time to try again. The coach stands with her hand on Jenny's back. Jenny walks on, without bothering about the coach.
Coach: *"I don't notice anything. You started walking again! Isn't it natural to turn towards the source of danger? Isn't it true that when you get attacked then you want to look at the attacker? Can we do this again, slowly? "*
Jenny: *"Yes."*

Again - the coach stands with the "dagger" in Jenny's back.
Coach: *"What do you feel now?"*
Jenny: *"I'm scared and want to go."*
Coach: *"OK, you're scared and want to go. What are you afraid of? "*
Jenny: *"I'm afraid that you are going to stab me in the back."*
Coach: *"You are afraid that I am going to stab you in the back".*
Jenny: *"Now I feel that I am getting angry as well."* She turns around to face the coach and says: *"I don't trust you. I'm afraid you will stab me in the back. I don't like it. I'm furious."*
After this, the work continues with how Jenny can raise this with Paul (Stages 3 and 4).

The Dialogue method in Phase 2

The dawning of awareness involves being able to identify and admit feelings and characteristics. Emotions are used to promote mental activity and motivation, and also to interpret messages contained in emotions. Awareness in itself solves nothing. Awareness is to being noticed, to be certain. Achieving an effect from emerging consciousness presupposes that the coach acts on the insight that consciousness provides. Coaching in Phase 2 develops emotional skills, or, in other words, develops emotional intelligence.

Change in Perspective

To change perspective is to see something or a situation from several sides. By using the projection chair the coachee can act as "the other person" and will be able imagine what it is like to be the other person. The perspective is changed. To put one self in someone else's shoes is a real, rational thought process.

One can choose to look at an event from two different viewpoints: from (as a participant) and from outside (as an observer). From inside is to take the subjective perspective, and to see it from the outside is to take the objective perspective. In business coaching, the ambition is to get both perspectives.

It is possible to use the 'I-You' approach to put words on subjective experiences, which can then be conveyed to someone else. In the coaching with Peter, the coach describes he experiences in relation to Peter's legs. The coach gives an 'I-You' perspective and the coach is talking to him. When the perspective changes, it becomes almost like a domino effect – the coachee changes his attitude and puts something else into the field. The field changes and everything that is in contact with the field must respond in a new way. Changes in perspective take place throughout the entire process of consciousness. Perspective changes at each step. This is something of a process of transformation.

Be more of myself

Developing awareness is to know oneself more. And getting to know oneself is also to become familiar with, recognize and make friends with emotions and characteristics. Diligently increasing the awareness of emotions develops emotional intelligence, EQ. Emotional intelligence is the starting point to experience, to think about and deal with the emotional patterns of oneself and others. It is also crucial in the creation of relationships and the utilization of human potential to the full.

Emotional intelligence can be defined as the ability to perceive emotions, to make contact with them, and to develop them in order to establish a better basis for thought. It is also about improving one's understanding of feelings and thereby gaining emotional knowledge. Authors such as Mayer and Salovey claim that reflection and the ability to regulate emotions promote emotional and intellectual growth.

A person is filled with conflicting forces. The self-image is related to upbringing and personal experience of an inner reality. The self-Image is also linked to conflicting internal forces, such as being stupid and kind. Change means to challenge the self-image by uncovering, identifying, and "making contact" with a characteristic, such as adaptability, and in due course to think what it "costs" and what it is "worth".

From Phase 2 to Phase 3

During Phase 2, the coachee used himself, more than others, as a source of information. In a way, Phase 2 makes the coachee more self-centred. This is intended to build up the individual for Phase 3, which is about seeing himself in an interaction with others at work - to be able to see himself in the team, group and organization. In the transition between phases, the employee or coachee often expresses phrases such as "this is the same as what someone told me earlier" or "that's something I recognize." Employees are now starting to listen to themselves and others in a different way - often in a more phenomenological way.

In business coaching the coach or manager has unconditional trust in the process of consciousness and is confident that the coachee will proceed to Phase 3 when the coachee is ready. Since there are always multiple forces in the field the coach is on the lookout for signals that may indicate a preparation to go into Phase 3.

THE EXAMPLE OF CHRIS AND JOHN

During Phase 2, Chris went with the help of his coach on to Phase 3.

Chris becomes aware that he feels dejected, indicated by his slumped body.
Coach: *"Dejected".*
Chris: *"Yes, dejected".*
Coach: *"Dejected ".*

After a moment the coach wonders if it is now time to move on.

Transition to Phase 3
Coach: *"Can you imagine an occasion where you can say to John what you just said now?"*
Chris: *"I feel dejected when the two of us "fight".*
Chris now realizes his contribution to the struggle that is ongoing. And he can put into words what is happening between the two of them.
Chris is ready to enter Phase 3

The process halts

It is possible that the coachee is not ready to explore himself regarding interactions with other working relationships. Or the coachee may be satisfied with the coaching at this point and has no need of more.

Dialogue Method Phase 3 – Choice of strategic intervention
Insight and maturity

The coachee explores how he affects, and is affected by, the workplace. The coach and coachee bring into focus what "really is". The focus is on patterns found in relation to managers, colleagues, corporate culture etc. There is space to reflect on his own integrity, personal ethics and morals. This concerns his own attitude to visible and invisible rules at work, and other figures of authority. How much does the individual want to, is able to, or has the energy to "resist" what is in the system? What is the price of always being obedient and what will the price be for disobedience?

Dialogue methods in Phase 3 include the projection chair, "sociogram", drawing, fantasising, and reflecting on metaphors.

The Projection Chair

Again an example from the combatants Chris and John:

Coach: *"Can you imagine a time when you can say to John what you just said here?"*
Chris: *"I feel dejected when the two of us fight".*
Chris changes seats and becomes John: *"So I feel the same way."*

Change can be achieved after Chris has worked with his role in the fight, his projections, and begins to be clear about his role in the fight. The next time Chris gets the feeling that the "fight" is starting, he can make an active choice to continue the fight, to feel dejected, or he can choose a different strategy, which can be the subject of experimentation during the coaching. During coaching, Chris has at least had the chance to experience how it is when 'John listens'. This is also something that is stored in the knowledge bank on the day at work when this hopefully actually happens.

Chris also realizes that he can never change John! He can only do something about his own attitude towards John. The moment Chris realizes he is forced to change his attitude towards John. Their interplay enters a new phase where the rules of the game are yet to be decided.

"Sociogram"

Eve is a secretary at an international company. She now needs help to sort out where she stands in the organization, who she should report to, her responsibilities, etc. Earlier, her department had a manager who did not work well either with subordinates, including Eve herself, or with superiors elsewhere in the organization. Finally the manager accepted severance pay and quit. Many in the department cheered - everything would be fine now. To survive in the department everyone had unconsciously developed an interaction whereby everyone did everything. In this way, they survived as a group and also produced good results. There were problems when the new manager began work. Everyone, including Eve, continued to do everything even though they now had new job descriptions. Although she was not an engineer, she had previously had to do some "engineering work". So what she was expected to do now - just secretarial duties? What did the manager and the rest of the group expect from her? Eve went to the personnel man in the HR department and booked a meeting.

The HR person had a coaching dialogue with Eve. Eve was invited to use the flip chart and draw the people in the department "in the way that you experience the department". Eve drew a chaotic pattern in which engineers and administrators ran around like headless chickens. Eve could put words to "interaction".

The next task was as follows: "Now draw on another piece of paper how the Department is structured hierarchically". Eve drew in a new way. The owner at headquarters was at the top, and then came the Chief Financial Officer, also at Headquarters. Under him came departmental managers, engineers and so ... the challenge ... where did Eve want to place the administrators, including herself?

Confusion. Eve holds her hands in front of her face. "I don't know where I belong." Again, the interaction feels totally confusing, and now the administrators stumble around like headless chickens, in Eve's head.

Coach: *"I see that you keep your hands in front of your face."*
Eve: *"I'm confused. I don't want to see. "*
Coach: *"You are confused and don't want to see."*
Eve: *"Yes, that's the way it is."*
Coach: *"What can happen if you look at the paper?"*
Eve: *"I can see where I belong."*
Coach: *"Well."*
Eve: *"I see, and I think I understand. Give me some time. I don't feel very well. "*

Making roles visible

Hello there! Which formal role do you have?

Linda was the store manager in one of a chain of fashion shops. As store manager, she also had the role of assistant to the Chief Financial Officer. Linda had got the job by rising through the ranks and at the same time attended a training course. She had many former colleagues as subordinates, and some were still her friends. She had now been put into a difficult position by an interview in the newspaper where she had been pressed on "what the managers really meant". She was now afraid that her popularity in the organization would begin to fall and she felt uncomfortable walking in the corridors and meeting managers – friends she was planning an autumn holiday with.

Linda went to her CEO to organise a coaching dialogue. There she was asked if she wanted to do an experiment. Linda had to put chairs in the room in places corresponding to how her relationships with colleagues looked. There were lots of chairs: the Chief Financial Officer's chair, her own assistant chair, a chair for those she trusted, a chair for the middle managers, a chair for a job- and neighbourly contact, and a chair for her friends. Linda reached a better insight into herself by alternately sitting on the chairs and talking about the people and their likely relationship with her, and then standing behind their chairs and talk about her own relationship to the people. She realized that she found it difficult to disentangle her own roles and functions, such as to be both a store manager and assistant to the CFO.

The most important insights came when Linda realized that the employees couldn't tell the difference between her various functions in her different roles either. They were confused. Who was Linda when she walked down the hall? Was she the assistant, friend, neighbour, or store manager? Who was she? Together with her CEO, she worked out a strategy to make herself clear in relation to her roles depending on what seemed most important to her. The goal was firstly to become clear towards herself so that this clarity could then spread out into the organization.

Experiences of an organization

Sketching

The HR department has trained several to be "internal coaches". In this case, it is a coaching relationship that has worked over a longer period of time. The company is international with a distinctly technological culture. The coachee is the head of a production department.

Coach: *"If you could sketch your department as a human being, what would it look like?"*

The coachee sketches and describes what he is drawing.

Coachee: *"When I think about it, the department has a big body. It is supposed to cover the whole organization. It has tiny arms and legs. "*
Coach looks at the artwork: *"It is very small limbs."*
Coachee: *"He needs a lot more muscle."*
Coach: *"So it is a 'he'. There really isn't much muscle on that man! "*
Coachee, *"No, and that reflects reality. We really don't have much money in this year's budget. "*
Coach: *"You've drawn a heart ..."*
Coachee: *"When I look at him, I see he has a very big heart. He wants to achieve so much. And people are happy. "*
Coach looks at the coachee and sees that he is studying the man's legs.
Coach: *"I see you looking at the legs."*
Coachee, *"I think that he (the old man) has difficulty walking. He is so fat. He has a sort of rolling gait ... What is it that makes me not believe that he is trying to lose weight? "*
Coach: *"And the ears?"*
Coachee: *"Yes, we hear a lot about what happens in the organization. The head! The head is small. We act probably more than we think ... We rush from one meeting after another. But the legs ...? And being overweight ...?"*
Coach: *"Yes, what is it about his legs and being overweight?"*
Coachee: *"I'm getting worried. He can't walk very far! "*
—
Coach: *"If you were to say something about how your department is in proportion to the rest of the organization, in light of how you have drawn, how would you summarize it?"*
Coachee: *"We deliver on target, but no more than that. We are sociable and we want a lot, we cover a lot in the organization, we have limited financial resources, and we have difficulties moving."*
Coach: *"How can you use this insight?"*
Coachee, *"I'll bring my sketch to a managers' meeting. Before I show up my sketch, I'll ask the others to draw their own picture of the department. That way I can see if others recognize the same things, and then go from there. "*

After the coaching dialogue, the HR person wonders if there are more departments within the company that look like this production department. What does it cost the organization when a lot of people are just walking around and clearly not contributing to the company's performance? And what is it that makes this department feel, in the manager's eyes, overweight and almost immobile, despite all the meetings? Does the department produce the right things? What work environment has been introduced into the organization? Is this the hidden side of a job that has felt so comfortable for decades? No one has been dismissed in the last twenty years. Doesn't everything just seem too comfortable? Is the sense of "urgency" gone? Do the employees know why they are employed and what is expected of them? How close or far away are customers and competitors perceived to be?

Without exposing information from any individual employee, the HR department can begin to clarify the corporate culture, the current situation, what is desired, and how to get there.

Fantasies - metaphors

When fantasy becomes reality

Gerry is a manager at the local council office. He has an appointment with the company doctor after his performance appraisal with his manager. The reason is that he complains that he has a sore back but he doesn't want to take sick-leave. The doctor has attended courses in business coaching and has had to learn a new type of counselling skill. Instead of simply writing out a prescription for painkillers and referring Gerry to the physiotherapist, she begins by asking him to alternately tighten and relax the muscles in his lower back. Gerry finds that "when he tenses the muscles in his back then he is on guard. It's just like when he stands out in a stream and fishes for salmon. "

The metaphor "standing in the middle of the stream and fishing for salmon" was the starting point for further dialogue:

Coach/doctor: *"You're standing in the stream. How far up does the water go? "*
Gerry: *"It comes up to the middle of my thighs."*
Coach: *"Can you say something about the water?"*
Gerry: *"Yes, there are torrents - it's a waterfall."*
Coach: *"How safe are you?"*
Gerry: *"I'm standing quite well. No, I feel rock solid. "*
Coach: *"Are there a lot of salmon?"*
Gerry: *"There's a lot of salmon and its hard work pulling them in. But I have to have food! "*

Coach: *"How does this metaphor fit into your work?"*
Gerry: *"It works almost too well. There is also plenty to do - like torrents. The tasks drop in all the time. It feels heavy. But I can't afford to work less hours, or be sick. The bills have to be paid each month. My back pain is probably something to do with the fact that I am tense the whole day at work. "*

Dialogue method in Phase 3
Identify, recognize and articulate interaction

Insight into a situation is not complete until one is fully aware of all the aspects of how one behaves in the circumstances. If anything is omitted, the awareness becomes less than complete. Insight follows a feeling of "owning" the situation. It means gaining control over the situation, experiencing freedom of choice in relation to ones behaviour in the circumstances. Insight includes an acceptance of oneself, a true confirmation of oneself.

Intuitive intelligence – self-awareness
In Wikipedia you can read that the word intuition comes from the Latin intueri, "look at, consider." In philosophy, intuition is "experiential belief characterized by its immediacy". Intuitive understanding is a clear and distinct perception, which is comprehensive and therefore does not need to be developed from a lower level of lucidity.

One person who was very interested in intuition was the 'father of phenomenology', Edmund Husserl (see also Chapter 3). He argued that intuitive intelligence is the ability to immediately understand and take advantage of complete or hidden underlying patterns, preferably faster than achieved with normal thinking. Intuitive intelligence can be seen as a "gut feeling", and is trained in coaching Phase 3.

A "GREEN SOUL"
Robert was the owner of a petrol station. After coaching he realized that he really was a strong believer in Mother Earth and nature.

Robert felt at loss and not honest to either himself or others while remaining at the petrol station. He decided to leave and take over his parents' farm where he started to produce organic dairy products.

From Phase 3 to Phase 4
The transition to Phase 4 is characterized by recognition and orientation within reality:

"I do not own the truth."
"I am a part of society, and I can affect and be affected."
"I am responsible for my own well-being."
"Yes, it fits together in this way."

Again, it is possible to refer to the combatants Chris and John. At the end of the story, the two sat in dialogue. Through coaching, Chris has become aware of the interaction with John. But how can Chris move forward:

Chris (back in his own seat): *"Okay, I see that John is also affected by the situation. I haven't realised that earlier. He is actually resigned to the situation. "*
Coach *(reality-orienteering): "Chris, we really don't know if he is resigned, he isn't here."*
Chris: *"Okay, but there is a possibility that he is."*
Chris now has a different attitude to John. He is more open to examining his relationship with John and listens to what John has to say.

The process halts
Phase four is about being able to impart knowledge and visions, and about decisive reaction. Insight and awareness are not everything. If the process stops between Phase 3 and Phase 4 then this could be due to a lack of initiative or an unwillingness to expose oneself to risks in life.

Dialogue method Phase 4 – Holistic overview and new perspectives
To be able, willing, daring, have the energy to change

So far in the dialogue process, the coachee's awareness has continually evolved and moved to larger and larger wholes, resulting in increasing comprehension. Phase 1-3 have focused on one thing at a time: "you", "I", "I / you / others". Phase 4 involves achieving insight into how everything is connected, and interconnected with other fields, such as social influence or existential issues. Phase 4 involves a holistic approach: that the whole is greater than the sum of the individual parts.

The steps in Phase 4 will also clarify the driving force and energy the coachee has to change. What does she want, anyway? What does she dare to do? Is it the right time just now to make this change? What will the consequences be for her and for third parties? Does the "good" and positive dictate, or not?

It is not enough with greater insight

To sit with lots of insight into how the system works is like the hermit who sits alone in his cave without sharing his discoveries with others. Contributions from the manager and employee are needed if the person or organization is to move forward.

"Fear" is a feeling that seldom comes up early in a dialogue. To talk about fear with another human being often feels like exposing a weakness. It may be one thing to talk to about fear to an outside party. It is quite another to talk about it with a person at work. Fear is an element of the existential questions in life that is often masked in other terms (such as aggression, a nervous laugh, clowning around).

Dare to accept reality

In the example of Chris, and John, Chris at least went to John and talked about his fear. John admitted that he felt that Chris intervened more than he needed to. John was also afraid - afraid of being excluded by Chris. Their conversation was the first of many. They realized that the best thing was to tell each other immediately when one of them perceived a lack of competence, the risk of being run over by the other, and so on. This marked the start of a genuine interaction between them.

The coach's perception of reality is no more valid or objective than that of the coachee. In phenomenological theory there are multiple realities. No perception can be said to be unreal. I create my reality and you create yours. I do not lose myself in the meeting with you but rather I lead myself and you lead yourself. Subjective realities allow for differences. If I have a dialogue with you, then we can jointly explore the "reality" that, for the moment, appears to be the same for the two of us.

In the example of Chris, he experienced a feeling that he had hardly dared to speak to a colleague. He was afraid of losing his job. John, on the other hand, was also scared - scared of involvement - that is to say, to lose himself. Two frightened men, with different perceptions of what was reality. Can we say that Chris's reality was more real than John's?

The only thing to note is that from the company's point of view it was essential to its survival that Chris and John could work together. What is good or bad is irrelevent. It is imperative, since the company can be a good solution for one person, but a poor solution for another. The question is whether this situation could be solved without outside assistance. In this case, the company got a major return on investment by investing in coaching.

TO BE AFRAID AT WORK
Chris has a dialogue with John, with the help of the projection chair.

Coach: *Chris, John is not here. You are here. I'm thinking now about what you want from John? "*

Chris: *"I need to talk to him because big decisions are being made that will affect me as CEO."*

Coach: *"How can you meet John's claim that you do not see his competence?"*

Chris: *"Shall I bring it up?"*

Coach: *"Yes, you could certainly do that..."*

Chris: *"Hmm."*

Coach: *"What is your attitude? What do you see that you are doing in relation to expertise? "*

Chris: *"Many times I think that John does not have an eye for everything. I actually have experience of that and then I get afraid that my job is in jeopardy. "*

Coach: *"So when John takes major decisions on his own as chairman of the board, then you're scared?"*

Chris: ... ...

(Coach feels that Chris is thinking.)

Coach: *"I am going to make an assumption and I want you to check whether it is true. You become afraid and lose the big picture when John decides on his own. "*

Chris: *"Yes, that's right."*

Coach: *"Is this something that you can talk to John about?"*

Chris: *"Yes."*

Phenomenological approach

A phenomenological approach requires that the coach and coachee renounce their "pre-conceptions" of how the situation should, or could be resolved, in accordance with accepted practice or experience. Instead, they create the present during the dialogue. For the coach it is important to have a cool head and have faith that there will always be a solution. For the coachee, this approach can feel languid, fuzzy, strange, and annoying.

Putting in brackets – to park

Unconscious feelings steer people in everyday life. By beginning to know what is happening inside emotionally, we learn not to 'get into a spin' too often. Having access to thoughts and feelings makes life more peaceful and stable, and we have the strength to make more of ourselves available to others.

Leadership is precisely this - to be available to others by inspiring, supporting, acting as a sounding board, and so on. The ability to put one's own process in brackets, as well as thoughts and feelings, becomes essential. These are 'put in brackets' for a while, and then picked up again at a more suitable time.

To put in brackets may also mean that the manager or employee is able to put their own needs aside in order to agree on solutions that benefit the whole. In a management team someone can say "I parked my comments for later so we can make a sensible decision that will benefit the majority. " The demands of the individual regarding their own work may need to take a back seat for the group as a whole to succeed. The Business Coach also "parks" his personal parallel processes to the benefit of the coachee. The whole is again larger than the sum of its parts.

Dare to be yourself

The existence

Existential problems can feel so overwhelming that many people become angry. In addition, the question is often raised about a dialogue regarding work can really take up such "fuzzy" stuff.

These issues are rather "harder" than the usual business-related issues. Sooner or later they come up, without the coach needing to drive them home. They may involve a conflict in a group, or adult bullying in which a person is blamed and designated as a scapegoat. This may involve a reorganization that means many are fired. And it may involve an offer of a promotion, which automatically results in loneliness at work. The wind is strong and it is lonely at the top.

Reorganization raises issues of life and death. People are forced to leave, which can be seen as a major crisis for all those involved, and a large or small "death". To lose one's job still feels shameful for many socially and it's easy to lose one's footing. Those who are left on the company often have feelings of guilt. "I'm not smarter than those who had to go. It'll be my turn next time." To say goodbye is to die a little.

Loneliness is also an existential question. How much can a human bear to be alone? If a person is alone in a special management layer or is a specialist, where are the colleagues who can be trusted - those one can be familiar with? If a person is not accepted by a group, how does this loneliness feel for the victim? And what holds the existing group together? What are the rules of the group? How does it feel to be labelled as a bully just to remain in the group and avoid the chill of loneliness?

It is not uncommon for a coachee to wonder what he's doing. "I run around like a scalded cat, travel the world like an industrial tourist have time neither myself, my friends nor my family. What I'm doing is beginning to feel rather meaningless." Another said, "Why should I become more efficient and do the job more profitably? It's only shareholders who profit from it and in the end I still think that the Chinese are taking over. It feels rather pointless actually. "
Existential issues represent paradoxes for many. Those who dare to explore them further can gain a security that can be a great support for both themselves and others in uncertain times.

Who exactly is a "good employee"?

The question can probably provoke different answers depending on whether the respondent is the company owner, an employee, or a relative of the employee, and will also depend on which culture the person comes from.

Anyone who perceives that they succeed in their job almost always works for more than just money. This is a person who has a vision that extends beyond the person himself. The vision often includes not only work but also life itself, as a private individual and in relationships with family and friends. Quite often the vision includes the desire to, for once in a lifetime, make an extraordinary impression. It can be totally work-related but it could also include other things, like writing a book or learning to play the organ.

The vision can be as concise and clear as a spring sky without clouds. But it can also be hidden and may need time to unveil. Some people are able to do themselves. Others decide to ask for help to mull things over without demands being made - to receive and give themselves time for reflection and interactive discussion with a coach or coaching manager.

Following chapters

In the following chapters, some of the scientific elements that can be regarded as most significant in the dialogue method are highlighted:

- Field Theory
- Perception
- Existential Philosophy

The reason that the authors have chosen field theory, perception, and existential philosophy is that these areas include everyone and everything, everywhere. Here there are also links between very old research and philosophy and the very latest in physics. It's exciting. It is useful for everyone who can, wants to, dares to, and has the energy to create an awareness and hence clarity in both his working life and private life. This is a journey without end ...

Reference literature chapter 1.

Please find below books and references applicable to the text. The English title has been inserted when found. When not found, the title is left in its original language (English translation in brackets), for the reader interested to find other texts by the same author.

Anderson M, Anderson D (2005) *Coaching That Counts*, Elsevier, Burlington, MA

Austheim K (2006) *(Gestalt oriented coaching) Gestaltorientert coaching*, Oslo, Norsk Gestaltinstitutt AS. The article is inspired by Gary Yontef from his text Awareness, Dialogue and Process published by The Gestalt Journal Press.

Baalen v D (2005) (Revised gestalt diagnostic scheme) Revidert Gestalt diagnose skjema, Oslo/Norway, Norsk Gestaltinstitutt

Baalen v D (2004) *(The cycle of will) Viljebuen* (lecture), Oslo, Norsk Gestaltinstitutt. Inspired by The act of will – a guide to self-actualisation and self-realisation by Roberto Assagioli.

Berg M E (2007) *(Coaching – enabling leaders and employees to succeed) Coaching – att hjälpa ledare och medarbetare att lyckas*, Lund/Sweden, Studentlitteratur

Buber M (2001) *I and Thou*, published in 1923, first translation into English in 1937

Colbjørnsen, T (2004) *(Leaders and leadership) Ledere og lederskap*, Bergen/Norway, Fagbokforlaget

Covey S (1990) *The seven habits of highly effective people*, Stephen R Covey homepage; 2011-09-24; https://www.stephencovey.com

Csikszentmihályi M (1992) *Flow, The Psychology of Optimal Experience*, New York, Harper and Row

Collins J (2001) *From Good to Great – why some companies make the leap... and others don't*, New York, HarperCollins Publisher

Crocker S F (1998) *A well-lived life – essays in gestalt therapy*, Cambridge MA, GIC Press

Edvinsson L, Malone M (1997) *Intellectual Capital – realizing your company's true value by finding its hidden brainpower*, Malmö/Sweden, Liber Ekonomi

Frager R, Fadiman J (1998) *Personality & personal growth*, Addison Wesley Longman

Greene R (2002) *The concise 48 laws of power*, London, Profile Books Ltd

Hatch M (2006) *Organization Theory – modern, symbolic and postmodern perspectives*, USA, Oxford University Press

Kaufmann G, Kaufmann A (2003) Psychology in organizations and leadership, Bergen/Norway, Fagbokforlaget

Kokkersvold E, Mjelve H (2003) *(Between us), Mellom oss*, Oslo/Norway, Gyldendal Akademisk

Lindberg B (2000) *(Leading organizations, non-profit societies and popular movements), Ledning av organisationer, ideella föreningar och folkrörelser*, Sober Förlag

Morgan G (1986) Images of Organization, London, Sage Publications

Nevis E (1998) *Organizational Consulting – a gestalt approach*, Cambridge MA, GIC Press

Nilsson P (1998) *(Become your own best coach), Bli din egen bästa coach*, Farsta/Sweden, Sisu Idrottsböcker

Parsloe E, Wray M (1999) *Coaching and Mentoring – Practical methods to improve learning*, Kogan Page

Follow the leader - no matter how or where?

FIELD THEORY

AN EXPERIMENT OFTEN EVOKES a strong reaction in all the participants. Afterwards the group gathers to reflect on what happened and a report is written based on proven scientific practices.

In this book, the experiment has been replaced by a story. The text that follows considers some of the phenomena described in the story. A theoretical discussion is also woven into the text to give the history, background and the names of people who have made major contributions to this research.

... and now the first story as an introduction to Chapter 2, which deals with field theory ...

KEYWORDS CHAPTER 2.

- Field Theory (phenomena in one place are often found in other places too)
- Unhealthy interactive development cycle at the organizational level.
- Group development: belong / do not belong to / opt out
- Be able to, want to, dare to make choices: keep quiet, agree with, belong to, or call attention to-reflect-risk

Part 1: The psychopath who inspires enthusiasm

I hurry down the corridor. The meeting begins at ten o'clock. Chris, Anna, Greg and I will be planning the new campaign. Chris has got off to a flying start with the reorganization. Talk about climbing in the ranks - from local manager to a regional boss within one week - but why not? He is both pleasant and driving - a true leader. In addition, he has visions. He would even make a good president. I might even tell him that in the taxi on the way to the airport. Adam can't really sit there much longer - he turns 63 next month.

It is a nice May-morning. The sun filters in through the wide aluminium blinds and the birds can be heard through the open window. It's too bad that we have to sit inside. Chris doesn't seem to worry. He works all the time, at work when we arrive and leave. Damn it, is he really going to draw the blinds now when we for once have a little daylight in this country lost in midwinter darkness, at least for six months of the year?

It's really fun working with someone like Chris. Bringing things into focus is just the start.

"Now we'll show the slow coaches in the organization what can be done if you invest a bit", says Chris. The whiteboard marker pen flies backwards and forwards and visions take shape. Pens fly over the flip chart. He has really thought this through. Impressive! I wonder how he thinks that we should proceed. There is no doubt about what we must do; I'm just wondering how? Well, we'll find out. It was smart to begin with the goal and step backwards. It is just like going on a trip: the arrival time decides when you have to start packing.

"Chris, I really like the way you begin with the end point, but to squeeze in six months work by August is perhaps a little too creative".

Chris looks at me. "You can if you are committed. You have to really believe in this, Robert. It is not possible unless everyone believes in this adamantly. We will succeed with this and everyone must be committed".

Chris looking straight at me and I look back. The others look a little tense. I have a vague feeling that something is strange, not quite as it should be.

"There is no doubt that everyone in this room is willing to commit", I say after a moment's hesitation. What I really want to discuss is how we will have time to launch in August. If we all understand the plan then the job will get done better.

"Understand and discuss it! Damn it, does everyone need to understand now? We don't have time for bickering". Chris is really emphatic: "It's all about faith!"

"I must at least be allowed to ask. What is this all about?" I wonder, both amazed and disappointed.

"What it really all about", says Chris with a low voice "is whether you are with me or against me". It is totally quiet in the room apart from Chris. "When I come back I want you to have made up your mind."

Then he goes out and gets coffee. The rest of us remain, sitting silently, each submerged in their own thoughts. What just happened?

Part 2: Three kinds of pride

God, Darwin or CEO/Managing Director
We are all ants in your stack.
Whence and whither?

The path runs first up the hill, but then starts to run downhill. I run on down, first through the thicket, then the pine plantation and finally the muddy area. It has dried up a bit but I but I have to jump over the parts that are still wet. Out on the edge of the long field, across the bridge over the brook and then up the waterlogged hill, over the crest with the oak and so on down the path on the eastern edge of the field. The field is shimmering sheer green in the backlight. The sun warms. Rounding the woods, I pass through the high grass and up onto the gravel road. On the other side: the old bunker that has turned into an anthill. The sun warms. The ants are out.

It's nice to stand and relax for a while. The panting subsides. My thoughts drift through my peaceful mind, not following any particular furrow, allowed to wander free. It is soothing to consider the bugs. The ants swarm. There! One is carrying a dead comrade. Should be heavy but does not seem to be. But hold on, there is no way that ants can be comrades! They have no feelings of nature.

Colleagues perhaps. They work together. Here comes another colleague to help out. Looks nice but is hardly caring. Rather a reflex. All are industrious, busily working by reflex. They carry pine needles, dead colleagues or food, signal for food, attack my shoes and bite me - the major threat, at least for now. Their reflexes steer them to bite where it is soft. According to Darwin, the species will survive better if they bite where it is soft, where it hurts so the intruder goes away on average more often than if they bite where it is hard. Those who do so will survive and get more offspring who, on average, do the same thing. Therefore, the ant bites my shoelace. I do not care but, instead, rather considerate, I stand there and avoid stepping on more ants than is necessary. If I wanted to I could stir up the stack. And to what purpose? Individual ants will die, but the society survives as long as the queen is still there. In addition, I have no quarrel with them. They give a relaxing break and are an integral part of the nature I enjoy. And by the way, the queen is a real example of top-down management. Everything depends on a single individual. All the others are negligible, each and every one. It is together that they accomplish great things, by their design and their reflexes. Hardware and software merged into one, coordinated by the queen's chemical signals.

I come to think of the article on chimpanzees. They are both similar and different to us. Why are we so many and they are so few? What happened six million years ago when we went our separate ways, leading to human domination? They were buffoons, we the crown of creation. Crown and clown by the way: well ok! Buffoons they may be in some people's eyes, and it is we who decide. Right now. On the sand grain called Earth - a particle in the universe. We have the ability to understand the essence of existence like a goldfish can understand French. We are simply not sufficiently equipped. We rely on faith - in God, Darwin, Love, The Big Bang, financial statements, Hennes & Mauritz, or all at once.

Chimpanzee groups are controlled by males. Their close relatives, the Bonobos, are controlled by the females. We humans are usually controlled by males. Sometime these are real alpha males. Peter talks about faith. But in what? He surrounded himself with a small sect: the inner circle, with the support of, if not God himself, at least the CEO. He got responsibility and took power. He put himself in the driver's seat and hit the gas as hard as he could. He saw a meter, we saw next year. But we sat in the back seat and could only scream.

"Damn it, you do not believe," was the standard answer to those who had objections, if ever so cautious. The four looked on at me coldly, taking note of everything that could be useful in the future, at least to make sure I noticed it. Perhaps they sent a copy of their blackmailing e-mails to the CEO if they suspected that I might have objections. And the CEO was asleep, or didn't want to know. Or he thought what he saw was good since sales went through the roof.

The rest of us talked to those who had been affected. Customers who cried when they had to pay for something they did not want. Some threatened with lawyers. There were salespeople who resigned and sued the company for harassment, and product managers who cried and cursed in turn. The financial manager saw that the sales figures were false: we sent out the goods without being paid, because no one wanted them.

We built for a future without Peter. We knew that one day the bubble would burst and then it will be better. That was what kept our spirits up. As long as the company doesn't go under in the process.

It's been a year. Peter has reassigned. Who knows, he might do some good. The product he was selling is dying. The sales curve that went straight up before, is now going down, straight as an arrow. We are back to square one. The warriors are scattered and to some extent de-programmed. The CEO realises, although he doesn't want to. He still takes a defensive position.

The replacement seems talented but hard-boiled. He does not accept help from those who were involved before he came. We need a new crew. Hibernators become minor players, or are thrown out. We must admit that Peter still showed that he needed us. Although we never got so much as a thank you, we were important to him - too important, because the expectations were astronomically unrealistic. Now, expectations are zero. We have to take care of ourselves without guidance and support while he is up to his neck in meetings. How tough is it, really, to think that you yourself have all the answers?

Was it really so awful under Peter? He and I might just have had a bad personal chemistry. He at least cared. He was charming and passionate but also a control freak and unrealistic megalomaniac. The new one is the opposite - sad and cold, without control or any expectations. Who should I choose? What shall I choose? The frying pan or the fire?

What is the goal of an anthill?
How did Charles reason? Charles Darwin.

Or God.
If he exists.

Or is there something wrong with me?
And the CEO continues to sleep and doesn't notice anything. Or maybe he's awake but just lets things happen. Why should he care about small problems when the company is profitable? That some people are in distress is perhaps something that he regards as inevitable, to be sacrificed so that we can achieve the goal. The goal is with a capital G - the goal of the company.

I look up. The ants crawl, both on the stack and on my legs. I brush them away. I probably trample some to death when I move. I start running along the road, take the route past the motorway, away past the forest lake. There I crouch down to see if the tadpoles have arrived yet. Normally there are hundreds in the warm surface waters. They just swim, eat, grow, and defecate.

Note 1: All persons described herein (including deities) are fictitious. Any resemblance to reality is pure coincidence.

Part 3: To break an organization
Information to a human resources director

Support words in the discussion: It is not "what" we are doing that is wrong, but "how" we do it!

Sect Mentality is our "code of conduct" and culture right now:

➤ *"You / they do not believe in this"*
➤ *"NN wants it ..."*
➤ Us and them ("it's only we who can and do right – everyone else is worthless")
➤ Often a cc upwards in the Organization, to put pressure on the recipient

- The individual will never be shown respect
- Micro management without any form of management by objectives
- Always sudden ad hoc decisions with no planning in advance
- New ideas which must be implemented immediately. The old is immediately defunct.
- No briefing for the person who will perform the work
- No one knows what the boss comes up with next time, resulting in discomfort and fear
- No questioning allowed
- The manager shows no confidence or trust in anyone outside the "inner circle". Compare child rearing with and without trust or confidence! What employees does the company want?
- No delegation - only central management and control, resulting in

unmotivated underlings. Again, what employees does the company want? It is obvious that competent adults are significantly more efficient than infantilized performers.

- Today "no feedback" means that the person has fought and won! No employees are allowed to prevail in public. Today, it is all about the whip without the carrot.

The result at this point

1. Nonexistent sales!

2. Damaged reputation with customers

– Have we promised our customers to get them customers?!
– Wasted meetings = sour customers
– 5000 products to customers who do not believe they have ordered = sour customers
– A customer returned products with a copy to his lawyer = angry customer
– Even the local media are telling us that our "stupid campaign" is insane and recommend more cost-effective solutions
– Bad reputation in the market makes it difficult to fill open positions.

3. Erosive organization

– 'Fire / hire ratio' high
– Sales force heading for extinction (Country 1: All have resigned the first week in December, even the good ones; Country 2: one salesperson is left after the New Year, Country 3: one salesperson left, Countries 4 and 5: a salesperson left per country)
– Spontaneous departures due to deficiencies in management / execution of decisions ("The staff are deprived of their own self-respect. This is not seen, and the extent not understood, by those who have not experienced it.")
– Affected employees put on a brave face and try to do a good job – it's possible up to a point, but if misrule continues then it is only a matter of time before more quit.
– An experienced Executive Secretary, hired in, breaks up crying after one day - "I've never felt so useless in all my life".

Reflections on psychopathy

What affects what? Who influences whom? How is it that some people in particular are given space and power in an organization? What does the

organization look like? What does society look like? Based on these issues, it is natural that the introduction to the chapter on field theory can be about psychopathy.

In a conversation between a coach and coachee, or manager and employee, both partners are always affected by the so-called field that exists in their surroundings. A powerful force in the field, a manager or leading personality, can therefore have an impact and deform the interactive development cycle. It is possible to handle this by re-focussing and being aware of the situation.

From being a non-issue and a non-debate, it has become more accepted to talk about the issue of psychopaths in organizations. Nevertheless, it is always perceived as a shock and even a near-death experience when a group or individual becomes a victim of the psychopath.

The victim often wonders first if he or she is sick, because the psychopath is phenomenally good at manipulation. In view of the section on projections, it may also be appropriate to reflect on the psychopathic features that even the victim might have. At the right time and under certain conditions, the vast majority can certainly exhibit psychopathic traits without being a "full-blown psychopath."

There is also the issue of which survival strategies the victim can use to survive the psychopathic situation. If it is a psychopathic chief then he or she is often put in "quarantine" without subordinate staff – as long as the human resources department have realized what has happened. If it instead involves an entire organization that is psychopathic then the situation becomes more difficult. It seldom happens that the organization itself can see the psychopathic behaviour. There will be a "blind spot", which is described later in the chapter in the model "Johari Window". A new employee can see it, as well as an external consultant. A strong management team can help to make visible invisible norms and highlight the core values that should apply. Everyone should realize what is going on and become aware of their own values and what they are able and willing to adapt to.

The story above is written by one person in a company that experienced psychopathic tendencies in the organization as a whole, in a group, and in some individuals. This person has considered their own behaviour and their own values in individual coaching with an external coach. Part of this reflective work was to read about psychopathy and to also write a story for their own learning.

Apparent control

"We know what we have, but not what we get."

These old claims signal a desire for control, calmness and stability in both everyday life and work. But ... Nothing stands still, life goes on, everything affects everything ... Any stability is short-lived. To catch the future is impossible.

Yet wise people in working life are forever creating new business plans that range from one to five years. Endless hours are consumed in the writing of these plans. And ... The smallest, at first seemingly uninteresting and unimportant actions, may constitute the first step towards a major change in the organization or its environment. But man does not give up but rather continues to try to gain control over their lives. She does so today. And she has done so since time immemorial.

$$B = f(P+E)$$

B = Behaviour
f = function
P = Personality
E = Environment

MATHEMATICAL FORMULA FOR BEHAVIOUR, AS DESCRIBED BY SOCIAL PSYCHOLOGIST KURT LEWIN

Behaviour is a function of Personality in the surrounding Environment, which can be set up as the mathematical formula, $B = f(P + E)$

Everything affects everything

Anything that affects the modern man becomes infinite if the perspective is the cosmos. But cosmic rays affect our skin, storms create chaos for railways, an argument with her husband often affects the women's work, and an event from the past makes itself felt today and affects events. Each and every one will thus remain in their own field and at the same time influence an infinite number of other fields.

The behaviour forms an overall picture of the person, with her background, culture and experiences and environment in the influencing and interacting field. The field can only be experienced, explored and understood in the present. Everything should be seen as energy and momentum in the field. A process consists of birth, development and change.

The mathematical formula is derived from Kurt Lewin. He borrowed physical force- and field-concepts from quantum physics and transferred them to psychology. He stressed that the self, individual and her behaviour can never be understood in isolation from the environment, or field, where they act, influence and are influenced.

Lewin said that every human being is part of a dynamic field and that any change in one part of the individual or part of the field will have repercussions on the entire system.

Chaos Theory to the Behavioural Sciences

Kurt Lewin

Kurt Lewin was born in Germany in 1890. He trained as a psychologist in Berlin. This led to aPhD in associative learning. Lewin came to the United States in 1932 as a visiting professor at Stanford University. He influenced social psychology as soon as he got there. He had already published several books before he arrived and wrote more during his life in the United States.

Lewin left Stanford for Cornell University and finally settled down at the University of Iowa, 1935 to 1944. Then he got a position as director of the new Research Centre for Group Dynamics at the Massachusetts Institute of Technology (MIT). Kurt Lewin is best known for the development of field theory.

Books he wrote include "A Dynamic Theory of Personality" (1935), "Principles of Topological Psychology" (1936), "The Conceptual Representation and Measurement of Psychological Forces" (1938) and "Resolving Social Conflicts" (1947).

CHAOS THE NEIGHBOUR OF GOD
(Friend, in the Desolate Time)

Friend, in the desolate time, when your
soul is enshrouded in darkness, when,
in a deep abyss, memory and feeling
die out, Intellect timidly gropes among
shadowy forms and illusions. Heart can
no longer sigh, eye is unable to weep.
When, from your night-clouded soul
the wings of fire have fallen, and you,
to nothing, afraid, feel yourself sinking
once more, Say, who rescues you then?

Who is the comforting angel, brings
to your innermost soul order and
beauty again, Building once more your
fragmented world, restoring the fallen
altar and, when it is raised, lighting the
sacred flame?

None but the powerful being who first
from the limitless darkness kissed to
life seraphs and woke numberless suns
to their dance.. None but the holy word
who called the worlds into existence
and in whose power the worlds move
on their paths to this day. Therefore,
rejoice oh friend, and sing in the dark-
ness of sorrow:

Night is the mother of day, chaos the neighbour of God.

Erik Johan Stagnelius (1793-1823), translated from the Swedish by Bill Coyle.

Social Psychology to Leadership

Lewin's Research Centre for Group Dynamics quickly became the leading training institute for social psychology. His research has helped to explain the conditions of leadership and the group dynamics that surround them in the organization.

Lewin's ideas about objectives and rationale-oriented forces were a development. He said that our behaviour has meaning. We live in a psychological reality and a social environment that are important to us. In addition, things that we carry with us from the past, upbringing and values, are important for motivation and our individual goals.

Lewin also showed that socio-psychological phenomena can be studied in reality. It was an important leap for scientific experiments in organization research. He also revealed that events must be viewed in context, for both individuals and groups.

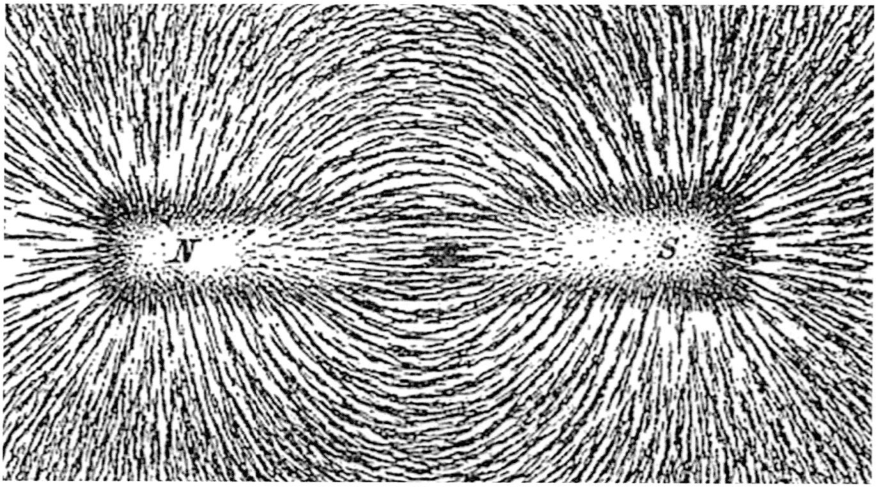

Electrical fields with atomic interactions

Lewin and Gestalt psychologists

Field theory is fundamental to Gestalt psychology. Gestalt psychologists work with wholes and the data included in the whole is known as the phenomenon. The dynamic systems or wholes affect changes in all the individual parts of the whole field.

Gestalt psychologists studied mainly man's cognitive side (thinking and perception, how the world is perceived). They cared less about emotions, personality, and motives for this or that action.

Despite this, Gestalt psychologists meant that the situation man is in, and his surroundings, have dynamic properties in addition to the structural. Some of the Gestalt psychologists of the 1930's joined the Nazis, arguing that the people formed the superior figure in relation to the individual. And the individual must be subordinate to the whole. Kurt Lewin, who did not share this view, emigrated from Germany when Nazism began to grow strong and developed Gestalt psychology through his research, including field theory.

Lewin's "system" and "field"

The terms "field" and "system" are used in different ways and can therefore create confusion.

- **The term "system"** is used here for something that is closed and is comprised of elements that interact.
- **The term "field"** is used to describe open, process-oriented wholes. Quantum Theory and Field Theory are also based on open wholes that interact with each other.

FIELDS
Fields comprise all aspects of the person and the person's surroundings at different levels and everyone carries them. All the fields interact more or less clearly with each other. Examples of fields in a person are upbringing, genetic inheritance, culture, and norms.

When the equilibrium is disturbed the systems regroup, interact with other systems and then regroup again.
A new structure arises.

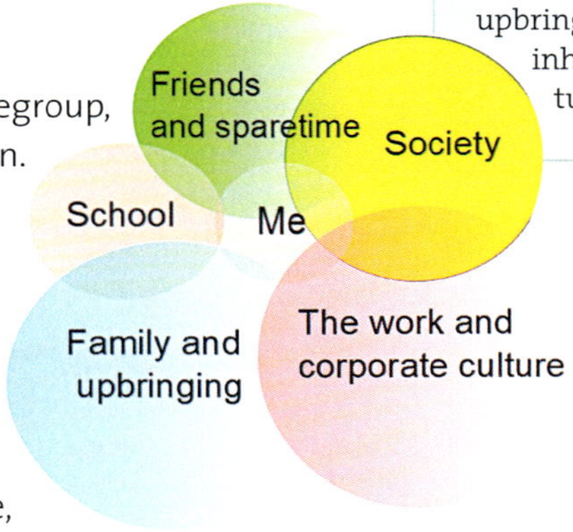

Life's Room

Life's room consists of subjective, more or less well-defined and available fields that interact with each other. They create pressure on individuals in different directions with demands from home, school, friends, and society.

The dynamics of life's room makes itself known by the different fields that have different values and importance for the individual. The individual fields mean that every individual is in different geographical, social and conceptual states. Incomplete events, things that are not complete, lead to needs that are difficult to ignore.

"Your perception of yourself and your relationship with yourself shifts as your life space shifts. How do you change your life space? If you're a member of a group, your life space as a member of the group is a development process."

Extract from "Notes on Kurt Lewin" by Laurence J. Horowitz

Behaviour determines in which field we currently find ourselves and what impact the surrounding fields have. Fields in these cases may be a relationship, work, or relatives. How far each and every one wants, dares, or has the energy to come in their relationship or their work depends on the ambition level.

The theory of life's room or life's field means that a person is motivated by temptations and threats in their surroundings and thus the individual's driving force comes essentially from the field. These surroundings (or environment) set off a chain of actions. Individuals taking shelter, start an education or get married. The fields around the individual determine what support he or she has to succeed in their goals and intentions.

POWER AND AUTHORITY

Power is the probability that an individual in a social relationship has his or her way despite opposition from others.

Authority is the probability that an order with a specified content is obeyed. This can be achieved in different ways, through democratic alternatives, or autocratic or hierarchical models.

An individual's power in the group

Democratic processes and leadership styles were important to Kurt Lewin. Through his field studies, he showed what it took to be a democratic leader and how to build a democratic group structure.

Proponents of networks and network field-theorists realize that the democratic or organic leadership that takes into account power in relation to rights lead to faster and more enduring survival strategies.

Lewin said that it was possible to choose between three styles of leadership in the organization:

Democratic leaders
Dictatorial leaders
"Let-go mentality" leaders

In this choice the Democratic leader was the most effective by far. According to Lewin, he gave the best balance between comfort and efficiency. Management has a changed role in a network organization and the employees' initiative is extremely important.

Lewin also pointed out how important it is that democratic leaders help to develop new leaders. Leaders in the network organization trust the process. A democratically controlled organization with open borders and clear leadership generates the best results. The self-organization of open systems leads to development and adaptation. The organization itself is aware of the surroundings and reacts to stimuli from outside.

Helplessness in several structures

The fact that everything affects everything else can be seen in society. An example would be helplessness and the "learned helplessness".

In 1975 a scientist (Seligman) found that a response to stress may cause depression which in itself can be the result of man realising that he is helpless. Everything seems hopeless and one may as well give up. This may lead to depression or becoming exhausted or overworked ("burnt out").

It is possible to think about where this feeling of helplessness comes from. Has it become more common today? One can speculate if it exists at several levels in society and, if so, how it unconsciously affects the citizen.

Help me!
Or support to help yourself.

Societal level: Social systems have been developed with the best of intentions to ensure that everyone has a measure of financial security. Communication and the pulse of society have been increased by developments in IT but man is still at the cave level. Many are struggling at a high rate, for a long time, and have no energy left in the end. Maybe, maybe a thought sneaks into the consciousness: "it is only right that I can stay home and get something back from my taxes". Perhaps many unconsciously "showing the finger" to society when they are experiencing helplessness and powerlessness in being unable to affect the large structures.

Family level: Much has been written about curling parents. Many parents have been sweeping clean in front of their children with the best of intentions. The children have not had to strive so much. The school bus has arrived - even if it is only 2 km to go to school. Courses are paid. The monthly allowance drops into their account automatically. Dinner is served. And the cleaning lady comes and cleans every room. WHAT the young do is often rewarded more than HOW they act in friendship, their demonstration of empathy through loyal actions etc.. How many youngsters have you met who lack energy, are listless or sad? Who don't see any point? Or say "I have no job - I just have to go to social security to get some money"!

Organizational level: Organizations reward all those people who work hard. Here are many of today's "curling managers". They sweep in front of their co-workers. Employees do not dare or care to make their own decisions, but go instead to their curling manager who "knows best". And employees quickly fall into a state of helplessness where they can work a lot but only under direct orders and without making their decisions.

People hold chaos in check

Organizational theory of creation stories in chaos

Chaos was the first ancient unit in Egypt. In Nothingness there was only compact darkness.

Energy lead to the generation of creativity and this creative environment gave birth to the sun and the cosmos. The darkness dissipated and order was created around the poles of darkness and light. All the time the balance between darkness and light was threatened by the forces of chaos. It was particularly critical at the precise dividing line between chaos and cosmos. This critical point was represented in several places as the Ouroboros, a snake which bites its own tail: the never-ending chaos surrounding the structured world of creation.

More than 5 000 years ago, scientists in Egypt thought not unlike Kurt Lewin, Einstein, quantum physicists, and chaos theorists.

Everyone who works with groups and systems that are in a state of flux in organizations can also learn from the Egyptian "organizational consultants". The Egyptians considered that life and existence are one: a whole in which everything is connected (holism). Creation is a force field where order prevails. Humans are in a system and the important thing is to try to keep the system in balance.

NEW ORGANIZATION

"Now it's been quiet in the company for quite a while and everyone has found their place. Finally, it's become peaceful here, but ...

The managing director called an information meeting in June. Now we have been acquired by an international company. The head office where I work will be moving to London.

Everyone should stay calm and everything will be OK. No one has been laid off yet, but the managing director is talking about rationalization and that we must increase our profitability.

I feel really deflated, empty. Others are sad, and many are really angry."

Coping with chaos

All cultures have had their own myths of creation. Most tell of different states of chaos or nothingness that eventually take shape. Often a superior force or forces are needed to gain control.

Taoism shows parallels to modern quantum physics in that their creation myth claims that it was precisely in the emptiness that there was energy and power for creation. About 2 500 years ago, Lao Tze said that, prior to the Tao ("the road to follow") there was this nothing and that out of this nothing came the power that created heaven, earth, human, and Tao. In Norse Paganism the serpent Jörmungandr held together chaos, while in the monotheistic religions the world was created by a god.

Chaos hurts

To be capable of change is a matter of survival for many companies and organizations. The challenge is to transform existing, inflexible and hierarchical organizations to those that can continuously adapt to new realities and new power structures. Future employees will be requested to embrace change already in the employment interview. Before the change is a fact many people can probably attest that this feels okay. But it feels often both unsafe and unpleasant when the organization is in the process of going from control (I know what I have) into a period of chaos (I do not know what I will get), followed by a new, brief period of stability.

People who were earlier considered to be wise, and had been employed because of their pronounced capacity for flexibility and willingness to change, lose their footing and can be steered by the reptilian brain in ways that they never thought possible.

Despite everything, chaos can hurt...

Robots or people

Many believe that groups work in closed systems - systems that live and develop in a predetermined manner. Here the view is often that "work is work and we do not mix in our personal life." And "here we can distinguish between facts and people". It would obviously be easier if people and groups acted as robots with no antennae directed towards the outside world. Then everyone would be prepared for anything that may happen in a group, with managers, or with staff, without irritating incidents.

The working group's "life" is not at all predictable when working with a field-theory approach. Everyone is interdependent and the group forms a dynamic whole. Anything can, in principle, disturb the working group's balance. Removal of a member affects the whole group as does the introduction of a new participant.

Every change leads to a new development cycle of change and interaction and new structures are formed. To lead a group with this approach is challenging, and success requires tools other than those for good planning.

People in transition

The goal is that organizations can continually adjust to meet the new criteria set by their complex surroundings. Companies want to achieve an organization that has the ability to change such that the employees do not perceive the change as a separate task, but rather as a regular part of work - in other word, more of an opportunity than a threat.

Continuous influence caused by large numbers of fields seldom allows stability over time and requires constant adaptation to new conditions for the organization.

Change in organizations provides new managers

The leaders who can lead their organizations through these constant changes and adapt to new realities will be successful in the long term. The leader can aid this by developing common objectives in a dynamic process. This is provided by the following:

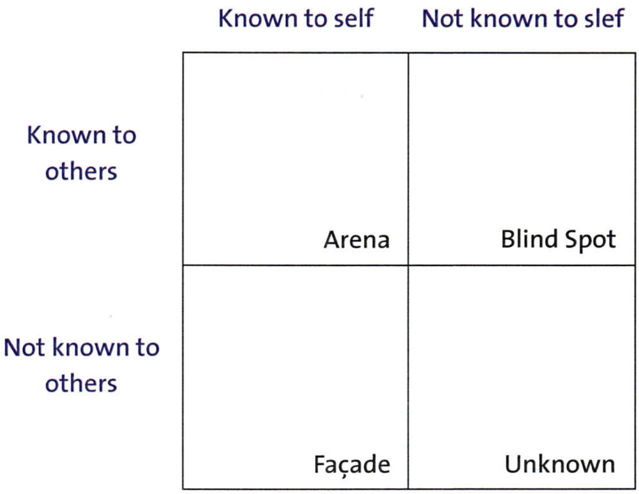

The Johari Window , on an organizational level. Joe Ingham and Harry Luft, 1950

A minimum of critical rules. If organizations and companies set up detailed rules then these will be circumvented if they do not fit the business.

Corporate culture can become blindfolded, making it impossible to stop a downward trend. Corporate culture might not allow criticism and the pointing out of shortcomings, even if it is an open secret at the company. And the shortcomings may be likely to drive the company towards disintegration. This behaviour is reinforced in autocratic organizations, as Lewin also pointed out. It will be the democratic leaders who help to develop new leaders.

AUTOCRACY
Definition:
government by one

Synonyms: absolutism, czarism, despotism, dictatorship, monarchy, monocracy, oppression, totalitarian government, tyranny.

Source:
http://thesaurus.com

Permeable boundaries (transparency). These limits will open up the surrounding fields and systems while providing a continuous feedback and can correct errors in discrete steps. The company must be able to observe its own development.

Open systems and self-monitoring with self-organized systems are field-concepts that are applicable according to Lewin. Sub-optimization, or at worst collapse, occurs when the organization is affected by what is called "The Blind Spot", described by Ingham and Luft (see figure). The organization cannot observe itself. That is, the corporate culture, myths and norms make it impossible to stop the machinery even if it drives towards decay.

Flexible and dynamic organization architecture. Proper knowledge is not sufficient to trigger changes; a climate must be fostered that makes this possible. The capability of change develops as a continuous and dynamic process. Companies build up their capacity in stages and gain energy to move towards a more "organic" ability to change.

Common goals. Common goals are the platform and also the prerequisite for the strategic work that drives companies forward and makes them competitive. They do not come as a result of resounding speeches and charismatic managers, but rather a persevering change over time. The corporate culture makes the employees feel a *mutual dependence* to solve problems and that they have a *common destiny*. (The italicized words are field-theory concepts that Lewin coined).

Leadership insight that the whole is greater than the sum of its parts. The leader gets a new role and is not solely responsible. The employees' initiative is extremely important. The organization strives towards cultural openness, which is a joint effort and there is recognition that the work arena has now become global.

Verification through chaos

"Everything changes, nothing is like it was last year ..." said the Egyptian Chacheperresenebs in his "complaint" during the 18th Dynasty, 1500 BC.

The only thing we know for sure, and may have some control over, is that chaos is really the only thing that is constantly recurring. Thus, we can also venture the idea that creativity in the world will never run out since it is in chaos that innovation often takes place – in other words, before everything has "landed" and the surroundings only want peace and quiet.

Influence of invisible roles

Everything is, as stated, moving at the level of the particle. Quantum physicists have shown experimentally that when a particle is in focus then it is the same time at three thousand other places.

Similarly, it is possible to study a person's various roles in life. The human is an individual but acts in a host of unseen roles. In the workplace, she can be a woman, project manager, policy maker, colleague, management team member, counsellor, judge, etc.

At the same time, she works in a lot of other roles in private, for example, mother, lover, cook, maid, shopper, friend, daughter, cat owner, shoe lover, etc. Roll reassignments are often unconscious and work seamlessly. But there can be problems sometimes if roles are not clarified. Is a doctor at a dinner party in the role of friend, free medical advisor or connoisseur? It is not always appreciated if your neighbour takes the opportunity to get a free diagnosis.

Similarly, a person who had been promoted to head of his group may have obvious problems at the next office party. Who is he a friend of now? Is it possible to have a glass of wine and talk the same way as before with his workmates, or not? And what do his old workmates think of him? In what role do they see him now - as the old mate, a capable manager, or a traitor?

It may often be wise to clarify the role in which a person acts - both for themselves and their surroundings. Then the surroundings know what they can expect from the person and can be assured that misunderstandings will be avoided.

Select or have a role

Lewin's formula for the behaviour of humans, and thus their roles, has been presented as: **B = f (P + E)**

- The **Behaviour** is the type of conduct
- The **Person** and her **Personality** is made up of emotions and feelings, intellect and ideas, and basic existential motivations
- The **Environment** includes people, events, objects, surroundings, values, sounds, tastes, etc.

The role or behaviour can therefore change depending on the emotions that every individual is driven by and/or the environment in which the individual finds them self. Awareness of the emotions that drive different roles and their implications on behaviour, can, in many cases, be valuable when conducting meetings and conversations. This example illustrates one such situation:

Josephine: *I was at a meeting yesterday that our subsidiary asked me to hold with the new customers. Two representatives of the subsidiary were also included, Patricia and Stephen.*

Manager: *How was the meeting?*

Josephine: *The customers were well informed. They asked a lot of questions at a level of detail that I could not cover. I feel that the customers were quite unhappy afterwards. Patricia and Stephen seemed crushed. Yes, it doesn't feel very good. If I was unsure before the meeting but that was nothing compared to how miserable I felt after the meeting.*

Manager: *What have you learned from this?*

Josephine: *F irst of all, I must always ask what the objectives are for the meeting. I realise now that I didn't really know what the customers wanted, just that their expectations weren't met.*
Manager: *And if you had known what the objective was? Would Patricia and Stephen have been satisfied with your efforts?*

Josephine: *No, I don't think so. Actually our own expert, Thomas, was invited. But as usual, he was fully booked and told me to go in his place. The customers probably thought that I was this expert. And Patricia and Stephen thought that I could play the role of an expert. And I was not at all clear - somehow, I had hoped that I could have functioned as some sort of expert.*

Manager: *Expert role? What role do you think you could have adopted and been clear about, instead?*

Josephine: *I'm comfortable in my own marketing role – it's something I can stand for. From that role, I have a pretty good understanding of substantive issues, without being able to go into details. If I had made that clear to the customers right from the start then their expectations would probably have been totally different. And if I had been clear to Patricia and Stephen that I actually wasn't an expert then they could have decided whether to invite someone else, or complement me in some other way.*

Manager: *So to clarify the role you take yourself becomes important to your surroundings, and not least to yourself. Different roles imply different feelings of discomfort or comfort. And these roles control both your behaviour and the response you get. Did that become clear to you?*

Josephine: *Yes*

Manager: *Good. I want to leave the role of follow-up manager, and instead move into the role of hungry colleague. Let's go and eat!*

The feeling creates a role that gives rise to action.

Event - Feeling - Role - Action

Democracy is voluntary

In his research, Kurt Lewin found that the democratic group showed more originality, group thinking and cooperation among team members. In the autocratic (absolutism) organizations, there was more aggression and searches for a scapegoat.

Lewin noted that the difference in behaviour between groups was not primarily due to differences between people but rather linked to the organization of the groups.

He pointed out that democratic behaviour in an organization is something that must be learned in the process and with active participation. He said that the goal of democratic leaders, therefore, is to replace themselves in order to bring out the new leaders in the group.

Lewin also said that understanding or knowledge does not automatically lead to changes. Consideration must be given to natural and cultural forces in the surroundings. He also found that it is easy to go from an open democratic organization to an autocratic or "laissez-faire" organization, but much harder to go back to a democracy.

This brings us to another of Lewin's theories. Democracy cannot be forced on people but must be learned through voluntary, active participation. This is something to take into account in connections with transitions in organizational development.

Democracy cannot be forced on people but must be learned through voluntary, active participation.

Experiment and Research

In later years, Kurt Lewin shifted his focus from research of the individual, with individual goals and actions, to the groups' interactions and interpersonal conduct. His research still concerned fields, tensions and conflicts and their settlement in a learning process as well as studies of group processes.

PHASE THEORY
- Unfreeze
- Change
- Refreeze and normalise

Phase theory

Kurt Lewin showed three phases of the organization and processes of change:
"Unfreezing" which means to thaw old behaviours and attitudes.
"Change"
"Refreezing" which means normalization and re-freezing through the assembly of forces. This includes acknowledgement and support.

Phase theory can be applied to groups, individuals and social institutions.

Action Research

Action research was developed, which was about trying to change where the problem occurred in groups and organizations. The research was conducted by practical experiments and evaluated by participants and researchers together. Lewin's theory of action research uses empirical research on social action and was therefore based on controlled evaluation.

EMPIRICAL
Definition: practical; based on experience

Synonyms:
experient, experiential, experimental, factual, observational, observed, pragmatic, provisional.

Source:
http://thesaurus.com

Kurt Lewin's field theory and the "action field research" has meant a great deal to modern social psychology, organizational development, and group processes. Most of this work found its way into the organizational world in the form of group exercises and processes in various management courses.

T-groups and fish-bowls

Lewin argued that we humans know too little about how we affect each other. Therefore, he wanted to resolve such conflicts by ensuring that individuals have greater insight into their surroundings. This could be achieved with different methods.

He developed, for example, a method that allows groups to study themselves during the work process in their **T**-groups, or **T**-raining groups.

T-groups were mainly found in universities where the participants and teachers exposed themselves to one another, got feedback on their actions, and evaluated their influence on each other. Feedback was also given in what are now called the "fish bowls". In these, one group sit together and talk about how they experience a situation, while other participants watch and listen, without actively participating in the discussion. The "other participants" then form their own group and talk to each other, while the former group sits by and listens.

Fight - Flight - Remain

The Fight-Flight phenomenon is also woven into the process of giving and receiving feedback, and this is a recurring phenomenon during the group's entire development. What is the first reaction of a group or person to the feedback: to "fight back" or to "get even"? Or does the group or person search for a quick escape route through words, deeds or attaching blame? Or can the group or person stay, take in the feelings that arise and do something other than simply flee or fight?

Lewin's field theory led to the development of genuine fieldwork concerning human behaviour. His approach has guided many experiments in social behaviour, social motivation and group processes.

Force field analysis

To raise awareness of the underlying conflicts and other obstacles to the development of new strategies in different groups and organizations, Lewin carried out a so-called force field analysis.

The method involves a group identifying together factors perceived as inhibiting or stimulating the activities they intend to change or develop in some way.

Force field analysis

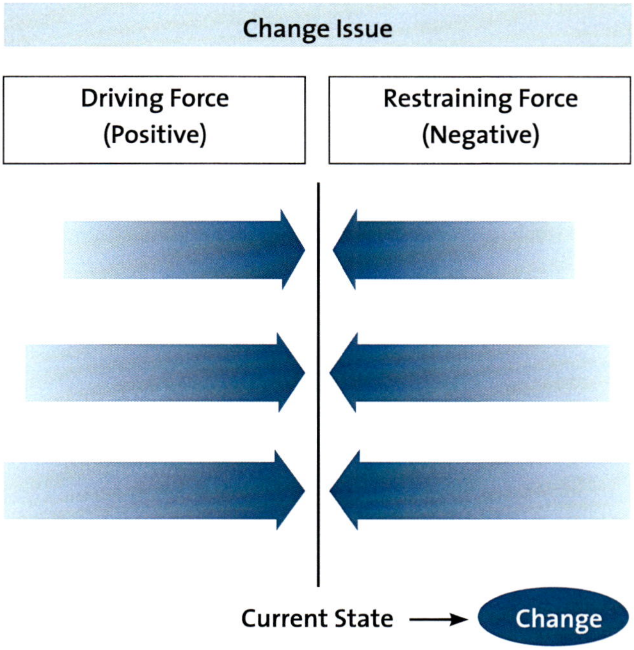

STEPS IN A FORCE FIELD ANALYSIS

1. Describe the current situation.

2. Describe the desired situation. Determine what the situation will result in if no action is taken.

3. List all the forces driving change in the desired direction (driving forces).

4. List all the forces that oppose the desired change (opposing forces).

5. Discuss and review all the driving and opposing forces. Are they valid? Can they be changed? Which are critical?

6. Grade each driving force and opposing force. Use a numerical scale where 1 is extremely weak, and 10 is extremely strong.

7. Identify the different forces. List the driving forces for change on the left. List the opposing forces on the right side.

8. Decide now whether change is possible.

9. Discuss how the various forces may be affected by reducing the strength of the opposing forces and / or by increasing the driving forces.

10. Break down all steps that need to be taken to counteract the opposing forces to the time-specific quantifiable tasks that can be distributed to those responsible. Repeat with the driving forces.

A force field analysis diagram demonstrates how positive or attractive forces in a group drive the ambitions of participants from a current level to a future desired level. The negative and repulsive forces pull in the opposite direction. By stepwise analysis of the content and tension in the various factors the group and the organization can form a more differentiated picture of the factors that influence in one way or the other. From this it is possible to design activities that strengthen the positive aspects and activities that minimize the negative aspects.

The strategies and activities can be broken down to a personal plan for each member of the group so that everyone experiences that they can contribute to the effectiveness of the whole.

UNFINISHED EVENTS
As long as the need is not satisfied then one strives towards the goal!

Conclusion of Kurt Lewin

The unfinished sticks in the memory

The unfinished creates tension

Sigmund Freud believed that most of man's problems are based on frustration. He said that frustration makes us incompetent as human beings. Kurt Lewin and the researcher Bluma Ziegarnik said rather the opposite: it is most likely that learning functions best when there is tension in the surroundings.

Learning expands the field. This will open up the possibility of new things happening. The risk of opening up a field is small even if the outcome of learning is unknown.

The idea of Lewin and Ziegarnik was, therefore, that man builds up tension in order to learn. After the learning process has passed, the stress is released. This has to do with the fact that something has been completed.

> *"We keep on learning throughout life, and what we learn we integrate into how we behave..."*
>
> Extract from "Notes on Kurt Lewin" by Laurence J. Horowitz

Or, as the Gestalt psychologists would put it, the unfinished figure can be terminated and the system (in this case, the person) can become calm.

Berlin experiment

Bluma Ziegarnik's experiments on recall of uncompleted tasks and experiments on tension systems were carried out in the period 1924-26. The experiment involved 164 children and adults.

Two groups were given tasks and one of the groups was stopped during the experiment. Thereafter, all participants had to recall as much as possible of what had been done. It was found that work-satisfaction depended on three things: firstly, the need to complete the task; secondly, personal goals, and ambitions and willingness to please; and, thirdly, to do as the leader of the experiment said.

It turned out that those who did not have time to complete their tasks remembered much more of what had been done than those who could complete theirs.

The experiment continued and it turned out that the critical factor was not stress in itself, but that one was not allowed to complete the task. The explanation was that the energy that was mobilized remained, making it easier to recall the task.

The same is true for uncompleted things at work or in personal relationships. What is it that remains and troubles the mind?

Field theory in everyday life

Efforts to change existing organizations in business from stiff, rigid and hierarchical structures to organizations that are able to change are a matter of survival for many companies.

The fundamentals of field theory are used in organizational development. Everyone translates stimuli from their own frames of reference and perception. This means that some things are stimulating, while others are not. Content and framework are important - that is to say, what the message is about and who delivers it.

Learning arises from the perspective and experience that the individual or population has.

The pedagogy in the above "change cycle" can be described as follows:

- A practical experiment or exercise is carried out.
- During the exercise, a person can act as an observer.
- After the exercise, participants reflect on what happened. The observer communicates his views.
- The theoretical concepts can then be discussed and formulated in an idea that participants can encompass and stand for.

- Concepts and ideas are tested in new situations to see how they affect others and other things.
- The experience is included in a new cycle ...

Interdependence in groups results in the group becoming a dynamic entity. Removal of a member affects the whole group as well as the introduction of a new member.

Biology, Field and Network

General, complex adaptive systems and models taken from biology are becoming increasingly common in interpretative models of network organizations.

Social science research and social development are gradually becoming more and more process- and system-oriented. As a result, network theory is now a tool for understanding and explaining complex processes of social, organizations and change in which different types of networks interact with each other.

The holistic approach in network theory, that the whole is greater than the sum of its parts, is also part of the field theory. Work on network theory includes the study of processes. Instead of examining smaller and smaller parts, the wholes are studied and how they interact with each other.

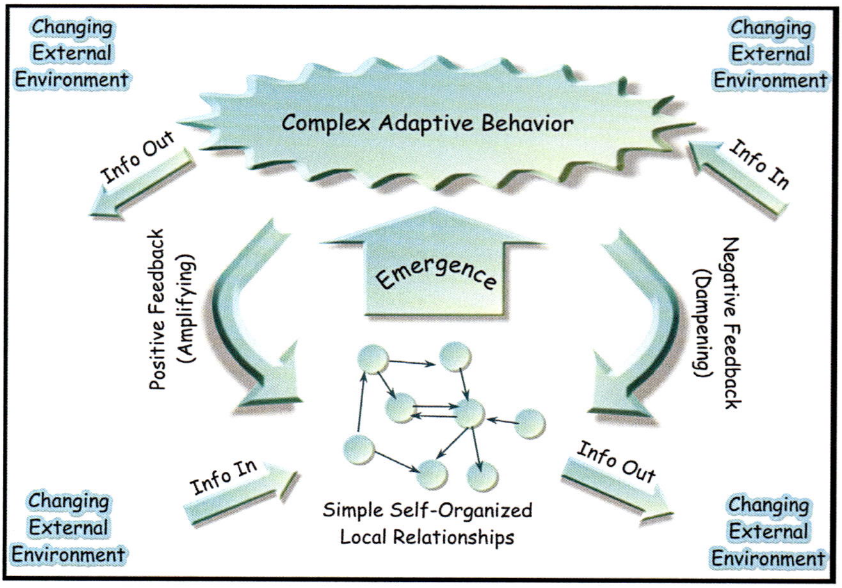

Different networks interact and influence each other

Complex network organizations

The Network Organization encourages work towards a common goal. It also encourages own initiative. On the other hand, it has the disadvantage of fuzzy decision-making, where responsibility and authority may be perceived as unclear. This, in itself, can cause stress since work and leisure blend together. Several studies indicate that network companies develop an ability to change "organically": that is to say, a built-in capability that exploits the power of, for example, "coaching" leadership. A genuine and fruitful interaction demands that the structures and people involved have very different obligations and rights than those that are most often encountered. Such enterprises are more flexible and the staff is involved in change process in a natural way.

Overall, it is usually said that employees in networking companies feel more involved. Employees of these companies are also more likely to embrace new technologies and have a greater willingness to relearn or adjust as a natural part of the work.

Fortune 1000 companies

"Top-performing companies concentrate on relationship-centric activities and growth while lower-performing companies focus on decreasing working capital, improving supply chain efficiently and spinning off non-core business."

..."More than two-thirds of top-performing companies focus their Organizations on meeting customer expectations and extending long-term customer relationships, a much higher percentage than among bottom-quartile companies...".

..."A model of success is merging that we call the Relationship-Centric Organization – a networked, agile and highly adaptive entity that transcends traditional boundaries as it develops deep and collaborative relationships internally as well as with customers, suppliers, alliance partners and increasingly, competitors...".

The quotations are from a study on "Fortune 1000 companies - Organization for Success in the 21st Century - The Relationship-Centric Organization" by Booz Allen Hamilton at the Kellog School of Management.

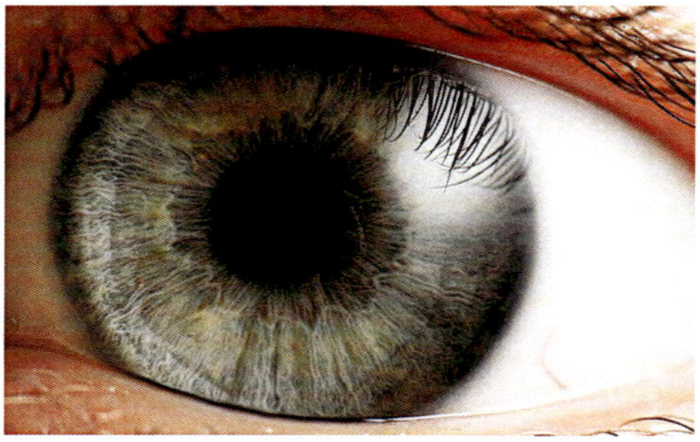

"Eagles Eye"; example of a network model

"Knowing who to turn to for what is ultimately the key to doing what you need to do quickly so you can go home to your family...

We have found social network analysis (SNA) – A set of tools for mapping important knowledge relationships between people or departments – to be particularly helpful for improving collaboration, knowledge creation and knowledge transfer in organizational settings... In this context, network analysis shows considerable promise for helping organizations handle a number of classic situations including:

- **Leadership selection** – who is central in the trust and respect network?
- **Task force selection** – how do we put together a team what is maximally connected throughout the organization?
- **Merger and acquisitions** – it's not just two cultures merging, it's two separate networks..."

The crisis that came after the economic crash of 2001 did not lead to any cutbacks at IBM, Cisco or Nokia, partly because of the strength of the network model, which creates robustness in the organization.

Field theory and network theory - a summary

Network theory and research into complex adaptive systems is an extension of Lewin's research on fields. According to Lewin, the prediction of behaviour must take into account the whole field, that is, all aspects of the person and the environment. Lewin argued that correct knowledge does not automatically lead to change; there is also a need to foster a climate that makes change possible. And it is important to understand the mechanisms that control this, based on the following important principles:

New steering methods, leadership and management structure

A minimum of critical rules is important. If organizations and companies set up detailed rules then these are circumvented if they do not fit in with the business. Lewin also pointed out how important it is for the democratic leaders to help develop new leaders. The leaders of network organizations trust the process.

Open interfaces and democratic organization

A company must have permeable boundaries and open up to the surrounding systems. When that happens, you get a continuous feedback from the surroundings and can correct errors in discrete steps. Companies must be able to observe their own development.

> *Culture, myths etc can make progress more or less impossible even if the organization is heading toward a disaster.*

Open systems, self-observation, and self-organizing system are field concepts that are applicable in Lewin's world. Sub-optimization, or at worst collapse, occurs when the company is struck by what is known as the "blind spot": the organization does not observe itself. Culture, myths, etc. make it impossible to stop development even if the organization is heading towards a disaster. This behaviour is reinforced in autocratic organizations, which Lewin also pointed out. The self-organization of open systems leads to development and adaptation. The organization is aware of its surroundings and reacts to stimuli from outside.

Flexible resource management and organization

Lewin argued that correct knowledge does not automatically lead to change; there is also a need to foster a climate that makes change possible. The company or organization, in the form of complex adaptive systems, will undergo crises, periods of chaos and confusion before the situation clears.

The theoretical aspects of this are described in Kurt Lewin's phase theory - "thaw" - "change" - "re-freezing" - which leads to normalization, and his concepts of feedback and self-observation. This process is facilitated by a flexible organizational structure.

Strategic work and goals

Common goals will not be reached through impassioned speeches, but as a result of a patient, long-term effort towards change. This can take time, often five to seven years. In this work, you cannot skip any steps. A democratic, steered organization, with open borders and clear leadership provides the best results. Common goals are also the prerequisite for the strategy work that moves companies forward and makes them competitive.

The concepts of Field Theory are mutually dependent when solving tasks: common destiny is associated with strategic management; power is the probability that an individual in a social relationship has his way, despite opposition from others, and authority is the probability that an order with a specific content is obeyed.

This can be achieved in different ways, through democratic, autocratic or hierarchical models. Both proponents and network field-theorists realize that the democratic or organic organization or company, leads to faster and more enduring survival strategies if one takes into account the issue of power.

Built-in willingness to change - versus power

In network theory there is the realization that the whole is greater than the sum of its parts. This holistic approach is part of field theory. Management receives a changed role in a network organization and the employees' initiative is extremely important. A cultural openness is worth striving for since you are in an international arena. It takes a long time to change an organization and it undergoes three primary stages as mentioned earlier, none of which can be skipped. Leaders who can drive the progress of change towards an "organic" plane give their companies a competitive edge.

A learning organization takes advantage of employees' knowledge and skills in order to become more competitive. The importance of being competitive is, of course, obvious. The increased competitiveness affects stakeholders, including customers, employees and shareholders. For customers this means, for example, that they get a better product. In addition to increased self-esteem, the employees get an excellent opportunity to increase their market value by

The ability to change and adapt gives a competitive advantage

constant improvement in knowledge and skills. From the shareholders' point of view, it means that the company reduces its costs and thereby increases profits. The increase in knowledge is an asset that owners see in the balance sheet. The constant development and adaptation of the company to the outside world improves security for the future and for all stakeholders.

A genuine and fruitful interaction demands that the structures and people involved have very different obligations and rights than those that are most often encountered today.

The ability to transform businesses to enable them to change organically has become very important, and it seems that networking organizations have the greatest potential when the needs of democracy are taken into account. Closed systems can therefore only survive by opening up and interacting with their surroundings.

Sequential or cyclic organization theories

There are really two main approaches within group development theory. One is a **sequential process**. This means that the sequential cycle is constantly interrupted and the group returns to previous core issues and themes in the process. This means that the groups go from A to B and then to C, in a given order.

The other approach is a **recurring, repetitive, cyclic process** that can also behave chaotically. In this case, Kurt Lewin's research seems to be far-sighted and visionary in that he argued that groups and systems are in constant motion. There are no fixed, sequential steps or frameworks that determine how a group or organization can be developed. Disruption of development occurs frequently and in each phase. The change is constant. The only thing that is constant is the chaos - not control.

FIRO-model

FIRO stands for Fundamental Interpersonal Relations Orientation and was presented by Will Schutz (1925-2002) in 1958. It was developed in the context of the war in Korea where Schutz examined how groups with equally qualified personnel and with the same information could act so differently. He divided the groups' development into three stages: inclusion (the associated phase), control (control phase) and affection/openness (open phase). Schutz found that the differences in efficiency between groups were due to the working relations within them and the members' way of communicating.

Nowadays this theory can be seen as sequential (see above), in contrast to Lewin's view of continuous processes and changing mindsets.

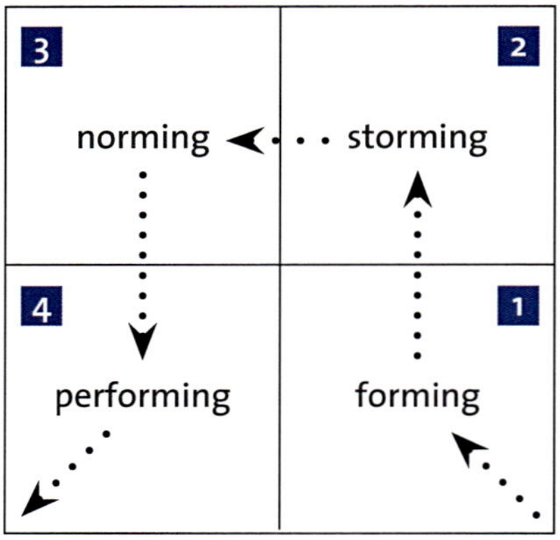

Forming, Storming, Norming, Performing

This four-stage model was developed by Bruce Tuckman in 1965 (in 1970 he added a fifth stage - adjourning). Tuckman not only took note of the group's development, but also described how the leader must gradually change his leadership style depending on the group's development.

It was a style that started with military-style 'forceful instruction' then coaching leadership, a participating leadership and, finally, a delegating leadership. In the final stages of 1970, Tuckman also included the step where the leader should step down.

Nowadays this model is regarded to be a sequential approach, but it has the advantage of considering both the group and leaders.

BARUCH LEVINE'S MODEL

Baruch Levine developed a group theory which interweaves the two directions, sequential and cyclical. He speaks of four stages:

1. Parallel phase
2. Including phase
3. Common phase (the group is a "we")
4. Concluding phase

Recurrent themes are apparent in these phases according to Levine. These themes must be solved to be able to move to the next phase.
Crises of different types are also in constant motion: authority crisis (between group members and leader), intimacy crisis (between group members) and separation crisis (when the group is terminated or changed by new members being included or old ones leaving).

There are other dimensions in the crises and the group's themes, including:

- The strength of the feelings that exist in every crisis theme (named for affective polarity).
- Codes of conduct and norms of the group.
- The role of the group as a whole, and those of individual team members. The role that is accepted by the group and group member.
- Group members' expectations for the group - what everyone wants out of joining the group
- Which relationships already exist when the group starts (couple, family, friendships ...).
- Power Relationships.
- Conflict management methods and approaches.
- Comfort and security for everyone in the group.
- Group Control versus freedom - how the leadership team controls the group, how much the group allows leadership to control them, and how much control the members have over each other.
- The goals of the group and individual.

The group thus goes through different sequences but there are recurrent crises and themes. Levine takes into account the positions of the leader and the group members and what is required of them to ensure that the team functions properly.

Barush Levine Model:

Kurt Lewin's field theory is still a powerful tool in the analysis of phenomena in the development of organizations towards adaptive complex systems that are able to adjust to the changing reality of globalization.

Transforming businesses in the direction of an organic capacity for change is high up on the strategic agenda. Everyone recognizes the value, but few are able to implement changes. Therefore, the capacity to change is a competitive advantage that can be measured, analyzed, acquired, built and lost.

The network Organization appears to have a great potential for long-term survival. Closed systems can only survive by opening up and interacting with the surroundings. An approach employing field theory can certainly be of value in the change process.

But, as in other processes of change, companies and organizations as complex adaptive systems also undergo crises, periods of chaos and confusion before clarity is achieved. It takes time for an organization to become self-sustaining.

Success for survivors

The leader who can bring the ability to change to an "organic" plan gives their company a competitive advantage. One CEO described this as follows: "It is as if the employees have become free. They think that it's fun, exciting. It has prompted some to liven up, but of course not all ... "

Reference literature chapter 2.

Please find below books and references applicable to the text. The English title has been inserted when found. When not found, the title is left in its original language (English translation in brackets), for the reader interested to find other texts by the same author.

Allvin M, Aronsson G, Hagström T, Johansson G, Lundberg U, Skärstrand E (1998) *(Work without borders or work with new borders, part of study), Gränslöst arbete eller arbetets nya gränser,* Arbetslivsinstitutet, Sweden, Arbete och Hälsa (Work and Health) 1998:21

Bredal D (editor) *(My transposition. Me and my job: how survive a business world in constant change), Min omstilling. Jeg og jobben: hvordan overleve et naeringsliv i konstant forandring.* Norway, Wigestrand Forlag AS

Capra F (2002) *The hidden connections. Integrating the biological, cognitive and social dimensions of life into a science of sustainability,* New York, Doubleday Random House

Capra F (1975) *The Tao of Physics,* USA Random House

Clipping III J H (1999) *The Biology of business. Decoding the laws of enterprise,* San Fransisco, Jossey-Bass

Englund G (1996) *What life was like on the banks of the Nile: Egypt 3050-30 BC.* Time Life Books

Gilad B (1996) B*usiness Blindspots – replacing myths, beliefs and assumptions with market realities.* Calne, Wiltshire, Infonortics Ltd

Granér R (1991) *(The working team. The psychology of the professional team.), Arbetsgruppen. Den professionella gruppens psykologi,* Lund/Sweden, Studentlitteratur

Hanson P, Voss C (1999) *Taylor to Toyota to Technology Manufacturing, article from Engineering page 11-14* (February)

Hopcke R (1997) *There are no accidents – synchronicity and the stories of our lives,* New York, Riverhead Books

Levine B (1979) *Group psychotherapy, practice and development,* New York, Prentice-Hall Inc

Lewin K (1951) *F ield theory in social science; selected theoretical papers. D. Cartwright (ed.),* New York, Harper & Row

Lewin K (1943/1997) *Defining the F ield at a Given Time. Republished in Resolving Social Conflicts & F ield Theory in Social Science.* Washington DC, American Psychological Association

Luft J, Ingham H (1955) *The Johari window, a graphic model of interpersonal awareness, proceedings of the western training laboratory in group development*, Los Angeles: UCLA
Marrow A (1969/1984) *The practical theorist: The life and work of Kurt Lewin*, New York, Basic Books
Mazur E (1995) *The Ziegarnik effect and the concept of unfinished business in gestalt therapy*, article in British Gestalt Journal, volume 5, no 1
Menckel E, Österblom L (2000) *(Health improvement processes in the workplace. About leadership, resources and empowerment), Hälsofrämjande processer på arbetsplatsen. Om ledarskap, resurser och egen kraft*, Stockholm, Arbetslivsinstitutet
Nilsson L (redaktör) (1998) *(Network companies – innovative, flexible and virtual), Nätverksföretaget – innovativt, flexibelt och virtuellt*, Sveriges Tekniska Attachéer (The technical attachées, Sweden)
Nordström K, Ridderstråle J (2000) *Funky Business Forever – How to Enjoy Capitalism*, Stockholm/Sweden, Bookhouse Publishing
Raymond E (1999) *The cathedral and the bazaar. Musing on Linux and Open Source by an accidental revolutionary*. Sebastopol/Canada, O'Reilly Media
Sarv H (1993) *(Behind success – change management in companies), Bakom framsteg - om förändringsarbete i företag*, Isberg och Sarv AB
Sherman H, Schultz R (1999) *Open boundaries Creating business innovation through complexity*, Santa Fe, Center for emergent strategies
Schutz W (1966) *FIRO: A Three-Dimensional Theory of Interpersonal Behavior*, Science and Behavior Books
Svedberg L (2006) *Group-psychology – about groups, organizations and leadership*, Earbooks
Tuckman B (1965/2001) *Developmental sequence in small groups*. The article was reprinted in Group Facilitation - a research and applications Journal, no 3
Uddenberg N (1993) *(An animal among others? Biology and man's belief of his place in nature), Ett djur bland alla andra? Biologin och människans uppfattning av sin plats i naturen*, Nora, Nya Doxa
Whitaker D, Whitaker G (1997) *Kurt Lewin; His dynamic and force field models in conteimporary research, management and practice.* Onsala, Samarbetsdynamik
Wolinsky S (1993) *Quantum Consciousness – the Guide to Experiencing Quantum Psychology*, Bramble Books
Wilber K (1996) *A Brief History of Everything*, Shambhala. Boston

What are they doing? A Swede will just know

PERCEPTION

LEARNING STARTS IN THE CRADLE and continues throughout life: at school, at work, through friends and media, etc. Some learning will already occur in the womb through hearing and nutrition; more learning comes with upbringing, siblings, or society. In the beginning, all learning takes place more or less sub-consciously. Eventually, learning becomes more tangible and evolves into a more conscious process.

KEYWORDS CHAPTER 3.
- Introject and projection (learning, interpretation)
- Be selected or deselected
- Authorities, adaptation or not

Even in adulthood, learning occurs on a subtle plane. Media, culture and group-identity play a major role. A good example would be the war in Iraq. Which view has the "world" about the war and about the Americans? Whose fault is that? What 'should' you, I, or our friends think in order to fit in? Media reports provide one picture. CNN and travel in the United States give another. Internet News from the Middle East provides a third. Well, how is each and every person affected and to what extent? From which viewpoint is the world considered and interpreted?

This chapter on perception describes how human experience is made intelligible. And that the "truth" for one person may just as well be "false" or be given a different interpretation by another.

INTROJECT = To incorporate (characteristics of a person or object) into one's own psyche unconsciously

The versatility of the Saga

The emperor was a vain man, in addition to having power and glory in his kingdom. Therefore, he hired the most famous tailors to sew his clothes. One day a new pair of tailors came to town. They said they had the most thin, delicate, wonderful fabrics to sew clothes that only suited an emperor. Yes, the fabrics were so thin that they were practically invisible, except for those lucky few who had the gift to see them in all their glory. The emperor immediately ordered a variety of garments to be sewn up. After a few weeks it was time to try them. The tailors helped the emperor to try the clothes, and exclaimed loudly how beautiful, strong, and perfect the emperor looked in the clothes. Yes, only a disloyal subject would dare say otherwise. So the emperor delighted in seeing himself so honoured - this of course was fantastic! And of all the Emperor's advisors, no one dared say other than that these clothes really suited their emperor and ruler - although of course the fabrics seemed very, very thin.

Eventually it was time for the emperor to show himself in the city, to all his subjects. He put on his new clothes and walked proudly out. And all the subjects said Aaaaaah, and Ohhhhhh, for they knew that only disloyal subjects would say anything else. But there was a little boy who saw the emperor for the first time. And he had not understood anything about the commandment of loyalty and how a subject should behave towards those in power. So the boy said: "But the emperor doesn't have any clothes on. He is naked! "The people began to mutter ... When the muttering could no longer be traced to a single person, the masses dared utter the words: "He's naked - he has no clothes on!" (Freely translated from Hans Christian Andersen, The Emperor's New Clothes)

Moral of the story

The story can continue to be a fairy tale only for children. Someone must have included the tale in the storybooks once upon a time. And a story book, we have learned from an early age, is for adults to read aloud to their children, and maybe tell the children how the story can be interpreted. The language has its subtitles and the adult reader makes interpretations based on their own knowledge and experience.

"Think that the emperor didn't realise that he was naked! How embarrassing to go out among a bunch of people and be completely without clothes!" The child's view would obviously be confirmed by their parents. Mum's or Dad's opinion puts itself into the child's consciousness as an unconscious truth. The child now knows that to show them self naked so that people can see is shameful. And this moral, from an innocent fairytale, can follow the child for years to come. The adult can, of course, have other opinions...

Rulers and the masses

What is it that prevents a whole group of people from spontaneously daring to challenge the power of one person? What is it that makes no adult dare to step out of the group and resist peer pressure - and only the boy dares? This 'emperor-and-the-great-masses' behaviour can occur in any organization. Each individual has, at some point, learned how characters are to be interpreted, words are to be understood, and how their own behaviour can be rewarded or punished. If the ruler / Director / CEO / emperor is lucky then most of the employees or subjects understand the organization's symbols and language. They also understand the unspoken rules, about what is permitted or prohibited, that are in the corporate culture.

If those in power are unlucky then there is a gap between what the manager wants and how employees interpret the manager's intentions. An order is not executed as it should. Not because the employee does not want to, but often because he does not actually understand, or does not dare ask.

The president or managing director can act with natural authority only when the organization manages to convey what the company culture really stands for, and ensures that most employees understand the culture in the same way. The people can rally around their leader or emperor and the task they have to fulfil.

Price of adaptation

The great masses are doing what they're told and do not question. They cannot help think that the authorities know what is best for them. They dare not saw off the branch they sit on - to perhaps be fired for an "improper" question. Why should they risk their income and social status when it is so much easier to disappear into the silent masses? It might feel better to just lay low. Perhaps some can consider talking on the sly in the coffee room about what feels wrong, but they would never be likely to summon up the courage to talk to the person who can really change things.

Through early experience, all too many know how it feels to have been bullied, to have been rejected from the group. It's cold to stand alone and feel like an outsider. Many will do almost anything to remain in a group and be accepted. It may feel better to blame everything on others and not take responsibility for one self - sometimes consciously, but often unconsciously. The previously bullied becomes the bully - an adult bully.

Lead or be led (Pieter Bruegel the Elder 1527-1569 - Parable of the blind

Lead or be led

To become conscious about one's own way of looking at life can make it possible to break old patterns. It can be a painful process to dare to look at life in a new way. The consequences can almost seem too tough. It does, however, offer an opening and opportunity to begin to lead one self - from a previous position of being led.

And what about in the organization, and the manager? Trust is something that must constantly be won. Daring to be aware of what makes people afraid, or what can strengthen trust, is a step towards changing the atmosphere at work - to become the workplace where everyone understands that conversation and contestation are allowed. This can be acceptable only up to the point where a decision has been made and is in force. After that the organization must adapt to the decision - to accept the situation. If this is impossible for an individual then there is rarely any other option than to quit. Conducting guerrilla warfare in the workplace is seldom a way to drive the business forward.

So many fearful

What punishment awaited advisors and subjects of the emperor's kingdom if they disagreed with the emperor? And why was it that, instead of firing the tailors, the emperor was so keen to believe what they said? What was the Emperor most afraid of himself? Even he was a product of the society which gave birth to him. Even he had received his own images of what was important and unimportant.

If an emperor (or president, managing director, or prime minister) is afraid himself, how can those in the surroundings be anything but afraid? If those ruling have a habit from way back of casting the blame on others, think how easy it is for their subjects and co-workers to do the same. We act, as you know, not like mum or dad say, we should, but rather as they do.

Who are you?

Who do you identify yourself with when you read the story of The Emperor's New Clothes? The boy? Are you really being honest? Could you, would you, dare to take the boy's role in larger groups at work? Or does it feel still better to be a part of the masses? Or maybe the emperor?

Nudity is nudity, or ...

What one chooses to see and relate to in everyday life, including working life, depends on how the world and the everyday life of its people, symbols, colours and features are perceived. It has something to do with learning, with memory and its storage capacity, and how well we sharpen the senses.

- A head injury means life in itself looks different.
- As does a problem with vision.
- A person from the United States also looks differently upon, for example, leadership and loyalty than someone from Uganda, India, China or Sweden.

Each person is unique. And we have our individual, unique way of relating to life: we have learned to deal with reality, through our own interpretations, in order to make life meaningful, understandable and bearable.

Perception in a historical perspective

Perception research has involved many and for several thousand years. It has been interesting to examine how shape, colour, sound, light and sensation are perceived. The word 'percept' comes from the constructivist school in the 1940s, which argued that humans from different, perhaps contradictory, sensory inputs construct 'percept' based on previous experience.

Recent research has sought to understand how people make their own reality comprehensible. In other words, how man himself from his early childhood, with or without the help of adults, has made his world tolerable to live in, with all the norms and values associated with it. The research in experimental perception began in earnest during the first half of the 1800's, inspired by the developments in philosophy. Two distinct branches of perception research developed during the mid 1800's.

The first built on an introspection method in which trained observers tried to study their own reactions and objectively analyze the components, such as how they reacted to a particular piece of music. Instead of concentrating on what caused the feeling they would describe how it felt. The methods are still used today to study certain cognitive processes.

The second is psychophysics, which involves looking at how our inner experiences are related to the physical characteristics that generate these experiences.

PSYCHOPHYSICS
How much heavier do we think that the shopping bag is when it contains two kilograms of potatoes compared to when it contains only one kilogram? How much brighter do we think that it will be in a room when one light bulb is exchanged for two? If a person can barely perceive a difference of 12 grams between two weights when one weight is 200 grams, then what is the approximate difference, compared to 12 g, that he or she can perceive if one weight is 400 g?

Additional screening is done, consciously or unconsciously, by taking in a selection of information and interpreting it in a personal way. The selection and interpretation is determined by both external and internal factors. External factors include intensity, size, contrast and frequency, while internal factors may be needs, feelings, expectations and past experiences. Even the level of alertness affects perception and attention.

- **Perception** = experiences that are understandable.
- **Experiences** = the immediate experience generated by the stimuli that affect our five (or six?) senses.
- **Cognition** = include intake, storage, preparation and use of information. Learning and memory will often be associated with cognition.

The western world's short history of perception

Empiricism 1850-1900	Experiences associated with learning. Sense of "deep", for example, cannot be perceived by a newborn. This perception is learned gradually.
Gestalt Psychology 1925 -	To see the things that organized the whole structure more than as separate, isolated islands. The whole is greater than the sum of its parts. The researchers of the day are still interested in what the original Gestalt psychologists concluded.
Behaviourism 1930-1960	Emphasizes objective descriptions of how an organism behaves. More interest in environmental determinants of behaviour than on mental processes. The Early behaviourists believed that thoughts were unnecessary, that man is probably not thinking what she reads, but rather speaking for herself, but so quietly that no one hears.
Cognition 1956 -	It consists of several specializations: psychology, philosophy, artificial intelligence, language teaching, anthropology, and neurology.
Direct Perception 1960's - and 1970's	Argues that man picks up information that directly specifies the world as a perceptual world in conformity with the outside world.
Information Process 1980 -	Psychological processes are identified which are linked together according to specific information flows (e.g. experiences pass through "short-term memory" and then "long-term memory" ...).

Birds and humans see the world differently

The eyes of flies and humans are built quite differently and therefore we do not perceive the world in the same way. The bird's eyes are on either side of the head, which also gives a different view of the world than ours. The same applies to cats and dogs.

Even the mind seriously affects experiences of the world. So, who has the right or wrong perception of the outside world? Sometimes even the real stimuli produce anomalous perceptions. This is about illusions or delusions.

Unlike the illusion, hallucination is entirely a creation of the individual's own brain, which produces self-stimuli that are perceived and give a perception in the absence of stimuli from the environment. Hallucinations can "strike" vision, hearing or other senses.

Interpret through the sixth sense

Sixth sense, or intuition ... How real is it?

No one has yet been able to really explain how someone can 'have the feeling' that something will go well or not, or whether there will be thunder. Perhaps this is as real or unreal as anything else that cannot be explained today. What is really the 'spark of life' or 'love'? But even if none of this can be explained, most people declare that "it's there" and have experienced it personally.

The ancient Greeks took up a phenomenon that they called the daimon (Greek for fate). We could perhaps call it the "visible soul" or some kind of tangible intuition. Daimons could be good or evil spirits, who showed humans the way in life. At that time, this was something that "was". When the Daimon was described in positive terms, it was a spiritual being that helped people in life, showing them where they can go without being harmed. People chose whether or not to listen to these Daimons, just as people today can choose whether or not to allow intuition or "sixth sense" to lead them.

A more scientific way to understand the sixth sense is to put it in the context of the brain and neurotransmitters. These transmit signals between cells and ensure that a cell reacts in a certain way by using the so-called endorphins and other small molecules. Today we know that endorphins not only relieve pain - they seem to be able to redirect the entire nervous system by increasing and decreasing brain activity so that the mind and body are kept in balance. This suggests that endorphins could constitute the sixth sense.

Aristotle's holistic view

Aristotle (384-322 BC) could not, as his teacher Plato did, see the mind and body as different entities. He saw, instead, that each needed the other and must be viewed as a whole. Entities are in constant change and constant motion, yet are wholes with their parts. He also said that the way of learning comes from experimentation and practice.

Aristotle tested ideas

Gestalt psychologists' holism

The term "figure" was originally coined by the Austrian *Christian von Ehrenfels* (1859-1932). For him, a figure constituted a form of a natural whole, which took shape when the field was organized (see also Chapter 2, Field Theory).

In his view, the scientific revolution was the observation that it is not the

THE WHOLE AND THE CONCLUSION
"The whole precedes the parts. The main characteristics of Gestalt formation are the functions of the organism and also individual movements towards the conclusion in order to reach a point of balance ".

Gestalt Psychology

analysis of the underlying elements that provides knowledge. He argued that a refined analysis of the parts not only fails, but even makes it impossible to learn more. Instead, it is man's own consciousness that forms the wholes, or "figures" (German "gestalten"). Psychologists from The Berlin School of Gestalt Psychology continued Ehrenfel's research.

The three most famous gestalt psychologists were *Max Wertheimer* (1880-1943), *Kurt Koffka* (1886-1941) and *Wolfgang Köhler* (1887-1967). But it was only when *Kurt Lewin* (1890-1947) formulated his concept that behaviour is a function of personality in relation to its surroundings that questions were answered. In other words, is it the individual's own interests, another person's input, or something else in the surroundings that organises entities in the field.

Create equality

A number of areas from the age of the gestalt psychologists live on in research and practice:

1. The law of how people want to group things (proximity, similarity, continuation, termination)
2. The law of discernment
3. Figure and Background
4. The wholes compared to the parts

'Gestalt Psychology' and 'gestalt therapy' are not the same thing. Gestalt psychologists were scientists who studied man's way to "take in" impressions while Gestalt therapists embraced elements of this research in its treatment of people, as a form of psychotherapy.

Grouping for understanding and meaning

It is natural to look for patterns in order to make sense of everything that happens and is done. The brain cannot accept that things just exist. The brain is looking instead for ways to group the data.

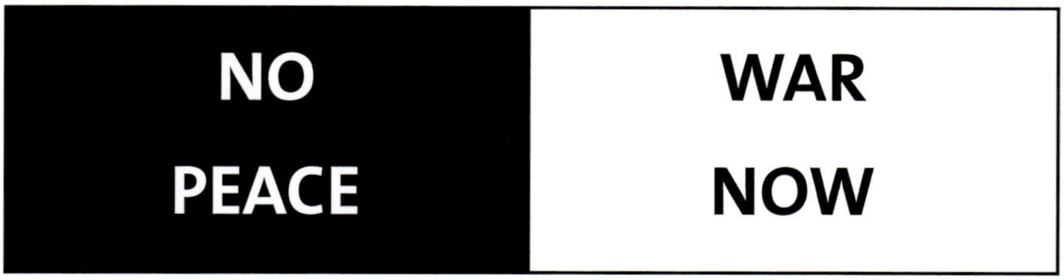

Make sense through row, column or colour

In a similar way, it is possible to think about what is seen at a restaurant. Are there a lot of women or a lot of men? Is there someone or something that "sticks out", e.g. a person with special clothes, or a different skin colour? So, how does each person's brain choose to group information that lies in front of them?

Positive closure

Every salesperson knows how important it is to achieve 'closure' to clinch a deal. Gestalt psychologists claimed that, in a similar way, the person wishes to finish everything before proceeding further (Kurt Lewin and Bluma Ziegarnik researched further on this - see Chapter 2, Field Theory).

The brain also wants to make closure. For example, the brain wants to finish a tune that it has noted the start of. Sing "Twinkle, Twinkle Little Star", and stop after a couple of tones. What happens to you or those who may be listening? Continue the song in silence, or sing out loud. The signature tunes of radio programs work in a similar way in that they associate with the program to be sent now or later.

In the dialogue method, closure is achieved in a different way. It envisages that there are unfinished phenomena (German: Gestalten) from childhood, or youth, which still hang on in the meeting with others and which affect the person negatively here and now. In dialogue, it is possible to find a way to these (often unconscious) memories, make the subject aware of them here and now, and then be able to finish them in a 'mature' - or at least conscious - manner.

UNDERSTANDABLE YET INCOMPREHENSIBLE

Airoccdng to a rseea-hecrr at Cbadmrige Ustvneiriy, it dsoen't matetr in waht oerdr the ltretes in a wrod are, the olny iaornmptt thnig is taht the frist and lsat letetr be at the rhigt plcae. The rset can be a ttaol mses and you can siltl raed it wthiout perlobm. This is bacseue the haumn mind deos not raed evrey letter by ilestf but the wrod as a wlhoe.

The brain can build wholes even if the text is, in fact, incomprehensible.

First impression

Gestalt psychologists believed that understanding comes when the brain experiences and meets a minimum of resistance. This is what every advertiser strives to achieve with a trademark.

Unconscious organization into wholes (or "gestalten") also occurs in social contexts. People are catalogued by external similarities, which often turn into stereotypes that are usually oversimplified, value-laden beliefs about people. One could say that humans each have within them their own catalogue of descriptions of people: the typical Dane, the typical Finn, or the typical Italian. We also have a picture of what the good, the bad and the typical culprits look like.

The image is dependent on experience, knowledge, or lack of knowledge, prejudices or expectations. In addition to assessing people by stereotypes there is also the influence by the so-called "halo effect", i.e. the tendency to make an overall assessment of a person on the basis of a single property.

The first impression of a person is therefore very important. A positive impression the first time stays, as does a negative impression. The ability to catalogue and systematize in this way orders things in the senses and it becomes easier to take in the whole picture. But it also means that it is easy to make mistakes.

Figure and Background

The Danish psychologist *Edgar Rubin* (1886-1951) was the first to seek to clarify what constitutes the figure, in contrast to the background - in other words, what, in each context, is quite clear, or important in contrast to what is barely perceptible in the background. Figure, in this perspective, can be the summary or key point in a discussion, one idea which stands out among a number of ideas, or the most obvious aspect of a relationship. Rubin came to the following conclusions:

What forms figure? What forms background?

- The figure has a clear form.
- The background appears to continue behind the forming shape.
- The figure appears to be near us (physically or mentally in the room).
- The figure is more dominant and impressive than the background.

The difficulty is in handling figures where you can see several things at once, depending on where you focus.

In everyday life, figure and background become important, for example, when someone tells a friend about a book they have read. How can the book be summarized in a fun and compelling way? What creates the figure is the sequence that the reader experienced as moving the story forward.

The figure Pablo Picasso

What forms the figure by the name of 'Pablo Picasso'? That depends on what everyone knows, thinks or believes. He produces, perhaps, the figure 'unknown'? Or is he just a man with a common first name and an uncommon surname?

Or a comedian ...? Author ...? Artist...? Someone might think that the figure is that he was married several times. Another is that he was religious.

Surrounding all these figures (giving different reactions in the listener) is a background. This might include one's own upbringing, or own values around religion or marriage. The background can also be a review of one of his paintings and so on.

The conclusion is that "reality" will vary, depending on who takes up the figure, and pushes everything else into the background. In a conversation between two or more people one can only hope that everyone says and thinks in the same way. In business coaching, one of the main tasks of the coach or manager is to ensure that this is, in fact, the case.

Humans tend to choose a very small amount of sensory data from the environment (the perceptual field) to concentrate on at any given moment. Anything that is directed towards us can be selected to be 'figurative'. This figure appears in front of all other sensory data, causing them to move back into the background. One example is the mingle party where everyone is talking at once but two people still manage to have their own conversation. The figure is this conversation, and mingling gossip forms the background.

The same thing happens when the focus is placed on a thought or a memory. Everything else disappears into the background. Only one figure is clearly perceived at a time. If several figures are perceived at the same time then they lose clarity and sharpness. The perceptive field becomes confused and unclear.

Choice of Figure

The person leading the meeting has the right to choose what the 'figure' should be. What happens to the figure in the meeting room when the director talks about the company's future ventures, while mobile phones beep and people both read and reply to text messages and emails?

How many legs does the elephant have?

Sometimes it seems that everyone is always choosing what should be in focus and what should have lower priority. In addition, certain gaps are filled in to match with preconceived ideas and experiences.

This is the way reality is constructed, based on past experience. Life would be extremely difficult if we couldn't take anything for granted; that is, if each day would require meticulous examination of shoe laces, the lock on the outside door, or the functioning of the toothbrush.

The bicycle and the working group

"The whole is always greater than the sum of its parts", says the person with a holistic view. In the example of the bicycle, the question is obviously how the user views his bicycle. Is he a repairman who needs individual parts to repair another bicycle? Or is he a cyclist who wants to ride into the countryside? Take apart one bicycle and the result is a pile of bicycle parts wheels, spokes, handlebars, tires, saddle, chain, etc.

All these elements, when combined, actually form the sum of all the parts, but they can scarcely have any function in themselves. It is only when all the parts are put together again and the bicycle is complete and functioning that a whole or function arises. The whole is then greater than the sum of its parts. It is often the same with the working group. The group consists of several individuals who each have his or her own responsibility. It is only when they gather in a common task, or strategy, or working platform that the group as a whole can reach the team's goals. Their surroundings consider them to be a complete group ("they seem to be a good team"). Individuals who only work according to their own personal agenda lead to a sub-optimization of resources.

Phenomena and data without interpretation

Previously we have considered that man creates a meaning and understanding of life by making use of knowledge and life experience. By putting people or events in one's own frames of reference one is continuously making personal interpretations of the world. Of course, this is a survival strategy that has been necessary for man over millennia. But unthinking interpretation of surroundings for oneself and others can cause problems.

The phenomenological research method can be used to slow down these hasty interpretations, even in everyday life. This method originates from *Edmund Husserl* (1859-1938). His view was that philosophy should not study the world scientifically, but should consider the individual - from the inside, including awareness and its structure, and how it is that things and experiences present themselves to the consciousness.

He pointed out that awareness is always awareness of something. Awareness is therefore referred to reality in an attempt to translate this reality in a way that is meaningful to the individual. He said that "we always experience something in some way". He worked with so-called phenomenological reduction, Epoch, or what in English is called "bracketing" (to put in brackets). What is perceived should be merely pure "phenomenon", one's purified mind or purified experience.

Nowadays, there is a recognized phenomenological research methodology. A phenomenological approach is useful even in ordinary conversation and in business coaching, as a way of seeing the data and avoiding personal interpretation. Even putting events, people or experiences 'in brackets' can be an effective way to focus, returning to what was put in brackets later.

Teaching and learning

Two schools of thought will be studied in detail in this section. Our ambition is to give the thought process the energy to consider how it can improve learning and also contribute to help people to adequately interpret what is seen, heard, felt and experienced by the individual and the group.

Learning is considered to be a process whereby the individual acquires knowledge by a variety of methods. Often, the individual is motivated by the need to pass exams, which then leads to some form of grade. Many argue that this is superficial learning that does not help the individual to incorporate the knowledge so that it can be used practically in conversation and action.

Learning, however, is the process whereby the individual connects the knowledge to past experience and thus can use this knowledge practically in conversation and action. For this process to occur, the individual must be motivated to work with and understand the exercises, experiments and materials in question.

Wise as an owl with the memory of an elephant

There are different learning methods within psychology:

- When an individual understands the link between cause and effect then this is called the probability of learning.
- Learning by imitating others is called imitation learning.
- When people learn through sudden insight (the bits of the puzzle fall into place), it is called insight learning.
- And people can also learn through trial and error.

Jean Piaget

Jean Piaget (1896-1980) was a researcher in the cognitive school. He was interested in how people develop their sense of reality and their thinking. Piaget was a biologist and translated biological models to intellectual development.

Jean Piaget

He believed that humans and animals must constantly adapt to their surroundings. He called this process adaptation, similar to the biological term. Adaptation consists of assimilation and accommodation. One assimilates, without any clear structure, an experience and moulds it together with earlier experiences. Accommodation has occurred when people change their old behaviour based on new experience. The individual has learned something and adapted. This process is part of human survival.

Piaget believed that children develop in fixed steps in which abstract thinking, for example, was linked to the final developmental phase from 12 years and older (towards the end of his life, Piaget changed his mind about this). He argued that child development is largely universal, that the process goes at the same pace for all children throughout the world regardless of their social environment.

Man steers herself through words.

The mental processes become conditional after having been unconditional.

From reflexes man has reached reflection and conscious action.

From being a victim of circumstances to being the creator of the conditions.

Necessity may become freedom.
... argued Vygotsky!

Lev Vygotsky

Lev Vygotsky

Another great figure in psychology, the psychologist and Russian, **Lev Vygotsky** (1896-1934), opposed much that Piaget stood for. Vygotsky argued, inter alia, that the child's development is completely dependent on the cultural and social situation that he or she grows up in. He studied the development of language and how it affected the individual's intellectual development. In connection with research in Uzbeckistan in the 30's he found that farmers who had not had the opportunity to develop their language had greater difficulty in making use of abstract concepts.

According to Vygotsky, the child's language development, and thus the child's intellect, requires the presence of adults who are interested and willing to supervise the child.

Supervisors should set requirements and challenges that children can manage by pushing themselves and testing their ability. The adult should arouse interest by asking questions without providing the solution. The adult must also provide feedback. Knowledgeable and experienced people are important role models for social and cultural development.

Vygotsky, like Karl Marx, took the stance that by changing the world man changes himself. The tools of materialistic production cannot serve human thought the same way as the tool's of social connections and language.

> *"The idea always represents a whole which is far more extensive than the individual word. "*
>
> Quote from Lev Vygotsky

Do not take adults at their word

Do not believe unreservedly in everything that is said, especially when so-called authorities claim something with great emphasis. Let the warning bells ring!

These opening words may be true for both Piaget and Vygotsky. Children might hear the words but they cannot put the words into the same frame of reference, and thereby give them true meaning as adults do. There are those, however, who believe that the same is true for adults. Do not think you understand what is being said just because it sounds intelligible. You have to check your understanding.

A step in the learning process can lead to 100 steps in development according to both Vygotsky and Gestalt psychologist Koffka. This is a more positive approach than to believe that learning does not give more than just what is learned. Or that a person of a certain age can only take in what just Authorities say that the person is mature enough to comprehend.

That would mean that anyone who trains spinning in addition to cycling will also gain insight into training, anatomy and that the body needs more than pizza and beer to cope. And it can mean that a 20-year-old can reflect on things that a 50-year old might not manage, regardless of what the actual human development steps "should" be.

Language subtitles

Lev Vygotsky was talking about a linguistic holism. A meaningful sentence, expressed by a living person, always has a subtitle, argued Vygotsky. So there is always something beneath the language, a hidden meaning. The reason may be that the idea is closer to the feeling. Thus, that beyond every thought there is an emotional-volitional context.

Do not think that anyone who takes a long time to formulate what they mean is a slow thinker. The thought does not dress itself in words but rather realizes itself in words. It means that behind the words there may be thoughts that are not expressed or understood.

TO BELIEVE OR NOT BELIEVE IN THE WORDS BETWEEN THE LINES

"In our company we strive for complete transparency between management and working groups ".

"The staff is the company's most important resource."

"Once we used benchmarking, we see that the positioning strategy is completely right and that we will exceed the objectives established in the scenario for the future..."

"If we are to understand what someone else says then it is not enough to merely understand the words, even their thoughts must be understood. But even an understanding of the idea, without understanding its motive, is incomplete", said Vygotsky.

If something sounds somewhat "fuzzy" it is everyone's responsibility to try to ensure that word and thought are consistent for both parties. The idea might be crystal clear for the sender, but if the words have not fully communicated it then the receiver will remain uncertain.

Language Box

Vygotsky suggested several tools to help teachers and parents. And these can just as well be part of the manager's toolbox:

- Writing organizes thinking.
- Beware of verbalism. Is there coverage for what is said?
- It is important that the context is clearly expressed.
- Do not look only at what you yourself, colleagues, or children can do alone. Also look at what can be achieved "with help". This puts into range higher goals than those the individual could manage on their own.
- Help to be creative to find helpful stimuli (tricks) to remember and learn.
- Think of the linguistic environment, social context and culture that the staff come from. Language develops in harmony with related parties, parents and siblings and also by peer groups, other adult groups, politics and parents' work situation, the cultural environment and social conditions, etc. Everything has an effect!

The memory as a computer

Those who advocate that the individual works like a computer mean that the way we process information is what primarily determines whether or not we will remember later. It is not about the number of times we repeat the information to ourselves. That is to say that quality, not quantity, is important.

The storage of information in the brain demands a great deal. When the information reaches the short-term memory, the information is processed to determine if it is to be sent for storage in long-term memory or discarded.

Entry of information in short-term memory can be visual (a mental picture), acoustic (sound) or semantic (based on meaning). Once there, the information can be repeated and thus stay longer.

Short-term memory has a limited capacity. It is often said that there are 7-9 storage compartments, that is to say it is possible to hold 7-9 units simultaneously. This varies between individuals. The best way to retain information in short-term memory is through repetition - that is to "train in the brain gym". Consciousness is occupied to prevent entry of new data.

Long-term memory is very spacious and there is no risk that it will be overloaded. It is not the amount of information that is problematic but rather the actual Organization for storing information. One could say that long-term memory uses different registers to encode and store different memories. It creates associations between different phenomena and thus we get different links to different memories. You could say that the encoding or storage of long-term memory is based on the meaningful structure of information stored within the brain.

Overloading "the computer"

When man works as a computer, a lot of impressions impinge on our senses. Some are filtered directly away as unimportant, while others continue to the sensory memory, i.e. the part of the brain where different sensory perceptions are made understandable. They remain here for a while and may be passed on should the need arise. The information that is passed on to our processor is the information that becomes perception and awareness. Finally, the information deemed important for various reasons is stored.

Our brains have not evolved very much since the cave man. However, the amount of impulses reaching the brain has increased significantly. When working at the computer, many people work in multiple windows simultaneously. Interruptions are many, with phone calls, people who drop in for a quick comment, text messages that must be answered immediately, etc. The question is how many beeps from mobile phones or pings from new emails can the brain cope with at the same time as trying to focus on a report that must be read and processed?

Some scientists believe that they are starting to see new types of attention-deficiency in adults. It looks like a type of "Adult ADHD" in which the person has difficulty in sorting all the impressions and stimuli, and cannot focus any longer. The brain has become over-stimulated and quits.

Which truth is THE truth?

The brain is triggered by simply looking at a questionnaire before it is completed, and even more when trying to make sense of the questions. What did the "author" to the questionnaire mean? What does a certain word indicate? Why are certain questions not being asked? What is the answer that the author is looking for? What is right and what is wrong in the respondent's cultural context?

Similar reasoning can be applied to all types of research. How much does the researcher influence the answers? How much impact does the sponsor have on the answers? Which questions are asked and which are not and how does this affect the outcome? Does it matter to the research if the researcher is in the U.S. or China? How are volunteers, or those who must respond to a phone survey selected? Are the scientists researching the hazards or harmlessness of cigarettes and who are sponsored by the Tobacco Company impartial? Or can the American scientists who investigate thrombosis and oral contraceptives have equal veracity compared to the Swedish researchers who investigate the same thing, but with a different pill? And where two different pharmaceutical companies stand for much of the research cost?

Similarly, the person "who just sits as an observer" can consider how much they affect what happens in the room. Coaching managers should ask themselves how neutral they are in the dialogue with co-workers. How much does the manager influence the employee just by sitting there?

Memories of childhood

To be able to remember and put an event into words requires the ability to reflect, not just react. Reflection is not fully developed in infancy, which means that a trauma early in life can persist today, often at an unconscious level. A new event in adulthood may be similar to the old one, and the body can react in recognition. The old feelings of full-blown stress, sweating and palpitations gain momentum.

Perhaps it is in coaching (for the "healthy") or therapy (for "the sick") that the reaction centre can be reached - in the experiment to re-experience it, reflect on it and above all be able to verbalize it. The body can complete the event in this way, or in other words... the brain can complete the "gestalt" in this way and make it consciously understandable. Emotion and intellect are in balance. It is possible to find peace with what has happened. History events and experiences no longer obscure experiences and perception. It will be a closed "gestalt", as Gestalt psychologists would put it.

The strange thing is that psychologists today can still tell us about children who have experienced traumatic events (such as the massacre at the school in Beslan in the Soviet Union in September, 2004) and indicate that the older schoolchildren should be helped to process their experiences, whereas the small children are too young to remember what happened.

This can be compared with the misguided belief that babies have no sense of pain and that surgery can therefore be performed on them without anaesthesia. This was a "truth" in Sweden as late as the 1960's. What might survive as unspoken feelings and reactions in these children when they reach adulthood? And when and how can these feelings and reactions be expressed?

To be able to remember and put an event into words requires the ability to reflect, not just react.

The experiment as learning

What is it that thousands of years of research have most in common? Rarely is it the case that the "word" or "intellect" alone have led to insight or awareness. These are just components or parts of the whole known as the human being.

Instead, it has been realized that exercises or "experiments" involving participants / researchers / students / audience / employees have the greatest impact.

The exercise is legitimate in the sense that it is performed here and now and everyone involved will have their own experience here and now. All senses, old personal memories, family values and so on are involved in the experience. Experiences will therefore automatically vary from person to person, but the experience itself is there, right on the spot. Reflecting on the results of the experiment individually, and in association with others who have performed the same experiments at the same time, will lead to personal development and new insights.

Each unit, or human being, with their own interactive development cycle, may contribute to the joint development cycle of the large group. During reflection, different experiences are discussed which results in a synthesis – a total figure for the group – that can be experienced. It becomes "the group's voice" and it can form the necessary "platform" that the group can stand for. It is the glue to unite the group, whether it is for a common set of values or a common market strategy.

> **EDUCATION FOR UNDERSTANDING**
>
> 1. Test, practice, experiment
> 2. Reflect yourself (itself, in small and large groups)
> 3. Discuss (all together)

The overall figure may be experienced and realised despite the fact that each individual also carries their own figure. Each and every member of the larger group chooses to what degree they will adapt themselves to belong to, or withdraw from, this particular group.

Historical summary

Body or soul? One philosopher after another has thought about whether it is the whole or the parts that is most important. What should we believe?

Emptiness as a whole

Most Western medical researchers today still study the individual parts, unlike, for example those studying Chinese medicine. Western medical research is therefore performed on the lungs, heart, ear or eye. The patient consults his doctor in the same way – the ailment that resides in a particular part of the body. There is rarely time to find out how the whole – the patient – is feeling.

- **The atom** was long considered to be the smallest unit. This unit has since been broken down into quarks, gluons, etc. It is also fascinating to consider that the component itself is a whole, and that the parts are in constant motion, in something larger.

- **Other researchers focus on the universe and the cosmos.** The question is when and how they include the parts. Or even describe what is between the parts – that is to say emptiness.

- **The void** is, in a way, the opposite pole to the universe. But on the other hand, emptiness is a whole that can also be described.

The part as a whole

The ancient Egyptian doctors 5,000 years ago realized that research must be conducted as an experiment in reality, i.e. by comparing real people with each other. They also established what is believed to be the first psychotherapy rooms, in one of the temples along the Nile.

Taoism described 2,500 years ago holism in which the whole is greater than the sum of its parts. Buddhism did the same. Spirit and body form a whole. It is also interesting that they described this whole as processes in which the entities are in constant motion.

Aristotle argued, over 2,000 years ago, that an arm is only an arm and only has significance when it is on the whole human being. And Aristotle, like the ancient Chinese, therefore considered that the wholes are in motion.

Leonardo da Vinci, in contrast to Aristotle, could perform autopsies on humans 500 years ago. He performed them in secret, because it was banned by the Church, who argued that humans were created by God and man could not in any way call into question God's creation. The whole was effectively designed by God, fixed, ready, and static and certainly not in motion. People could not take the liberty of investigating or questioning God's creation.

Gestalt psychologists developed on Aristotle's theory 75 years ago, among other things.

Field theorists took over and today quantum physicists and network researchers ponder further, using new technology. The part, the "figure", can be broken out from the background. But the one is dependent on the other. The part is in itself a whole and cannot live without the whole. Everything is in constant process, in constant motion. Similarly, human behaviour is a function of personality and the environment the person is in. One is dependent on the other and everything is constantly changing.

In the big whole

Everyone in the meeting room has his or her own interactive development cycle around the phenomenon that, for now, can be considered as the figure. At the same time, a lot of unfinished gestalts and figures circulate about the "room". The person is surrounded by the group's interactive development cycle, family development cycle, the company's development cycle, the country's development cycle

FRACTAL- a reduced copy of the whole
A fractal is "a rough or fragmented geometric shape that can be split into parts, each of which is (at least approximately) a reduced-size copy of the whole," a property called self-similarity. Roots of mathematically rigorous treatment of fractals can be traced back to functions studied by Karl Weierstrass, Georg Cantor and Felix Hausdorff in studying functions that were continuous but not differentiable; however, the term fractal was coined by Benoît Mandelbrot in 1975 and was derived from the Latin fractus meaning "broken" or "fractured." A mathematical fractal is based on an equation that undergoes iteration, a form of feedback based on recursion.

Wikipedia 2011-01-31

and that of the world. Everything is connected, even here. What can be seen right now is the truth - at least for the observer.

The small parts are in the larger whole. The small part can duplicate itself forever as fractals. Similarly, it is possible to see the larger whole in the smaller part. The Cosmos is huge, and each person is part of it.

Is it the whole truth that humans are totally alone? Or is it so that, by being part of the cosmos, the little person is part of the greater whole? And that the greater whole that can be called the cosmos, or perhaps God is not a separate entity, but also a part of every human being, of you and me? We are the same thing - in which case everything is connected, again.

Perception of Right and Wrong

For anyone working as a manager it is essential to consider one's personal viewpoint and the truths that, as a manager, one has adopted.

The only thing that is certain is that employees and the management each have their own viewpoint. It is possible to give everyone the chance to learn and relearn, using different methods. To explore through questioning and establishing clear, common values and a work platform is a way to really succeed with communication.

The issues of perception and how the world is perceived is something that is topical every waking hour of every day. It is a short step from the child's sand pit "You are stupid and you are kind" to the statement that "Those at headquarters don't know what it's like out at the subsidiaries - sometimes I wonder if they are stupid!"

The issue is how everyone should act in everyday life and still find ways to cooperate, despite the many thoughts, prejudices, expectations and everything else that is in the room, unspoken for the most part.

The associations of recognition

"John is an unpleasant type. I cringe every time he is at a meeting. Actually, he hasn't done anything to me but it's something in his manner... I don't think he likes me. Somehow, he just wants to provoke. Every time my music teacher got mad he inhaled in a special way, making a whistling sound. When that happened, I knew that the shit would hit the fan, even though I hadn't done anything. And then I see that even John breathes with a quick breath. I know that he is allergic and when he wheezes that much he has to get out his inhaler.

It actually has nothing to do with me. He just has the misfortune to resemble my music teacher. "

"Ah, how nice! You also have a Dutch name! And you're also an engineer. You must agree that the Dutch education system is something special. They really invest in maths and science. It's not like that in laid-back Swedish society. Sure, it was probably a bit authoritarian in Holland, but look at the talented people who got through! "

"When we have meetings with the French they always have to kiss you on the cheek. And I really don't like it. I think it's sleazy. Why can't they shake hands like ordinary people! "

To be associated with a partner, friends, family, business or working group is a basic human need. The question is, what constitutes the "glue" in this cohesion? Is it an activity, something to do together? Or is it about relationships, solidarity, or loyalty? Or is it simply better than being alone?

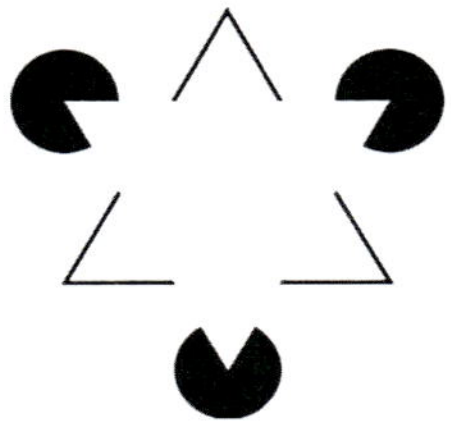

Understandable wholes

In the group or groups that one belongs to it may be relevant to ask what is required to be a 'member' - from the perspective of perception. What is it that everyone must accept and what is it that everyone must ignore? It can also be put like this: which wholes are comfortable to live in and which must be considered as a 'figure'? What is chosen to be put in parentheses - in the background?

The brain wants to coalesce incomplete forms, whether it is concerns marks on a paper or corporate culture. This is despite the fact that what are really visible are only marks that represent a pattern, based on the viewer's experience and expectations. The brain wants to determine in which compartments objects, phenomena, people, opinions and relationships belong. This is often done without searching for more facts. Perhaps it is not possible, or it seems unnecessary or scary. But, for whatever reason, the brain still forms a whole based on this incomplete information and communicates this "opinion" to a conscious thought.

It becomes difficult to let things, people or events stand on their own or to just be there. Everyone sorts and categorizes in their own way, in a more or less rough and ready way, and more or less in a hurry.

"Did you understand what the CEO said?

I think he meant that we are on the marketing side should be left as a unit. He did not say that explicitly, but because he did not mention us at all and mentioned all the other changes which will take place, that's probably how it must be. That is what I understood, anyway."

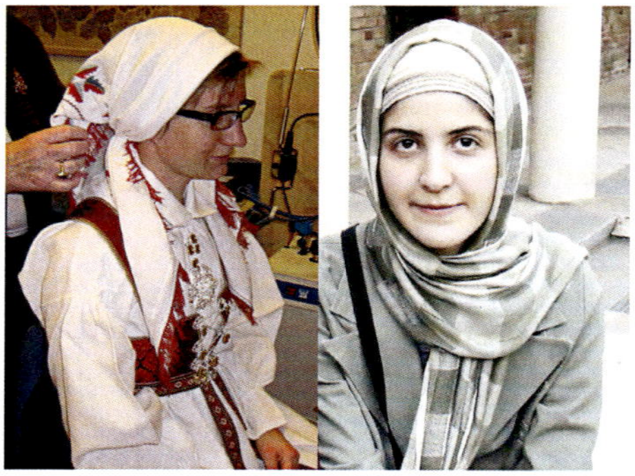
Trends, culture, prejudice and headscarves

Which questions will give the right answer?

Everyone has their own viewpoint from which they consider the world. It is not possible to really say if any viewpoints are right or wrong. They just exist. However, everyone can reflect on their very own viewpoint and find out why they have this way of considering the world. Which "authorities" has the person accepted to impact on their personal views, feelings, or prejudices?

When opinions and viewpoints adversely affect the company's or group's effectiveness, it becomes important to address the root of the problem. It may be that the subsidiary staff feel that the staff at head office are unfriendly, or vice versa. And there may be customers who report salespeople because they give a slovenly impression or do not know how to behave.

- What prejudices exist in your country? In the northern part of the country? In the family? In one's own family? In England, regarding your nationality? In China, regarding your nationality? Does it matter?
- What is true and false in the newspaper? Do the newspaper owners influence the journalists simply by paying their salaries? Or is there self-censorship because of "terrorism"? Or because of the federal defence?
- How much should we believe in scientific results? Or in polling agencies when they interview "all citizens" - those with a telephone landline, but missing all the young people who "only" have a cell phone or Skype?
- What will it take for you to make contact with, and take action in a culture other than your own? What will you talk about when almost everything is new and strange? How should one behave at a job interview in the U.S.? Where do you look standing in a full lift in China? Or on a crowded subway train in Tokyo?
- What do you think about the woman with headscarves in Sweden today? Or about the woman with a headscarf in the painting from 18th-century Sweden?

What psychological tests ask the right questions?

Many companies these days insist that job candidates undergo psychological tests before being considered for employment. There is a belief that the "neutral psychologist" with the help of a "neutral test" has a better insight into the individual than the regular HR person or manager does without the support of such a test. If something can be weighed and measured then the results are perceived as true. Few, if any, wonder who created the tests, what is behind them or how they have been evaluated.

Even fewer can or dare to ask psychologists about what affects their interpretations. With which eyes do they view the results and the person being tested? What is their experience in business or being employed in a large corporation? It takes a lot to challenge a strong authority, especially if you are looking for a job, or have to pass a test to further your career in your company.

Those who expose themselves to additional testing may often be given a result in written form, and meet the psychologist who has interpreted the results. All too often, the individual who has been tested feels that it is best to lie low and not challenge the results. There is rarely room for personal growth or development but rather the test-subject sees them self as stuck in a box, or on a chart with no apparent route out.

Sometimes the subject of the test recognises himself - "okay this is how I am" - but sees no potential for development. Sometimes the results are perceived as being strange or frightening: "I had no idea about that - and now someone who knows said this is how it is." All too often the results or discussions are perceived as offensive.

Get into a dialogue

Many tests purport that the sole purpose is to start a dialogue. The aim is admirable but even so many will say to their coach afterwards that "I now know how I am in black and white." Something happens between the good intentions of the tester and the perceived outcome of the respondent.

Some tests are designed so that it is the respondent who first gets to talk about them self and report whether the responses from the test feel true or false. This builds up awareness and the respondent has the opportunity to either accept or reject the results. The respondent therefore owns the truth but can never know how answers will be used and who has the final, "true" answer.

MYERS-BRIGGS: 47 % RELIABILITY

"One investigation (conducted by Indicator proponents, no less) found that the percentage of people who achieved the same four-part type across two administrations of the test was only 47 percent. In other words, more than half of those who took the Myers-Briggs were given a different type when they took the same questionnaire a short while later."

Source: The Cult of Personality, 2004

WHICH TEST IS TRUE?
A person who has been dismissed from an information job says:

"During the last 6 months I have been *called to several interviews. I have had to take four different tests for four different companies. It is quite remarkable that I cannot use the test results from the first company at the other companies. They all use other psychologists and other tests that they think are better. Why should they be? I am the person I am. If the tests indicate the "truth" then all the tests would be in agreement, but they aren't. I can see that and just have to accept the situation and go through the tests they propose, without comment. I really need to find a new job and I'm at a disadvantage. I cannot question either the tests or the competence of the psychologists."*

Tests used to supplement, not substitute for, other ways of obtaining a picture of a person's ability may function well. A humble tester from Europe also takes into account all the "architecture" behind the test and will not be satisfied with reports of, for example, the number of "Americans in the Midwest" who have used the test, making it statistically "true".

Filling in questionnaires

- **Intelligence Tests** claim to be able to measure verbal ability, abstract thinking, spatial ability, complexity, social skills, emotional skills, etc. They may consist of "drunkenness exercises" such as drawing, and interpreting shapes and patterns.
- **The Personality Test** is designed to tell what type the respondent is and the type of tasks the person may be capable of. Some tests even claim to determine if the respondent is an addict, or a psychopath.

Behaviour = function of personality + environment

By simply recalling Kurt Lewin's formula **B = f (p + E)**, anyone can see that the test results always depend on environmental factors and how the patient feels at the time. And yet, regardless of test type, respondents are asked to "take their time", or that everything should be done on time. It is often good to come unprepared. The person may sit alone in a room or office with his computer. Or the person can sit in a room with several others, with or without an interested or indifferent test manager. Environment counts and should be taken into consideration when interpreting the test results.

The test can be done at different times of day and the subject may be more or less tired, upset, performance-focused etc. Does the test subject understand the test, or is there a risk that the test shows more about language comprehension than intelligence, that the language is easy but can be interpreted in different ways, or that the test has become outdated so that a younger generation gets worse results than an older generation?

Practise and be prepared

In most circumstances one has to be prepared. It's about knowing the product or service. It's about being an expert in data management or purchasing. Courses and extensive training are on offer.

But when it comes to personality tests the "subject" is asked to "come as you are." And "you do not have to prepare yourself at all." One may ask, why? It is perfectly acceptable to prepare for the test just the same as for other tests and exams.

There are tests on the Internet that you can try. There are books to read. There are also recommendations for the best way to do the tests depending on the position on offer. The tests are made based roughly on the same templates, and they can be learned. There is, in many cases, even a standard answer. The truly interested and motivated can contact mentors or coaches to seek support from, and train with.

The goal is to be neither thrilled nor terrified by either the test or tester. It is possible to keep track of who one is, and that one can develop, and keep self-esteem intact. This minimises the risk of feeling offended. One does not lose ones identity.

An ethical approach for testers who have found a good test is to be clear about one's own identity and personality in various contexts. This may be achieved through their own personal coaching or by interpreting the results with the help of someone who already has self-knowledge. This will reduce the risk of confusing oneself with one's own projections of other people.

ATTITUDES TO THE TEST

1. See the test as an "experiment" and an indication of how each person is right here and now. Tests NEVER give an absolute answer.

2. Since everyone's behaviour is a function of both personality and environment, then the location, attitudes and events surrounding the completion of the test are all relevant to the outcome.

3. In a similar way, the tester and the test-subject are influenced by the same things in the feedback situation. Again - test results never measure "how a person is" but only how the person responded, associated and interpreted at a particular moment in his life, in a certain situation.

4. Everyone is always in a process of development and in "motion", and therefore constantly acting and interacting in new ways with others and other things. Nothing stands still.

5. The tests are narrow in their view, and never consider the whole person. The test focuses on a specific part of man, e.g. the "person at work", and then a certain role at work (e.g. does the applicant fit the job as personnel manager at this moment).

The art of the dialogue - Phenomenological feedback

In the Nordic labour market it is nowadays considered de rigueur to have performance reviews. It is also in the manager's role to communicate both positive and negative criticism to employees. This is often communicated in the form of "I think that you ....".

To "think something about someone" always involves a person pointing at them self at the same time. To "think and believe" are actually fantasies and guesses that the conveyer has concerning someone else. The guess may of course be right, but when it is expressed as a truth it is often perceived as painful, unpleasant or incomprehensible, especially if the criticism is negative. On the other hand, it may be embarrassing if the criticism was positive.

The goal when giving feedback is to be clear, without instilling a feeling of discomfort. It may be easier if the feedback can originate from the manager instead so that the employee can understand the source of the fantasy. The employee may, for example, get the chance to say that the fantasy/guess was wrong and that it was about something else. Alternatively, it may be correct up to a point but there is more behind the fantasy.

To concentrate feedback to the "phenomenon", facts and data - that is to say what is seen, heard or felt by the sender - makes communication clearer. Couple it with your own emotional experience and then create a fantasy/ guess about what that might mean. Then no one can experience what is being said as an accusation.

This is the structure of a phenomenological feedback dialogue:

When I hear... see...	...I feel...	... and I get a fantasy that...
... that you get red cheeks when you are to talk in front of the team...	... nervous...	... you are embarrassed in these occasions. Is this true?
...that you get your coffee at 9 o'clock when the team have their coffee at 10...	...both worried and irritated...	... you are not comfortable with the team and want to keep yourself to yourself. Is my guess correct?
... that you arrive at work every Monday morning smelling of menthol...	... uncomfortable...	... you drink too much during weekends which now effects your work. I would very much like to have your comments.

Tripartite dialogue for the difficult dialogues

When two people have had a serious argument and cannot resolve the conflict then a so-called "tripartite" dialogue is arranged. The two combatants will then meet under controlled conditions, that is to say not alone. The dialogue between them will be headed by a third party who sets the framework for the discussion and coaches the combatants.

The goal is that each must give and take something in order to resolve the conflict. The coach ensures that each talks in turn and that both really listen to what the other says. Instead of dwelling on old scores, the coach should drive the discussion in the context of the present. The dialogue can look like this:

Coach: *"I want you to sit opposite each other. I'll sit a little on the side. Maria has something she wants to tell you Tom. Off you go Maria. "*

Maria: *"I have repeatedly drawn up the sales plan for the following six months. You accept my plan but after only a month or so you tear it up and say we have to take a more creative approach. I know you have many ideas but this means that I will be off balance the whole time and don't know how I should act. I get stressed out of my mind. "*

Coach: *"So how are you feeling right now Maria?"*

Maria: *"I feel stressed. And I feel "over-run".*
Coach: *"Tom, what did you hear Maria say?"*

Tom: *"I heard that Maria said she was feeling stressed and that she feels over-run."*

Coach: *"What happens to you when you hear that Maria feels that way?"*

Tom: *"I am surprised. I thought that we always understood each other. A plan is just a plan that is current for the moment. Things happen all the time and the plan must be revised. I know I often go to Maria and bounce new ideas with her. But that doesn't mean that they should all be implemented. I'm just thinking aloud ... "*

Coach: *"Maria, what did Tom say?"*

Maria: *"He feels surprised ... I understand that we must deliver results. But I really don't see when Thomas means that new ideas are to be implemented or when it is just brainstorming. How should I know? And another thing, there's no point of me drawing up plans if they're not going to hold for more than one month."*

Coach: *"What do you say Tom?"*

Tom: *"No, I see that I must be clearer about what is brainstorming and which activities should really be carried out. I'll try to remember it but, Maria, I also want you to ask if you feel uncertain. It is the same thing with plans. As I can see, they will remain unchanged for the most part, and we are only talking about minor revisions ... But even here, I want you to check with me if you are unsure. "*

Coach: *"What did you hear now Maria?"*

Maria: *"That Tom will try to be clearer. And I have to ask if I am not sure if the ideas are activities to be implemented or if they are just ideas. And I have to ask if the plan is to be revised or not. Would it be okay for you if we have a meeting every month, just you and me, when we can go through this? Then I'll get the chance to prepare and we can focus better - if nothing really special happens, of course."*

Tom: *"Sure. We can plan the first meeting right now if you want."*

Coach: *"Okay, then do it and we will finish our meeting."*

What to say and how to interpret

At work, it is rarely what should be done that is discussed. That has often been based on a board- or management decision that has to be adapted to. It is possible to have opinions about the major strategies, restructuring, and ownership changes. But when the options and impact assessments have been made and decisions have been made, it is all about getting everyone in the company to "march in step" as soon as possible.

More often than not, opinions differ on the impact of the strategies and how staff will be able to "march in step", and how managers should communicate the changes.

The CEO may perceive that he or she has given very clear guidelines on how the business should be run, but because it is about perception, there will be as many interpretations of these directives as there are managers and employees. The CEO or Manager must therefore devote time and resources to ensure that the words of the CEO, management team and manager will be understood exactly as intended.

Some companies work hard to try to get everyone to adopt the common values of the company. They are not just produced as mere words. They are also implemented throughout all levels of the company, to be "lived" and therefore understood and accepted. All employees demonstrate their understanding through their own measurable actions every day. IKEA is a good example of such a company.

Written rules

The written rules are often documented in a personnel policy that covers most aspects of HR issues, such as the physical safety and psychosocial work environment. To have this on paper is all well and good. The question is how many people have read the material. And who has understood.

It is not unusual that groups who are in conflict, and in which even adult bullying can occur, can relate to the psychosocial document. But they do not realize that what the group does is entirely contrary to the intentions of the document.

NOKIA HAS WRITTEN RULES ON THE WEB WHERE TEXT DESCRIBES THE HEADLINES, MENTIONED BELOW, IN SOME DETAIL:

- **Vision:** " Nokia will empower everyone to share and make the most of their life by offering irresistible personal experiences.
- **Slogan:** "Connecting People to what matters..."
- **Values:** Engaging you – Achieving together – Passion for innovation – Very human – Professional and personal growth – Commitment to Self-development – Coaching – Learning solutions and training – Management training – Internal job market – Performance management

The quotations are from Nokia's website in 2010, www.nokia.com.

Unwritten rules

The unwritten standards are more elusive. Is it possible to know in advance if shorts are allowed or not at work during the summer ("it can hardly be something for management to care about - the CEO goes around in slippers and that's accepted"); if it is acceptable to tell the neighbours that the company is going badly; where in the company restaurant your group will sit; whether it is permissible to use the corporate card for private purchases on a business trip; whether it is okay to surf a little bit privately during working hours (what is "little" and what is "too much" and who has decided this); if the coffee break can be 15 minutes; if the smokers can go outside and take a puff every time they feel the need, no matter how often?

There are always unwritten rules and the question is how quickly they can be adopted and what is healthy or unhealthy for the company. If something "feels wrong" for the new employee then a conflict of loyalties could quickly arise. Does the person have the energy to resist his colleagues for the company's best or is the easiest way to do like "everyone else"? What does it take to be included in the group, ostracized, or kicked out?

Personal Ethics

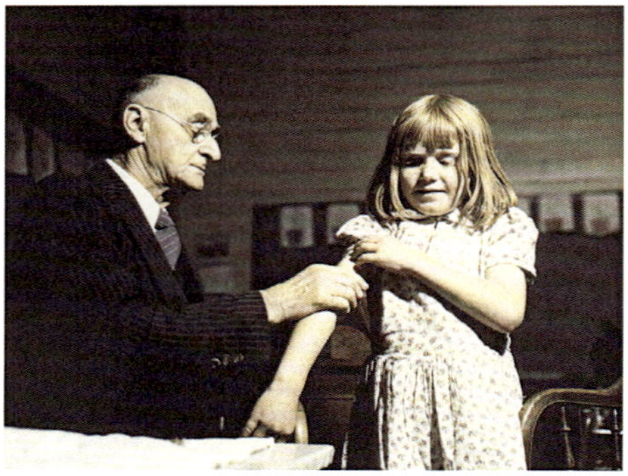
Decision: adopt and adapt

Ethics are perhaps obvious when they are written down: the responsibility of everyone to reflect on what their own ethical rules are in order to feel content and not harm others. They must also be aware of what the rules of the company, organization, group or family really mean, including what is spoken and what is unspoken.

The question becomes how far from their own ethical rules can the employee work and still be able to see them self in the mirror every morning and feel good. A person in a leadership position must also clearly communicate the company's desire without swaying, even when, or if, the company does not share the manager's own perception and values.

Who benefits from positioning ...

Making yourself heard... transforms to ... Taking you forward
According to Pia Gideon, the press service spokesperson, the sentence exudes the group's core values "professionalism", reports the Daily Media, 29/1 2007.

The new slogan has been thought up by the British agency Publicis. It replaces the old one from 1998, which became no longer current when Ericsson stopped making phones a few years ago. The "Taking you forward" campaign will be presented in connection with the February telecom trade show in Cannes, France.

New slogan for Ericsson (according to Dagens Media 2007-01 -29)

Today, we talk about how much it will cost to change a brand or slogan, thus re-positioning the company: to go from one perception of the company to another, to try to get customers, analysts and the outside world to adopt a new point of view from which to consider it. Actually, even entire countries and citizens of countries position themselves. As with commercial marketing, it can be interesting to know, for example, what position the Swede has in the eyes of people, and whether there is a need for re-positioning. The question regarding re-positioning is the importance coupled with cost and time needed. Is it worthwhile?

What did the United States stand for in the 19th century when many Europeans emigrated to the "promised land"? What was the U.S. in 1945 when World War II was over and the victors wrote history? What does the U.S. stand for now?

Who has positioned whom as a "terrorist"? Is the terrorist Palestinian, Israeli, the Kurd in exile, the American in Iraq, all Muslims, or a person with the wrong name and who used the wrong word in a text message, or someone who took nail scissors onto the airplane?

What was social democracy in 1920 and what does social democracy stand for today? And where were China and India 25 years ago and where are they today? Who is positioning whom, when and how? Who gains what?

"The truth is in the eye of the beholder," says the proverb. "The winner writes history," says another proverb. Which position is most true in that case?

... And re-positioning ...

A strong brand is worth its weight in gold. Getting a brand or company name that rings the right bell in as many environments and cultures as possible is a must in the global marketplace. People must get the right association regardless of language or history. They must at least not get the wrong idea.

Vishnus beams

Some concrete examples concerning symbols, which might as well be trademarks, dress, etiquette, and so on are described below. Several symbols have changed their meaning.

Nazisymbol

Sun Sign, or ...?

What is the sign above? It's the Nazi symbol, isn't it? A clearer re-positioning of a symbol of modern times is hard to find. It is a great shame for all the Hindus because this symbol is an ancient symbol of luck, which can be found in holy places, in print and at religious festivals. The word "Swastika" comes from Sanskrit and means "well" - a desire for success. The swastika represents the sun of the god Vishnu. Without these rays there would be no life.

The serpent's knowledge, or ...?

The snake is now used as a symbol for, for example, medicine. And a snake evokes many feelings and thoughts and is therefore a complex symbol. It has been re-positioned several times. Here are some examples:

COLLECTIVE UNCONSCIOUS

Collective unconscious is a term of analytical psychology, coined by Carl Jung. It is proposed to be a part of the unconscious mind, expressed in humanity and all life forms with nervous systems, and describes how the structure of the psyche autonomously organizes experience. Jung distinguished the collective unconscious from the personal unconscious, in that the personal unconscious is a personal reservoir of experience unique to each individual, while the collective unconscious collects and organizes those personal experiences in a similar way with each member of a particular species.

Source: Wikipedia

- The snake stands as the eternal symbol of the so-called ouroboro, in an eternal cycle of self-destruction and self-reincarnation.
- It represents both the female and the male and is often self-generating
- It symbolizes death and destruction, but also life and resurrection.
- It is an attribute to a number of female deities and is either coiled around them or carried in their hands. The snake is an ancient symbol of female knowledge and power over life itself.
- In Nordic history the serpent Jörmungandr embraces the world and the abyss. The Celts also associated the serpent with good, including healing springs and water.
- In Christianity, the snake acquired an ambiguous meaning: the wisdom of the tree of life, and at the same time the devil in the underworld. In monotheistic Judaism, the serpent represents evil, temptation, sin and sexual passion.

Uraues was a cobra in ancient Egypt and, unlike in Christianity, symbolized divine and royal wisdom, power and knowledge. The snake could also represent chaos.

Both the Greeks and the Romans were influenced by Egypt, which may be the reason why, in the Roman Empire, the snake was one of the attributes of Minerva, goddess of wisdom. In the same way, the Greeks saw the snake as a symbol of wisdom, new life, resurrection and healing. The serpent is represented in various ways in Greek mythology: there are women with serpent hair, and there is Askleipos, god of the healing arts with the sign of the snake.

The serpent of Hinduism, as in Egypt, stood for chaos, the formless and invisible. And it also stands for Shakti - nature and cosmic power. The cobra is also seen, for example, as the bearer of Vishnu and represents knowledge, wisdom and eternity. In the Buddhist tradition the snake is in the middle of the wheel of life and represents anger.

And what does the snake represent to you as a reader? What snake do you imagine when you think "snake" and why should it be so? What can be conscious and what may be unconscious? Can any knowledge be universal and belong to what Carl Jung called the "collective unconsciousness"?

The various faces of Truth

This is the story of a company that reorganized. It's more specifically about the marketing department, including two major business areas and the groups around them. Some people recount what they heard and what they experienced after this meeting.

This shows the impact of perception at work. In other words, how many wise individuals interpret the same event in entirely different ways? Of course this affects efficiency in the workplace.

Peter, MD

OK, I have just held the information meeting. I don't like to stand in front of people but I had to bite the bullet again. I had, at least, dressed a little more casually so that everyone could feel that I am one of them. I know that I presented what I wanted to say just a little too quickly. The fact that Lisa could stay is good. Whether she is a good manager is questionable but she obviously thinks so, at any rate. No one has as much experience as me. Then there is Bridget ... She has had a baby and we can assume that she is having another. It was a bit stupid that I forgot about her but she is a bit beige ... even if she has been around for a long time. Yes, I'll have to fix that another time. Stefan is on the ball and that's needed in the job I thought for him. And then we have the others...

I said what I planned to and it went pretty well I think. People were quiet and attentive. No questions came so everything was undoubtedly crystal clear. I have never liked Power Point so I did like I usually do - a bit more spontaneous. And then I left. It is best to let this kind of information sink in. It feels like I put my foot down, but in a friendly way. Everyone has also been up to my office individually so I have really given them all the time they need. Management by listening, that's what I believe in.

I remember when I started the company. I had been fired from the big company and got a good severance pay. I got together with an old friend and got hold of a product that we could live on for a while, but I saw before me the business idea that would make me rich. And ... I have succeeded. Now the company will be going public and I'm still there, leading nearly everything. This is my baby to cherish as long as I can. I don't know when I'll quit. I know people speculate, but as long as I think it is fun, I'm going to stay. It's a great feeling to that, as an old soldier, have the chance to now to try a lot of different roles. Perhaps the employees feel that I put my nose in too much. But it is after all my business. And I mean no one can complain. I have a good pay policy, there will be Christmas gifts for everyone every year, they get bonuses, we have a masseur at work, our own restaurant, free fruit ... But I do not know how grateful everyone is! Anyway, they seem to feel secure since we still don't have union representation. In fact I think they believe that the personnel department is there for the staff!

Now, the marketing manager had to take another job and I have gone in as acting marketing manager. I have read a bit about marketing and think I know a lot about it now. It annoys me when I see from the marketing department's figures that the money seems to just pour out. Expensive conventions with no result in the sales figures, pure industrial tourism when the whole group goes off abroad, a massive organization at headquarters where I can't see that everyone is working with the right things. It's fun with all these young people in the organization, but they are inexperienced. It's a question of who to bet on. My wife has in fact had something to say about this. She has seen more than me and she usually has a good understanding of who is good for the company and who isn't.

Lisa, Group Manager

I have just been in the strangest meeting ever. Of course I know that our managing director is a bit special and that it is always he who decides everything. But this was the limit! He just went into the room and sat down. He avoided everyone's eyes and we just sat there, feeling terribly nervous. I had also had a meeting with him and told him what I want but I don't think he listened. I actually suspect that he dropped off for a while - he had just come from the United States and was jetlagged. During this meeting, it was like sitting in a classroom with an old schoolmaster, waiting for punishment. And you know what he did? He turned to each and everyone and, just like a pompous Santa Claus, gave out presents: "You can do this" and "You may do something else". I was at least allowed to keep my job, "yes, you yourself think that you are a talented manager," he said, and what did he mean by that? As usual, I sit here with a lot of guesses about what Peter mean - and very little facts. Peter even said I should go on an expensive course - not the course I have been asked to go on, but quite another. This is a good thing in itself, but it is definitely based more on his needs than mine.

Then there was Stephen. He had at least made it crystal clear what he is definitely did NOT want to do and that was exactly what Peter now says that he has to do. You should have seen Stephen's face! He sat poke-faced and couldn't utter a word.

But the worst bit was that when Peter had finished, he had forgotten to give Bridget her 'present'. Peter just went out, without a word. Bridget just sat there and everyone in the room was silent. And then Bridget began to cry. It was really embarrassing. It's a shame about Bridget but what am I supposed to do about this? The ball is in my court. The HR women looked completely drained so I can't expect any help from that direction. I wonder just how much she knew in advance. And now I'll be having private discussions with everyone! And Peter expects me to be loyal to him and the company. How easy will that be? And somehow I must get the group to keep working and not lose momentum. It is really important that they don't start signalling a lot of frustration to customers. Things like this can of course even affect the IPO if it gets out.

Bridget, Project Manager

I have worked in this company since it started. I was one of the first hired, and I always think that the job has been fun. There is always something happening. Maybe it's been a bit chaotic but we have been growing so fast so it isn't surprising. In recent years I have been working with the product. We have invested a lot in it but the sales haven't taken off yet. We have had a lot of setbacks for a while now. The subsidiaries are critical, customers keep find problems, and Peter complains that too much money is being spent. But he himself was involved in setting the budget! It's as if he forgot that.

Anyway I had a baby a couple of years ago. It was nice to have a break. When I came back a lot had changed. Many seemed to have taken a beating over the year and a half I was at home - there was something in the air. The happy atmosphere was gone. Nobody had coffee breaks together - they went back to their offices with a coffee cup instead. A silence descended over the place. It took a while before I found my place again and I got back responsibility for the product. I have worked like a dog to get everything to work.

And then we had this meeting with Peter. It was so awful! Like everyone else I had contacted Peter and told him about my dreams and what I think I can do for the company. As usual, he stared at the floor more than he looked at me and then he started talking about other things, so I don't really know what he heard. At that meeting with everyone in the group he just stood there and said something about the future and that the marketing department is too big, inexperienced and expensive to run. And then he started talking about what people should be doing in the future. He talked to everyone in turn and no one understood anything. It was as if a great dark cloud descended over the room. And then he said "Well, that's all then. And yes, yes, we have you Bridget - I'll talk to you some other time". And then he left the room.

I sat there and just felt my heart pounding and became all sweaty. Everyone looked at me and looked as if they felt sorry for me. But I think that most of them were relieved that they hadn't been victimised. And then I started to cry. If only I could have held back the tears. It was absolutely awful. But what could I do? What did Peter want? Was he going to support me anymore? Was this a signal that I should quit? If only the personnel department could help! What use are they? It felt like being in a vacuum, and still does.

Stefan, Product Manager

Oh, and I got to know that I'm inexperienced and haven't done my job well, which I have had for four years. Not that Peter said so directly, but you can read between the lines. A new experienced person is being appointed and I was assigned a job that I have said that I absolutely do not want. And I'll be working together with a person I don't want to work with. How much fun is that? And I know, just like everyone else, that it's no use trying to do anything about the situation – just put up with it or quit.

Right now I'm really fed up. And he is the boss! How does he think he will get the loyalty of the staff when he does things like this? And then it will be back to business as usual. Everyone goes into their room and broods. I'm beginning to wonder if I should sabotage work and pretend to be happy. Just drop a comment here and there around the company.... I will at least ring around, at least to the central union. I wonder what the law says about what the manager has a right to do. Can they just hand out jobs like this without being told anything in advance? Revenge is the word I feel most for now. Just because Peter goes around and looks like a cuddly uncle he thinks he can fool everyone.

And then when he said to Bridget that "we should talk about that later" ... There she sat! We should at least be glad that we didn't end up in that position. It was really embarrassing when she began to cry. I can't stand it when people cry. It's pretty poor behaviour actually. She lost our respect. It might be alright at home, but definitely not at work. Here it is a case of fighting, but also about being smart. I wonder just how much Peter's wife had to do with this. No one says anything, but everyone knows.

Summary of perception

Reality is perception whether it is for research, private life or work. As such, a "truth" is only as true as perception allows, in each and every individual. The process of interpretation is ongoing in all of us. It is a natural survival mechanism even if the interpretations are sometimes inaccurate. That is the challenge of working together. This is the creative, challenging, and sometimes frustrating reality that the conscious coaching manager and business coach meets, every single day.

Reference literature chapter 3.

Please find below books and references applicable to the text. The English title has been inserted when found. When not found, the title is left in its original language (English translation in brackets), for the reader interested to find other texts by the same author.

Ander J-E (2003) *(The third language – communication with all senses), Tredje språket – kommunikation med flera sinnen*, Bokförlaget Arenain collaboration with Bild och Ord Akademin, Sweden
Andersen HC (1837) *The emperor's new suit*
Andersen J (2008) *Dos and Don'ts – conflict resolution at work*, Idrinia Publishing
Andersson L (2005) *(Jesus the sect leader), Jesus sektledaren*, article, Stockholm/Sweden, Ordfront (October)

Andersson L (2005) *(Jesus – self-righteous and arrogant), Jesus – självgod och arrogant*, article, Stockholm, Humanisten forum and publication for culture and the philosophy of life (no 3)
Armstrong K (2005) *A short history of myth*. Edinburgh, Canongate Books
Bengts M, Brund U, Nilsson-Puccio S (2003) *The Swedish Code*, Stockholm/Sweden, KnowWare Publications
Bowker J et al (1997) *World Religions*, NY, DK Publishing
Clarkson P, Mackews J (2000) *Fritz Perls*, London, Sage Publications
Cooper JC (1978) *An illustrated encyclopaedia of traditional symbols*, Thames & Hudson
Cotterell A (editor) (2005) *The ultimate encyclopedia of mythology*, Bath, Parragon
Engström C, Kvant U (2002) *(Explicit and implicit attitudes towards brands – a study to find if attitudes in awareness or non-awareness coincide with the behaviour of individuals), Explicita och implicita attityder till varumärken – en studie om huruvida medvetna och omedvetna attityder samt beteende hos en individ samvarierar*, Lund/Sweden, Psykologiska institutionen (the department of psychology, University of Lund)
Frazer R, Fadiman J (1998) *Personality & Growth*, Addison Wesley Longman Inc
Frick L (1975) *(The liar), Lögnaren*. Rabén & Sjögren
Goleman D (1995) *Emotional intelligence – why it can matter more than IQ*, New York, Bantam Books
Hwang P, Nilsson B (2003) *(Developmental psychology), Utvecklingspsykologi*, Stockholm/Sweden, Natur och Kultur
Johnson E (1948) *(Krilon – a novel of what is plausible), Krilon – en roman om det sannolika*. Stockholm/Sweden, Albert Bonnier Förlag
Jung, C (1968) *Man and his symbols*, USA, Dell Publishing
Klingberg T (2009) *The overflowing brain information, overload and working memory*, NY, Oxford University Press
Kolterjahn M (2002) *(Everything is my fault, of course), Allt är mitt fel, förstås*, Stockholm, Tiden/Norstedt & Söner
Kvale S (1996) *InterViews*, SAGE Publications
Magnusson H, Åslund M (2002) *(Handbook in research methodology), Handbok i forskningsmetodik*. Institutionen för informatik/Mitthögskolan i Östersund
Mahfouz N (1998) *Akhenaten – Dweller in truth*, New York, Anchor Books
Mayer, Salovey (1997) *Emotional Intelligence*, New York, Dude Publishing
Maslow A (1987) *Motivation and Personality*, 3rd edition, New York, HarperCollins Publishers

Matlin M, Foley H (1997) *Sensation and perception*. Needham Heights, Mass., USA, Allyn and Bacon

Morgan G (1989) *Images of organization*, Sage Publications Ltd UK

Nadel B (1988) *Inspector Ikmen Mysteries*, London, Headline Publishing Group

Patel R, Davidson B (1994) *(The basics of research methodology. To plan, go through with it and report a research project), Forskningsmetodikens grunder. Att planera, genomföra och rapportera en undersökning*. Lund, Studentlitteratur

Paul M A (2004) *The cult of personality*, New York, Free Press

Perls F, Hefferline R, and Goodman P (1972) *Gestalt Therapy*, London, Souvenir Press

Perls F (1992) *In and out the garbage pail*, New York, The Gestalt Journal Press

Peters T (1999) *Riding the waves of cultures. Understanding cultural diversity in business*. London, Nicholas Brealey Publishing

Polster E, Polster M (1974) *Gestalt therapy integrated*. New York, Vintage Books

Ray J (2002) *Reflections of Osiris, lives from ancient Egypt*, New York, Oxford University Press Inc

Schön E (2004) *(Folk beliefs A to Z), Folktrons ABC*, Stockholm/Sweden, Carlssons Förlag

Sjögren L (2001) *Sigmund Freud – (the man and his work) mannen och verket*, Stockholm/Sweden, Natur och Kultur, ref Internet Encyclpedia of Philosophy – a peer reviewed academic resource, http://www.iep.utm.edu/freud/

Sjölund A (1973) *(Group psychology) Gruppsykologi*, Stockholm/Sweden, Rabén & Sjögren

Skogeman P (1986) *(Archetypes – psychological monsters in a new world), Arketyper – psykologiska monster i en ny världsbild*, Forum

Svenhard H (editor) (1995) *(Manipulation is on-going. Disclosure and experience from ex sect members), Manipulering pågår, avslöjande erfarenheter från tidigare sektmedlemmar*, Stockholm, CKM

Söderberg J (2003) *(Some thoughts regarding research methodology), Några funderingar kring forskningsmetodik*, Sweden, Avdelningen för byggnadsekonomi LTH

Vygotskij L (1999) *Thought and language*, MIT Press

Wide K (2005) *(The healing power of the illustration), Bildens helande kraft*, Stockholm/Sweden, Mareld

Wood J, Nezworski T, Lilienfeld S, Garb H (2003) *What´s wrong with the Rorschach?* San Fransisco, John Wiley & Sons

Zetterholm T (1983) (The red Buddha), *Den röde Buddha*, Höganäs, Sweden, Bra Böcker

EXISTENTIAL PHILOSOPHY

How fear can control a group of adults

ALL LIVING THINGS EXIST IN COEXISTENCE WITH OTHERS. This is clear, straightforward, and concise. People today want to measure and weigh what is happening in life - it may feel good to lean on statistics and research.

Adults in leadership positions can go on courses in personal development at serious training institutes. And just there, in provocative situations, sides of senior executives can materialise that are frightening both for the person himself and for those who become victims. No statistics or research can help to answer the question "how one should be." It simply happens.

KEYWORDS CHAPTER 4.
- Contact Zones: outer zone, intermediate zone, inner zone
- Figure and background
- Groups, group dynamics and peer pressure in relation to an "I"
- Authority and power - Chaos

Extract from a college essay - an introduction

This paper has as its origin just one event that a group of people considered provocative. The consequences became clear to all. Rational thought, logic and reason were no longer applicable. Basic questions about existence came into focus instead. This makes it difficult to be human and to act in a so-called "professional" manner.

Similar events also occur at work under conditions of stress and pressure, for example during a reorganization.

Colleagues who used to be wise seem to overreact. They may start to behave "strangely" and no one understands what is going on. A new situation at work can be "triggered" by an old event.

It is therefore important that both managers and staff are aware of this to be able to respond, manage and move forward in a sensible, humane and responsive manner.

The theme and team development

> *"When one hundred heads are merged into one group, the result is one big fool, because every individual is hampered by the fact that others are different."*
>
> Carl G Jung

My overall theme is to connect thought and feeling, but the underlying theme of this year has been my vulnerability: to protect it, dare to show it, and dare to have the courage to allow myself to be dependent on someone. This theme came to a head when my relationship with Emma became public, the process that started, and its consequences. It affected the interactions and relationships between almost all levels of the organization. Even the teachers and their relationships to us students were affected. Questions concerning authority, norms, peer pressure, and power issues came to a head.

We have different approaches that manifest themselves in the need for security versus chaos, i.e. how much am I willing to throw myself into chaos to learn more about myself? There has been a big difference between those in the class who see the course as a professional and university education and those who see it as group therapy.

Breaking the rules has its price. I will try to show what it has meant at different levels for me and how I have handled it.

The school and I

The background that evolved into a figure was the school joining the university world. The rules that apply in the university world were compared with the rules and standards that were, and still are in place in schools. All organizations develop open and hidden norms and rules. This has consequences for the individual to violate, and it is the same in school. One of the standards was

that if there is a romantic relationship developed in a class then one of the couple would have to leave the class. This standard came to a head when the relationship between Eve and me became public.

Can a university education have such standards or recommendations? My answer is no, and it was also indicative of my conduct when I took the consequences of my position and demanded to continue. It is, however, important to stress that norms, rules and laws are constantly evolving. This is also the case in the school.

"Our concept of what is normal has evolved from an acceptance of certain standards of conduct for individuals in a particular group, who force those standards onto their members. But standards change with the times, cultures, social classes, and sexes, "writes Kurt Lewin.

The great group, subgroup and I

All phases in the development of a group will coexist in the group's life. But some will appear more or less clearly on different occasions.

The question of our relationship became a clear figure. Group identity was important and the dynamics of who was 'out' or 'in' became clear. Contact styles within the group and between its members became visible. When the discussion of our relationship came up in August, I felt that we did not speak the same language. I felt particularly challenged by the people from the supervision group that had been called the "rigid, inflexible" group. It made me terribly angry and sad.

Socio-Psycho Needs

Paul Moxnes uses the terms social and psychological needs. People with social needs look for the situations and activities that are characterized by a high degree of structure to balance their "operation anxiety".

Order and control are key principles for these people and formalisation and tranquillity are key words. For me it seems that those who reacted most strongly against us and our relationship were such people, i.e. the majority of the 'rigid' group. But I on the other hand am a person with psychological needs. I am reluctant to being captured, managed and controlled since it activates my "system anxiety."

This has led me to taking the role of the scapegoat, a role that part of the group has also wanted to give me. *"That someone stands outside the group can be a personal choice ... but it can also be due to the fact that the group's tolerance for diversity is limited,"* says Moxnes. *"Fragmentation may arise when the alliances that arise during the conflict in the group are made permanent. The Anti-Group develops during the conflict phase. It is characterized by attempts to settle conflicts in relationships within the group by projecting them onto an external enemy, or a scapegoat in the group,"* says Rolf Graner.

> *An open group with flexible boundaries appreciates input and also shares with the world around it. In a closed group, however, the group keeps to itself and distances itself to those outside.*

I feel that I was designated as a scapegoat by part of the 'rigid' group. I think there are several reasons for this. An important factor controlling a subgroup's ability to absorb change is whether it is open or closed.

An open group with flexible boundaries appreciates input and also shares with the world around it. In a closed group, however, the group keeps to itself and distances itself to those outside. Such a group considers itself to be self-sufficient. It is clear that when I am in the group I feel something else because I interact with the group members. From outside, others and I can see something quite different. The outside perspective that I and others share in our subgroup is not shared by the group members themselves. They do not understand the way I and others describe them.

Group identity in the process

The attacks on me, as I saw it, were initially a result of my feeling of hatred for large parts of the group. I asked myself, why should I be subjected to this? The issue of group identity became a figure for me. Can I meet these people, I can manage it, do I want to meet them at all, or do I want to remain excluded? The answer was yes, I can meet them and no, I do not want to stay outside.

Insights

While I wallowed in hatred for Sture, Linda and others I got an insight into fear and vulnerability, not only in myself but also in them. I thought of Sture's relationship with his mother, the need to succeed and to please, about Anna's father who betrayed her, and Marina whose father never allowed her to become involved, forcing her to stay in line. And I myself who do not like to appear weak and helpless!

"The members of the big group are all anonymous and in a sense more charged relative to the group ego; the presence of heaven and hell is, so to speak, more apparent," said Rolf Graner.

It has also become clear that the will and desire for unity within the group varies, and that the subgroups are the strong entities. Each force seeks expression, whether it is an individual, subgroup, or dyad, and the needs are expressed in the development of the group. The subgroups of the conflict phase remain but there is a high degree of interaction between these groups. Most avoid secrecy and make an effort to show as much openness as possible.

I realize that I will never have close relations with everyone, but that's ok. It will not prevent me from meeting these people or prevent us from cooperating to solve various tasks.

I feel grief and vulnerability. I, like the group's members, have my entire field in the group. Here, feedback and encounter sessions loosened up the one-sided picture that the group assigned to me, and I to others.

Such a large group has a large number of relationships that are difficult to survey. There is therefore a lot of exposure and vulnerability. In a large group there is higher charge and polarization, which makes it difficult to be seen as a complete individual, and this becomes even clearer when the power issue remains unresolved. I mean, if there is no balance, which is often achieved through the struggle for the roles in the group, then the group would fragment. And that is what happened! We create through the power struggle new figures. This also creates a new equilibrium.

One very clear conclusion for me is that if possible I will work with small groups (up to ten) in processes of change. Problems have been much less, or minimal, at the level of the support group and individuals.

Dyads and subgroups

Dyads and subgroups affect the group. As a couple, we strongly influenced the group, but less as a couple than a power base because the group has several self-appointed informal leaders. But no one has been allowed to steer the group or has been given leadership. This also demonstrates the importance of meetings involving individual members of the group to loosen up the roles that individuals take, or are assigned.

A dyad among many others

I realize that I could not have acted in any other way because of the extremely vulnerable situation I found myself in. But the work of the group could have taken other forms. I could have turned to Sture and any of the others and asked them about their reaction and the basis for it, and tried where possible to defuse the situation through discussion.

I felt misunderstood, offended and bullied. Therefore, it was difficult for me to reach out to the group instead of seeking revenge, but I managed. I could approach my group despite the risk of rejection.

The key as I understand it has not been what has been said, but more who said it. An example of this was when Linda pointed out those who had views on our membership in the group. She was given the task of picking out those who said or thought something about us and our relationship and forgot Louis, who was the person who spoke first. This was strange in itself, but it became even clearer when Louis accepted it! We assume and are assigned different roles and Louis got the role of 'does not respond', I got the role of scapegoat, and Linda took on the role of "self-appointed representative".

Opinion swung at the end of the week and it shows how important it is to trust the process, and dare to remain in what is important to me. Individuals in one group are often linked by the group's power, and that power can be so strong that the individual's will is dominated by the group's will. I also realize how strong the forces are to keep the team together. Sometimes it can be allowed to demand a high price including exclusion, assigning scapegoats, and bullying.

Reflection in the house of mirrors

Balance

The group needs balance (homeostasis) and this is achieved by openness and trust. I realized that the group's power structure was changing. The question was whether standards in both the group and the school had changed leading to a change in the power structure within the group. I had played a major role in this. This is part of the "rigid" group's frustration and fear, as they have had an extremely strong need for each other.

"A paucity of alternative or complementary groups can result in a strong dependence of the group which can perceive threats as being very strong," say Olav Sletta and Svein Steensaasen.

I was a part of the group and the group was a part of me, the individual and the group are interwoven. But everyone has an opportunity to break patterns of leave, open up or give in to the group. We can make a choice, and the choice I made was to try to meet the group. It led to the development of me and the group.

The teachers' relationships with me and the group

The issue of trust in leaders and others in the group came to a head. What also scared some of the 'rigid' group was that the designated authority in the form of our educational leaders and school was challenged, and thus felt threatened by us. I think Cecilia expressed the group's view when she said that – *"we have four teachers in the group"*.

I and individuals in the larger group

My feeling was that it also concerned a power struggle, at least in the case of some of the other men. Then I think of Steven, Eric and Louis. Steven had for some time said that we would have a conflict, and then he got it! I myself had felt surprise of his way of talking. For me, this was an expression of a power struggle rather than the pursuit of power. The mutual support and interdependence were lacking in the group then. For me, the power struggle had a lot to do with fear. Who can I trust and who wishes me well?

Me in relation to groups?

You have to rely on the group process in itself. If I, as a process manager, allow a group time to fall into confusion and chaos then, sooner or later, the group will solve the problems themselfs and a new equilibrium will emerge. And this was what happened in our group. This lead to openness and exploration within the group, in which group-interaction was the basis for new experiments that could bring the group forward.

What I also found was that the process surrounding our relationship and the group development at various levels had followed Lewin's three phases of organization development:

"Unfreezing" = unfreeze old behaviours and attitudes
"Change" = change
"Refreezing" = normalization and recovery through the assembly of forces, confirmation and support before the next thaw.

How have I functioned in the group?

I realize that I am willing to violate the rules if they deviate from what I regard as right and proper. With regard to the conflict that arose, it was not necessary for me to take the wrenching debate with the whole group.

I chose to go into the discussion, which I often do in similar situations. A new lesson for me was that I might not do this as casually next time. I could have taken into account and protected my vulnerability by simply saying that I do not debate about our relationship in the group.

I could also have said that the school had respected our decision. If you want a discussion then discuss with me alone or with the school! I made it clear that I had made my decision and intended to remain and face the consequences of my choice. I was willing to meet anyone who was interested in listening, to explain and help them understand the situation.

I can ask myself whether it was worth the effort, which for me has led to increased awareness. I also realize how important it is for many, especially during times of change, to belong to a group and belong to the same system of norms. One would rather take anxiety personally than confront the group.

The working points for the future

Questions that came to me about group processes and group dynamics were as follows:

1. Dependence and independence
2. Who can I trust and who can't I trust?
3. Community and alienation
4. Who gets power and who takes power?
5. Who can I influence, and who has influence over me?
6. Mobbing / Community
7. Confluence / Egotism
8. Rigidity, fear
9. Anxiety in the case of violating norms
10. Power struggle
11. "Trust the process"
12. Peer pressure

My overall theme and the underlying aspects are still relevant - to dare to stand there and maintain contact. "The contact boundary is the point where I feel "my-self" in relation to what is not "my-self ", says, for example, Polster, 1973.

It was important to realise that the contact boundary was neither me nor any individual in the group. It is expressed or created through our joint activity. This common contact is for me an expression of the group's voice.

It was a victory for me to dare to explore while I was searching contact with those who demanded that one of us should leave, to try to understand and get them to understand me. I wanted to belong to the group but not at the expense of my identity.

REFLECTIONS ON THE ESSAY

The fact that adults, established in their jobs and often in high positions, are not only driven by rational thought but also by feelings, is made clear in the essay. When people feel threatened on a deep level the reactions can be formidable and sometimes destructive. But, the same events can also provide a starting point for reflection, insight and learning at a "higher plane". This may take time, maybe require a sounding board.

The conclusion is that, despite everything, those events that most appear to be "setbacks" may be the main source of learning.

Ignition of life and emotional state

To experience something as being true can demand statistics and science. The question then is, what about concepts such as "vitality" and "daily form"?

Some industries and businesses have, in principle, claimed a carte blanche control over the human side of humanity, which can be referred to as the "soft side". There are priests, therapists, medical providers, social workers and HR specialists, to name but a few.

But all humans coexist with each other, in private life and at work. How is it possible to hand over such a large part of our life to others? It concerns the big questions in life, all the fundamentals on which all stand or fall. These issues are everywhere, more or less visible, even in the workplace: existential questions about loneliness, fear, the beginning and end, how to create meaning, how to make choices, and issues related to freedom.

Authors such as Jean Paul Sartre and Astrid Lindgren have formulated their ideas on existential questions in articles, books and fairy tales. A manager who is able to do the same thing can be regarded as having insight.

Nothing fuzzy

The priest takes on the "big issues" in his or her own way. He or she is related to a higher power, uses a special language of dress, and is in need of a particular house (church or mosque) and his or her own book (e.g. the Bible or the Koran). The priest, therefore, relates to themselves and to their fellow human beings based on their own interpretation of the existential questions and with the "glasses" that come with the priest's background and training.

Similarly, other movements, organizations and sects consider existential issues in their way, expressed and accentuated with colours, language, symbols and special codes. These can attract, and they can repel. Nothing will, however, be more fuzzy or concrete than the transmitter and receiver make it. To work and to be with others at work is neither fuzzy nor odd. All employees, senior or junior, act consciously or unconsciously according to their existential codes in order to feel a sense of belonging and not feel alone.

This chapter will highlight the existential questions, primarily from a job perspective but in relation to historical material. The introduction to contact styles is a direct continuation of the same topic from Chapter 1. The angle of this chapter is to look at contact styles as so-called "coping strategies" to cope with life.

The challenge

Gnosis means knowledge. To acquire knowledge is really the only thing that everyone can take responsibility for. To find knowledge in one's self is to find one self more and more. This in turn provides greater security and greater self-support - despite the fact that the knowledge can sometimes be hard to accept.

Being an "A-Gnostic" is to not know. Some issues are so large that they cannot be weighed, measured or known with one hundred percent certainty. And yet it is possible to create one's own view and have an opinion.

The more a person dares to challenge himself with existential questions, the more that person can meet others. It is, in principle, not possible to meet a person on a deeper level than that which one has managed to reach. In this chapter there are reflections from a "reptile" perspective, i.e. from the fundamental emotion which is shared by all peoples of all cultures but which often takes different forms. It's about seeing the whole person and not just his various parts. It's about giving everyone, including him- or herself, a chance.

Contact is to meet

Being in contact with "you" or "it" creates context and "meetings". It means that something happens with "me" when I meet you. And at the same time, something happens with "you" when meeting me. Instead of first getting to know the other person it may be wise to look at yourself. Instead of guessing what the other likes or dislikes, or is afraid of, it may be time well-spent thinking about the same thing with regard to oneself. It is hard enough to change oneself. It is almost impossible to change someone else. The person in question must decide to do that them self.

Almost anything can happen in the meeting between individuals or groups. What seemed simple at the start can become difficult. The person who seems most open and likeable can ultimately be most self-contained and quite unsympathetic. In business coaching, awareness is built around meetings in various forms.

The fragile thread

To be confronted with death, meaninglessness, sadness, betrayal. To be confronted with the choice to leave someone or something. To break the ties of friendship. It can go quickly. And it creates anxiety! Habituation is difficult when emotions like loneliness, guilt or shame arise. But personal attitudes and courage to face these feelings leads to the realization that this is something that is part of our existence as humans. This is not something unique to just me ...

"In the beginning was the relation" ... Well, this may be the case since "religio" is Latin for both religion and relationship, relationship to oneself, to others, to nature - and existential values.

But who has time to think about it now? Time or not, the existential questions are around us, if we choose to see them. *Only you can save yourself by your own insight*, says the Buddhist.

Old is the oldest

The Taoist philosophy has been expressed by Lao Tze among others. The scriptures, Tao Te Ching, have been rewritten, translated and interpreted a large number of times. But the original appears to be about 4,500 years old.

In Taoism there is an existential orientation without gods, with the enjoyment of focusing on joy and an open acceptance of life, an acceptance that sees the universe as fundamentally good. No other spiritual direction has combined art, mystery, laughter and joy as Taoism has done. The Way (tao) can only be understood by walking it, by living it. Life is not created. It is.

JOY AND BEAUTY DESCRIBED BY A TAOIST POET

"It's midnight. All is quiet in the house.
The water clock has stopped.
I cannot sleep because of the beauty of the trembling characters, with spring flowers which the moon throws against the blinds."

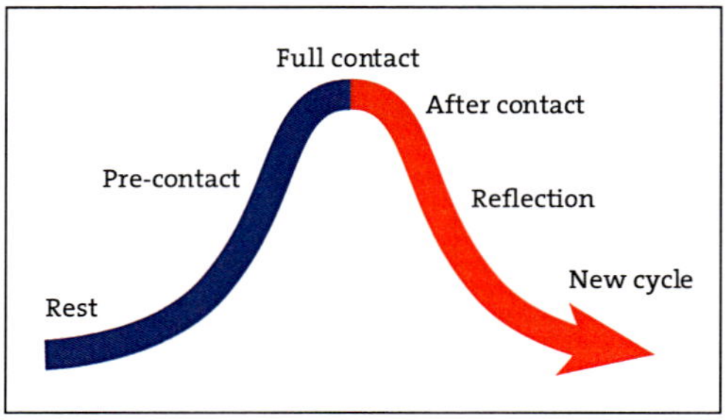

To be in "contact"

In Chapter 1, the general features of the interactive development cycle were described and how it is always present in the coaching conversation. It occurs in all meetings and in all conversation as a natural "life cycle". To be in or out of contact affects not only individuals, groups and the manager. It also affects the efficiency of the organization. The integrated method of dialogue aims at a more efficient communication in order to generate a more efficient organization. It is about transferring the responsibility to employees while at the same time making decisions in the right way and communicating these in a clear manner.

It is about being aware of one's own behaviour, first and foremost. The dialogue method, together with theory, provides both a secure platform to act from, and clear communication tools. This is not a case of learning by heart, but rather an integrated leadership and communicative ability based on the individual's will to dare to do more.

The business coaching dialogue actively involves both coach and employee. They influence each other and both share responsibility for this conversation. Each conversation has its own structure and follows a pattern. The relationship between external business coach and coachee rarely involves a pre-agreed agenda. The structure of the main features can be summarised as follows:

Initial contact: This is the start of the conversation, a little "small talk". Both participants will come into focus and make contact. If a person always wants to skip this initial contact ("I have no time for this bullshit") and wants to immediately start working, it is something to note and take up as an observation. Is there something a person wants to avoid? Or is there something they believe they gain?

TO BE IN CONTACT
Our contact is always NOW and changes constantly. We are always in contact, consciously or unconsciously, with someone or something:

Existentialism: I am my actions in this moment
Field Theory: B = f (P + E)
(Behaviour is a function of the Person and the Environment)

The contact area is a "creation", a "we" in a unique "now".

The contact boundary is a border that is constantly moving and is not fixed.

Contact Interruption is when two people are talking but the conversation suddenly ends due to, for example, an argument, that one gets up and goes out without saying goodbye, or that the feeling of closeness and consensus ends up in a vacuum.

Full Contact: The coaching manager uses his conversational methodology to put questions and feel their way forward and search for possible figures. This can take time and it is important to stay calm and be confident that sooner or later the figure will come up in the conversation.

It may also be that at this point the employee brings up what he wishes to take up in this conversation. It is possible that this is indeed the figure, but the manager continues questioning to ensure that this is the case.

Finally, both parties have agreed on the figure that they are to work with. If it is still difficult to find the figure then the coach should see a warning light. The experience may be such that a figure has almost emerged from the background, but then it slips out of their hands. It happens not once but repeatedly, meeting after meeting. The question is whether the employee is healthy. Is there someone else in the company's healthcare department who could talk to the person instead? Or is it that the employee does not dare open up concerning a topic that is perhaps controversial for the manager?

The manager is involved in creating the field and the employee's behaviour may hang up because of this (the manager is a part of what field-theorists call the employee's "surroundings").

The moment of truth may be that the manager wonders whether it is he himself who is sick, and thus takes back a projection which he has on the employee.

After Contact: Either the meeting time is running out or both begin to feel that the figure is now fully worked out. It is time to round off the conversation. The manager can then ask what the employee will take with him or her from the meeting. Is it a thought? A feeling? Or anything else that has become clearer? This is an affirmation of the tracks left by the meeting.

If the employee wants to raise an additional figure at this point then it is best that the manager asks that "we put it on hold for another time". The manager thereby ensures, in a friendly way, that they avoid starting a new interactive development cycle.

Some people find it difficult to conclude the conversation, and carry on. They can linger at the door, not rise from the chair, or keep coming up with something new to say. The manager must conclude the conversation, but in a friendly way. On a later occasion, the coach can bring this up as an observation that can be investigated. The manager can also ask the employee to come back in a few days time with a comment or reflection on the meeting.

REFLECTION

Both managers and staff will have residual feelings after the conversation. Perhaps this will involve some passing thoughts, maybe some reflections at the dining table in the evening. It may even take several days or weeks before a sudden explanatory reflection - a relic of the conversation – pops up. The conversation is only truly completed after this new insight.

Contact in or out of step

In the company, all people in a group are at different starting points in their development cycle. Often, management is one or several steps ahead of the rest of the employees. Management may find that employees are "stubborn"

COMPANY INFORMATION

The staff have just been informed that the company has been bought by a venture capital company. The CEO has said that the company is now steered by globalization. Profitability must increase. This in itself means that 30% of staff have to leave, but the company will remain in Sweden. The company will have a fantastic development, with lots of very exciting things in the pipeline.

The CEO is happy and full of optimism. He asks if anyone has any questions, but there is deathly silence.

The staff go back to their rooms, and smoulder. No one has realised that something this big was going on. Who has to leave? And we all know what a venture capital company wants - to make money. "The good old days" are gone. Has no one appreciated what they have done so far?

Some decide to resign immediately. Others feel sick. Some continue as usual and do not want to talk about the new situation. Others begin to slow down, taking longer coffee breaks, come late and leave early. Nothing is like it used to be.

and "resistant" while in fact the employees cannot keep up. Management is several steps ahead and see the goal while the staff have just been made aware that something new is happening.

The goal is that all employees will eventually end up in the same energy phase simultaneously and have a common figure - to be able to succeed in their work. In a working group, the manager takes the initiative to ensure that the whole group meets to jointly decide on next year's business plan. It becomes a common platform for the group to stand on. If the group has developed the plan together then it can be hoped that everyone is at the same stage in the cycle and the group members therefore "walk in step". This requires adaptation of the group members towards the common good. Individuals must therefore see the big picture and not be restricted to personal preferences.

If one or more persons have difficulty getting into the same phase, they may be perceived as playing the Devil's advocate. If you instead see it as just symptoms of the different phases then the goal becomes to identify the phases, raising awareness among those involved about the requirements that must be satisfied by all in order to seek out a "figure" that can be accepted by all. Only then is it possible to mobilize new positive energy in the team.

Healthy and unhealthy at work

The interactive development cycle can be used at the individual level, group level, and Organization or company level. Each phase in the development cycle has a positive and a negative side - sides that can variously be viewed as healthy or unhealthy. In each phase, it is possible to do specific interventions to clarify, enhance, reduce or activate at will.

If the manager, human resources, or the external consultant can see the state of the different levels within the company then everyone can get all the help they need as quickly as possible to arrive in the same phase, and in a healthy manner.

The CEO and top management team are often a step ahead. This is perfectly natural, since they have more information that has had time to mature for some time. The management are fooling themselves if they think the rest of the personnel can get into step immediately, for example through holding a fun kick-off.

A re-organization will seldom or never work out by cheerfully extolling the workforce to "knuckle down, forget the past and let's get on with it".

A re-organization can move relatively quickly from the old to the new state if management permits the workforce to complete their development cycles in a reasonable manner. It may require one or two "wakes" and may demand time for reflection on the good old days. What positive aspects of the past should you bring with you? And what should be left behind?

NIHILISM
Existential Nihilism embraces the notion that the world lacks meaning or purpose. All existence itself – actions, suffering, feelings – is senseless, nothingness.
The existential nihilist regards all thoughts and feelings as merely the effects of prior causes. In other words, free will is denied. Neither heredity nor environment is attributed to the nihilist's futile existence.

NARCISSISM
An excessive interest in, or admiration of oneself and one's physical appearance. Narcissism is distinguished by exaggerated sense of importance and superiority.

Phases	**Healthy** attitude at work	**Unhealthy** attitude at work	**Intervention** by manager or coach
Pre-contact Mobilising energy	Creativity, enthusiasm, understanding that things take time	Manic-depressive. Cynicism, do not want to, passive, chaos, fear	Concrete activities. Stimulate.
Contacting	Get ideas, managers go around, realizing plans, define goals, create meaning	Psychopathic. Acting without direction / goals, uncritical	Define goals, create meaning.
Full contact	Understand patterns, take responsibility, make decisions.	Perfectionists. Blame others, workaholic.	Define boundaries.
Post contact	Celebrate, learn, integrate	Narcissistic	Learn to let go.
Conclusion **REFLECTION**	Let go in order to start	Nihilistic. Lonely, bitter, indifferent	To be able to finish and reflect / learn for the future

The interactive development cycle from the perspective of 'healthy/unhealthy attitude'

The time required for this re-adjustment varies from company to company. There will come a day when hopefully everyone who is left is truly "on board" and have managed to adapt to the new situation in a relatively quick, practical, rational and effective manner. Those who are still in the old mindset and unable to let go will probably not be able to remain on the company. Hard? Perhaps, but so is reality. The safest route is for the staff is to know this from the beginning and that managers dare to be clear.

The ideal situation is that everyone who is involved in a meeting or in a planning process can recognize the phase that she or he is entering and determine if they feel positive or negative. Then it is a case of waiting to see which figures come forward and which choices for action are available.

For the organization that takes in a consultant, it is also a question of which phase the consultant likes to work with. The consultant who has a "caring" background may be tempted to stay in the mobilization phase ("What do you feel now?") and never reach the solution. The company-orientated consultant may instead be tempted to jump quickly to the clarification phase to promptly (and erroneously) find the 'solution'!

The company needs external help that can, and dares, identify and work their way through all phases.

Contact through power and influence

The word "power" is clearly open to analysis. When asked spontaneously many will say "I am not a person who wields power – I don't like people who do". But if the question is asked in another way, the answer may well be different: Who influences you? Who do you allow to influence you? And who do you influence? It is actually more or less the same thing. Anyone in senior management knows how it feels to make a decision. The question is what power and authority must accompany the decision for it to be followed.

It is possible to be influenced in an infinite number of ways that are perceived as being more or less pleasant, and are more or less effective. It can be a formal exercise of power by the formally appointed manager. And it can be power exercised in an informal way by various subgroups, networks or informal leaders in their own working group.

It may be easier to see how others exercise their power than to see one's own behaviour. One can also consider if the style of power is conscious or unconscious, and if it is reflective or reactive. Power Style and exercising power can be seen as another form of formal or informal role that each one takes or receives.

Who influences you? Who do you allow to influence you? And who do you influence? It is actually more or less the same thing.

Power and integrated dialogue method

It is possible to handle the situation for a particular person in an acceptable way irrespective of whether the person is a practitioner of power or used to being exposed to power. First and foremost one must be clear about oneself, one's own power needs and the driving forces that control through personality and external factors.

When a manager has attained self-insight, he can interact with others with either his old or new " style of power". By practicing and working consistently with the integrated conversational methodology, employees can be allowed to develop while the manager can remain calm and clear, without getting into unnecessary conflict.

Power, the exercise of power, and being exposed to power can be seen through several filters. One filter involves viewing power from the perspective of Kurt Lewin's theoretical field-model: Behaviour is a function of everyone's Personality and their Surroundings (read more about this in Chapter 2 on Field theory).

Personality and power

Many psychologists argue that the human personality is inborn and can basically never be changed. Possibly, they believe, there may be a personality change if a person falls into a deep crisis.

It is, of course, perfectly acceptable to maintain the view that man in principle is unchangeable and that only her behaviour can be adjusted. But, since most people will experience major or minor crises sometime during their life, almost everyone is faced with the possibility of choosing to experience life in a new way. Many also feel that they have lived through others and have acted and adapted according to the needs of others. This started with childhood, when the child learned to adjust to their parents. The child swallowed a number of introjects that integrated into the "depths of the child" and were then perceived as "personal views" during the course of life. In a crisis, the individual can realise that their position is actually nothing more than an introject and that it can be "spat out" and discarded. Instead, the individual experiences something else, something that others regard as more true.

If a person has "trained" to react and act through the old introjects for many years then it can take perhaps just as long to train to react or act in new ways. Does the person have the desire to change? Does the person have the energy to achieve change? If she does then her personality will seem to have changed. Viewed in another way, the true personality will become visible.

The true personality?

It is possible to simplify the personality by dividing it into four pure personality traits. Of course, people consist of a mixture of these, and many more besides. The following rough categories can be used to clarify the different ways of looking at power and the exercise of power:

1. The relationship-oriented
2. The creative
3. The result-oriented
4. The structured

THE FOUR PERSONALITIES OF THE GREEKS

Hippocrates in Greece (460-370 BC) was one of the first to describe the idea that four body fluids give rise to four personalities:

1. **Blood** (sanguine individual)
2. **Bile, yellow** (choleric)
3. **Bile, black** (melancholic)
4. **Phlegm** (phlegmatic)

The various personality types were assumed to possess different characteristics.

Hippocrates' descriptions have since been renamed several times, but the basic form is still heavily used, especially in many personality tests. Four-field diagrams are often used to describe personalities, management styles and group processes.

All of these personality types can be found at both the personal and organizational level. They are therefore within the person himself, as well as in groups and entire companies. These personality types react differently to stress, they look at job satisfaction and affirmation in different ways, and their power styles differ. Self-awareness about how one acts in different situations enables one to act in an opposite, or different way. The person grows and "becomes more of them self".

The relationship-oriented personality builds their network based on interpersonal relationships. It is important to have meetings to meet people, to find a consensus, to talk in the 'we-form', and to ensure that as many as possible are in favour of the decision. This makes this personality afraid of conflict. By talking in the "we-form" we will make it harder to say "I have made a decision". Responsibility is often fuzzy because everyone feels involved but no one takes personal responsibility. It becomes difficult to follow up the results of a decision.

In a tight spot different power styles arise. It is easy to put the blame on others because "I in particular" did not feel responsible. It is therefore easy to designate

VICTIM

"If only Jenny and Matt had filed the report then I wouldn't be in this mess."

MARTYR

"I have worked so much for this company and worn myself out with so much overtime. And this is all the thanks I get!"

scapegoats: those who should have acted. Personality types who are relationship-oriented quite often consider themselves to be unjustly treated and act with the power style "victim" or "martyr".

INDOORS IN THE WARMTH OR ....
"Now, our creative director has decided that the previous group did a bad job. So they are now out in the cold and may as well start looking for another job. Instead, he has decided that in the future all regions will report to a single function. He has asked Catherine to take care of this and build up the function. Catherine can only accept, but she's thinking about just how much longer she can remain in the "warmth" ...

The creative type is full of ideas. In the normal run of things these ideas are often both fun and realizable. In stressful situations, however, this personality type can pepper their environment with more or less brainless ideas. "If only the company can find a new slogan then sales will take off". Or making new give-aways. If this individual has strong formal power then such ideas create chaos and confusion in the Organization. Exercise of power takes place by "pulling the rug from under" individuals or groups. Just when they feel they know what they're doing then they get a counter-order. Or a new idea means recruiting a new group of people and appointing a new head. They may work as long as the manager thinks that it feels right. But a new idea pops up, the old idea is gone and hence the head and grouping. The style of power can be "if you're not with me, you are automatically against me".

The purely performance- and result-oriented type is driven by results, goals and supplies. They are so-called do'ers. They often have a certain inherent impatience with things, convinced that it must be possible to do everything better. If these personality types are exposed to negative stress then they can begin to pick up on everything that moves, without prioritising. If they have no power themselves, they may burn themselves out by allowing all activities to be equally important, both at work and at home. With power, the whip can crack among the subordinate staff. Targets become tougher, demands increase, and there can be zero tolerance to going home at the normal time. The staff are perceived as either under-achievers or sluggish. The business is given priority at all times while the company atmosphere and relationships become uninteresting. Such a power style can also involve micro-management rather can goal-orientated management. The employees can find post-it notes on their desks in the morning, specifying what should be done or prioritised.

The structured personality type is required by an organization to maintain discipline and order. The organization needs project processes, purchasing procedures, a travel policy, and so on. Everything is fine until something happens at home or at work that affects the person negatively. It is then necessary to fix belt and braces for everything. The power may be exercised by demanding that the regulations are followed to the letter, reporting the people who do not follow rules, or feeling that minor details have not been checked properly and returning work for comments and adjustments over and over again. "Square" is what many tend to call such a personality and the question is, what makes the person have such a need for extreme control? What is she or he is afraid of? What happens to this personality type if there is complete mayhem?

The surroundings and power

Everyone lives and works in different surroundings. These surroundings can also be expressed as living and working in different "fields", according to field theory. So even though "I am me", I am acting, or perceived, differently depending on the surroundings or field "I" am in. The person may be perceived in various ways when they are having a cosy evening at home with the children, on a sailing trip with their partner, at a presentation in the boardroom, picking mushrooms in the forest, doing the weekly shopping at the supermarket, or having a beer or two with colleagues after work.

CHANGING THE SURROUNDINGS

"Before next week's performance review, I suggest we get out of the office. How about a walk? Or shall we go to your place? Or mine? What feels most comfortable? "

The surroundings are therefore affecting the person. And the person affects the surroundings. The question is, what fields, or surroundings, does a person have with them to work in the morning? If they have scolded their partner, or if their child has been crying uncontrollably when left at kindergarten, then the employee will have a few things to think about when they sit down at the morning meeting. The manager wants them to focus on the job. How will the manager ensure that the company's surroundings or field is in the spotlight as quickly as possible? Would it be wise to first have a cup of coffee with a little small talk before starting the meeting?

A power style that works well in one arena could be completely wrong in another. If the manager is used to an authoritarian style of management in their dealings with their Finnish owners then this could prove devastating to the Swedish office. Or if the manager plays the caring, responsible parent to get their children to do what they want then may prove to make them totally passive and dependent - like their employees. This personifies the friendly power-style called the "curling parent" or "curling manager" - to know best, answer all questions, and appear to be able to get things cleared up quickly.

GET PROMOTED
Patrick has worked in a team for five years. He now finds out that he is to be head of this group. His old buddies will therefore become his subordinates. When Patrick is out playing football with the group, the question is what attitude he should take. Can he tell them that his wife just left him? Can he say that he thinks that the management's latest decision was bad? Who can he talk to? It feels lonely, despite the increase in wages.

Behaviour and power

Behaviour can be seen as a role that everyone plays, with more or less insight. But, as we have considered above, behaviour can be seen as a combination of personality and environment, which are always "moving" and changing; behaviour can change in a similar way.

To act in different roles

Behaviour can be seen as an act in professional, personal and private roles. There are advantages and disadvantages in all of them. The question is really when does the person play which role. It is about being able to distinguish between different fields and having the courage to act according to the situation. How personal can one be without being too private? How private does one want to be with subordinate staff or colleagues? What happens if someone only acts professionally at work and never in a personal manner?

- **Professional roles** include Project Manager, Consultant, Human Resources, Government employee, colleague, employee, board member, shareholder, officer
- **Personal roles** include brother, sister, girlfriend, neighbour, an only child, horse rider, football player, toastmaster, friend, patient
- **Private roles** include philosopher, "witch", know-it-all, crybaby, Cassanova, clown, seducer, "police", fundamentalist, mother hen.

Power may be wielded in various ways as a kind of more or conscious behaviour. In the literature, these are sometimes referred to by different names, such as the "queen bee". It is also possible to make people invisible, minimize or ridicule people, threaten, withhold information, or knock their personality – to name just a few.

Many times it is about taking the tools that people recognize and signal to one another – closeness or distance. People with certain designer clothes can instantly recognize each other and know roughly where they are in the hierarchy, and whether or not they will allow themselves to be influenced by that person. Money can represent something else, such as name-dropping, the tone of the voice, a laugh, snort, age, old achievements, sex or gender.

Power as stereotypes "top dog" and "underdog"

It is possible to find the so-called characters "top dog" and "underdog" in all organizations. They can be of either sex, although the modes of expression may vary between them. When the characters become stressed or provoked, the result is often an insidious game, usually at an unconscious level. No one wants to be called "manipulative" or "victim". But this is what it is about. It is an invisible power game, which, when driven to extremes, involves "surviving" at work in a manner that they have been learning for many years.

It is not just "others" who fall into these character roles, but also "I" or "you". It is only a question of which situation starts the pattern. By identifying the feeling of being top dog or underdog you can charge yourself with new feelings and hence make a role change, if it feels appropriate. Sometimes it is a good idea, and even feels nice, to be top dog or underdog. The important thing is to make a conscious choice.

Story 1: Manager and Sales Manager

We can call the Manager, Peter, and the Sales Manager, Anne. Anne has been Sales Manager for almost three years now. She was recruited by Peter and it felt really good from the beginning. Peter did wonder why Anne had to finish rather abruptly in her previous positions. But Anne gave plausible explanations. Over the years Anne has put together a talented group that delivers sales over budget. The Manager has asked Anne how it is possible that she can always go home so early when the group obviously has a lot to do. But of course ... She is always available by phone. And the young salespeople absolutely adore her. She is a manager to their taste. She is always pleasant, always prepared to sound out ideas, and is a real party-person when needed.

Now the company is facing a big change in the marketplace. Both the customer and the competitive situation have changed. An innovative approach is needed to prevent sales from dropping. Peter asked Anne six months ago to both recruit new staff with different backgrounds and to propose key activities. But nothing happens ... and this week a key customer called and asked what Anne was doing. She visited them, promised the moon and then ... nothing. Peter is clearly worried.

During the conversation between Peter and Anne, it appears that recruitment "is underway" but some problems have arisen during the recruitment process. Some candidates have dropped out and the profiles are not the right ones. But it is clear that the problems will get fixed ... But when?, asks Peter. Yes, it's a bit hard to tell, says Anne. As soon as we possibly can, of course.

Peter says that he is expecting a new "action plan" for the next six months but hasn't seen it yet. Anne says that it has been rather hectic recently. A salesperson has been ill and she herself has had to take care of her sick child a number of times. But, says Anne, Peter should stay calm. She, Anne, has everything under control!

Peter does not feel calm. How will he get Anne to understand? He thinks that he is clear enough about what he wants and why. But still, it is like a slippery eel that he can't get hold of. It slips away all the time.

Story 2: Group Head and co-workers

The group was formed just a few years ago and comprises nine people. It is the group manager's first management position and he really wants this group to be something special. For safety's sake, the manager has been on leadership training courses and knows that group processes are ongoing and that he, as head, must learn to act in the different phases.

In addition to all the plans for the group and each individual, the group has also been able to go away a couple of times for team development. The group is positive and really wants to do a good job. They have, among other things, developed ground rules for how to act towards customers, partners,

and towards each other. After six months the manager wonders why Linda, in particular, always complains, saying that she does not understand the group's role and not her own role, either. She thinks she has too much to do and that nobody, especially the manager Robert, appreciates her situation.

Robert sits down with Linda to go through the objectives and deliverables. Linda's work is restructured so that she gets a more limited number of tasks. Robert encourages Linda and says she is doing a fantastic job, and that customers really like her. But ... Linda should not immerse herself so much in details - "Good Enough" is enough. And she does not need to call all her customers in person. Sometimes email is enough, especially if it is difficult to get hold of the customer. Linda would otherwise risk being delayed in what she needs to do and will feel failure and stress. Linda says she is pleased with the meeting and that it now feels like everything is under control and a little more comfortable.

Time passes. Robert sees that Linda often goes into the office of one of the other employees (Neil) and closes the door. She comes out with red eyes but says nothing.

During the next team exercise, it appears to everyone that Linda has not succeeded in achieving her goals. Robert and the group begin to draw up a plan for the group as a whole to deliver as promised. Is it possible to help each other? Some in the group don't feel that this is okay. It cannot be that those who do not have children should do the job for parents who are away a lot, including Linda. It's ok, but only up to a point. Neil also believes that Robert has been unclear about the situation and the role the group should have. He and Linda have spoken and they are in complete agreement that Robert has good intentions but that their jobs are not clearly defined. Others in the group protest, saying that this is not the case at all - everything is now crystal clear.

Neil takes Robert aside. He feels that he has been a little hard on Linda. Robert should understand that she has a difficult situation both at home and at work. Time after time, Linda comes to Neil and starts crying. He has no longer any desire to be a counsellor. Robert does not understand anything; he feels uneasy, he feels that there is no-one in the group to whom he has given so much time, energy and support as Linda. He wonders where it all went wrong, he thinks that everyone works a lot but that only Linda complains ... Robert chooses not to say anything more just then.

Back in the office Robert's manager contacts him. He has learned that Robert is apparently very harsh and requires too much of his employees. Several in the department have come and told him that Linda often sits in someone else's room, crying in desperation. She feels unfairly treated and that Robert does not listen to her. The manager also tells him that Neil, who is perceived as both serious and credible, has reported that Robert is tough on Linda. What is the true situation? Perhaps this manager job is a bit too much for Robert?

The role of "top dog"

This is a person who listens and sees little or inadequately, talks a lot, and wants others to do what he or she says. The person may seem to be loud, repetitive, nagging, insistent, or otherwise assertive in trying to get their way. The person may be perceived as "loudmouthed" or opinionated.

This person often experiences that, however much he or she may nag, beg or threaten, nothing happens. Sometimes it feels easier to perform the tasks that he or she asked others to do - to really ensure that they get done. The angrier this person is towards an underdog, the more evasive the underdog becomes - or takes to their weapons. There is even more talk, putting the blame on circumstances that appear to make sense (at least at first), or outbreaks of crying. The result is that the person who acts as top dog feels guilty and miserable, while the surroundings may say "well you really went over the top this time".

Unhealthy behaviour for a "top dog"

This person has ended up in a character role that can be difficult to get out of. He or she may feel like a frustrated villain but has the gnawing feeling that there is something wrong. The underdog doesn't meet up to expectations. The top dog feels manipulated, but does not know how, because "everyone" smiles and appears friendly, or cries and is sad. If this person gets stuck in his or her loudmouthed top dog role then many will avoid him or her. If the strategy is to entice and cajole his or her colleagues to do things then the person can be seen as nice but also a vague wimp.

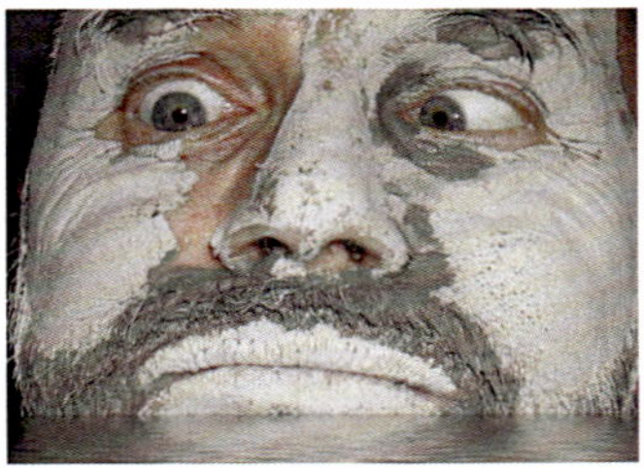

Healthy dialogue method for an ex "top dog"
There is only one way to escape being labelled a top dog - it is to set clear limits on what applies, what is expected, when this should be completed, and what is permitted or prohibited. For safety's sake, this can be written down to avoid confusion. The application of this framework includes an impact assessment of the consequences of deviating from the rules. The so-called underdog may be allowed to formulate both appropriate alternative approaches and appropriate consequences if the chosen path is not followed. It then becomes a case of simply getting on with it and following up on the agreement. The consequences of non-compliance must be fully implemented.

Underdog
This is a person who listens, sees a lot and holds a low profile, even if he or she is chatty and social. The person seldom delivers result but rather finds something or someone to blame for delays or even total failure to deliver - "a lot of talk but little action". The person may seem very nice but also as someone who just glides around.

This person may be an employee or a manager. In the case of a manager, the person can survive, provided that there are loyal employees in his or her group who do the job. It is only when these people either become sick from too much overtime, or quit for any other reason, that it becomes visible in the rest of the organization that something is wrong. There may also be customers who call and ask why promises are not fulfilled or why some commitments take so long to implement.

Unhealthy behaviour for an "underdog"
When forced into a tough position this character often see them self as being treated very unfairly. One of the following management strategies are applied, most often unconsciously:

- **Underdog 1:** This person says "if it hadn't been so, I would ...". "I am dealing with that out right now, and I have encountered some problems, but I'll sort it out." "I will .... I will do it, but ... ". He blames others, or other things: that they have not delivered, it was vacation time, that he has been ill, that the organization is too small, the budget is not enough, and so on. He is deeply unhappy and signals "I'm nice, I mean well, I'll do my best - if only ...". Of course, the surroundings feel inhumane if and when they run him over. Not infrequently this person gets fired and does not know what really happened.

- **Underdog 2:** This person designates scapegoats, and often feels like either a victim (of circumstances) or a martyr (How I work, and I don't even get a thank you, only complaints). One thing is certain - it is definitely not this person's fault fault that her or she cannot hold earlier promises. A young, cute co-worker can often get sympathy. But as the years go by, those in her surroundings become increasingly tired of her and that she complains so often. She risks becoming bitter and alienated.

Healthy methodology for an ex "underdog"

Stalemate

If the person has, in a positive way, been made aware that they often end up as a victim then it is possible for them to work them self out of the role. One has to learn to recognize the feeling before the role falls into place. Is it perhaps a feeling of being "misunderstood" or "exploited"? When the feeling has been identified then the person may wonder what is happening.

The person can signal their feelings to the manager and ask for help with interpretation. If the relationship feels like it is linked to the manager then the 'victim' can contact the personnel department, or another person who can act as an effective sounding board - for example, an external coach. Here, one can get help to act in an active way as employee. This involves being able to recharge oneself with "new" feelings and thereby make new choices (for example, go into new roles), with new consequences and responsibilities. This can then be expressed to the manager, with the mutual objective to resolve the situation, for the sake of the company and everyone involved.

An "oblivious victim" uses strong force

- Others, often managers who want to set limits towards the "underdog", feel guilty and that they are "cruel and harsh", although the "guilt" in the form of non-delivery, lies with the" victim" him- or herself.
- Since the underdog or victim is often a nice , relation oriented person, he or she often has a large social network at work and elsewhere. Such people often drop in on others, or drag out their coffee break, sad and misunderstood. They talk about how they have been treated and get sympathy. A manager of such people has difficulty in handling this, either because they may know nothing, or because the manager doesn't talk about their employees with other employees. The result can be that the managers can be positioned as heartless and unfairly harsh - without the managers being able to defend themselves in public. This easily becomes a virus that infects the working climate. This is about experiencing "a stab in the back".
- Cliques, or subgroups, can form around the victim / martyr / underdog. A shift in power can occur, more or less imperceptibly, and may result in a "kill-the-leader" syndrome. It is very important to slow down and realize this in time to ensure that the manager can, and has the energy, to remain.

Respond directly through clear integrated counselling skills

As soon as a manager finds out that the employee, the underdog, is going round and gossiping then the manager should call in the employee for a discussion. The manager should tell the employee that they know what is going on and that this is not okay. If something is wrong then the employee should discuss it with the manager. If this is not possible then the employee should go to someone in the personnel department. Limits, conditions and implications should be sorted out in a three-way discussion between the manager, the employee and representative of the personnel department (or other third party). In other words, everything should be put on the table at the meeting - all choices and responsibilities - instead of misleading information being spread like a virus as the result of coffee-break chats.

Power and pleasure

Power does not need to have negative overtones. Everyone is affected in some way every day without any adverse effects. It is possible to happily allow oneself to be influenced by a loved one, or by a compliment. There is good news to celebrate and be influenced by. A positive charismatic person can affect an entire group to work willingly and with commitment.

In one particular environment, a power style can be perceived as extremely negative, such as a laugh. While in another environment, the laugh can be perceived as relaxing and agreeable. The question is what is the feeling that fills the person at that moment when she or he is acting? Does the person have good intentions, or not? Is there a strategy to have fun or to laugh at someone's expense? Who perceives what? If the starting point is positive, then it is easier to give and receive feedback, and take it in.

Contact as a survival strategy

For humans to survive, they learned early on how they should behave relative to their fellow human beings - in good times, but especially in adversity. These so-called contact styles have often been crucial to survival – in a group of siblings, as a single child, or in relation to parents and teachers.

In developmental psychology, people such as Maslow, with his "hierarchy of needs", and Sigmund Freud, with the child's stages of development, have influenced the science of how man develops. Many things were considered earlier as being "sick" and needed to be "cured". The old schools of thought are constantly being challenged. Some of the old ideas are retained, others are scrapped. There are bookshelves filled with discourses on various schools of thought and development models.

This chapter, on the other hand, exemplifies how contact styles can affect people at work. Nothing is "sick". It is rather about different types of "coping strategies" to survive as a human being. Some strategies have been suitable at an early stage in life, others are better suited later. It becomes difficult for the man who is stuck using a contact style that was excellent at the age of six, but that is easily passé at the age of 40.

A human's defences should never be despised or destroyed. Instead, they can be scrutinized by the person who is affected. Each person should be allowed to quietly ponder whether other contact styles could be developed in place of, or alongside, the old ones. They provide new forms of protection in the adult world. It's all about developing selfesteem, in a new and insightful way.

Everyone has a whole range of contact styles. It is quite natural for a person to be better at some contact styles and worse at others because, even in this, "practice makes perfect". Contact Styles are projection, introjection, confluence, deflection, and retroflection.

CONTACT STYLES
Projection: To believe

Introjection: To learn

Confluence: To join

Deflection: To keep at a distance

Retroflection: To keep within

PROJECTION

To act as a projection screen for others is to allow others to think and feel things about you, things that primarily concern themselves. This contact style means that I see signals in you that give me a lot of fantasies about you. It is common to "think" about others and other things.

PROJECTION AT WORK
"I have met the new boss. What do I think about her? She has authority and appears to be completely clear about how she wants things. I know that she is divorced, which is probably why she works a lot and may want us to work hard, as well. Does she seem nice? Well, I don't know. She laughs and smiles but does seem a bit cold. She's probably been involved in a few scraps and has to be careful in the beginning."

HEALTHY CHOICE

Give the new manager a chance to show even more of them self before giving the "final verdict". Realize that an important part of one's job is to ensure that the manager succeeds no matter what opinions one might have about them.

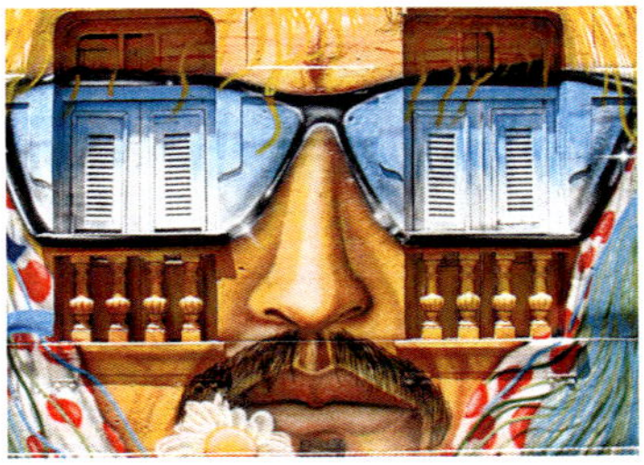

Friend or foe

UNHEALTHY CHOICE

To act just as cool as the new boss seems to be, stay on the fence and criticise the new person. It can result in the new manager feeling insecure and preferring to have another person in "your" position.

INTROJECTION

You must have the ability to absorb information to learn something. This contact style will mean taking in knowledge in the form of facts, attitudes, social norms, values, musts, roles, rules and regulations that are not your own but belong to the world outside. After having consciously or unconsciously reflected upon the "knowledge" that flows in, the person will both accept the "knowledge" and take it into their own system, or reject the "knowledge" - that is to say, spit it out.

INTROJECTION AT WORK
"At our workplace we take immediate charge of all new employees. They get a copy of the staff handbook which presents the equal opportunity plan, psycho-social policy and so on. After a few weeks they attend an introductory course which introduces "The Ten Commandments" that apply here. Everyone has to work in small groups and practice the commandments so they know how they affect their work. Twice a year we have performance reviews according to a template that everyone must use. Our working environment? It is characterized by clarity about what counts! "

HEALTHY CHOICE
The new employee quickly takes into account both the spoken and the unspoken rules. The adaptation feels natural and clarity from the company providing security. The Commandments are easy to relate to since they can be related to in the employee's job. The person does not feel that their own ethics suffer.

Taste and take in

UNHEALTHY CHOICE
To unthinkingly swallow everything can develop a leader with tunnel vision where it is not permissible to even breathe something approaching criticism. Orders are issued and shall be enforced immediately, without discussion. For the employee, an uncritical behaviour can, in the worst case, lead to them having to do the dirty work and then risk being labelled as "guilty" when the dirty laundry has to be cleaned.

CONFLUENCE
To become confluent means to come together, to merge. At confluence, you cannot separate out what is "me" and what is "other". The WE-form is often used. The royal 'we' and the patronizing 'us', as if addressing children, should also be included.

Advertising often plays on confluence, where WE will identify US with the celebrity or the inadequate role-model, do what they do, and thus almost become like them.

CONFLUENCE AT WORK
"I work in an incredibly exciting project. We are probably 50 people involved in total and the project will last for several years. We work, in principle, all the time. These aren't just my colleagues. They are my friends - they are almost like my family. During the week, for example, we often go out together and talk about the project and what is important right now. Every Friday we have a pub evening, which is often both boozy and late. Quite naturally many people meet here and become couples - where else would we meet? "

HEALTHY CHOICE
To be associated with a group in a positive way gives one a kick. This is all fine and good as long as new people are welcomed into the group and the informal subgroups work constructively. It is possible to consider what it is that the binds the group together. If you can't come to the pub evenings and still feel welcome in the group then the permissive attitude is okay.

Feel intimacy

UNHEALTHY CHOICE
When the project starts "demanding" that everyone is involved all the time, and when it is perceived as a disloyal act to switch over to a new project, then many will start attaching guilt to the person who has finished, and the situation begins to smell of sectarianism. When someone feels that it is impossible to get home to their own family, and when divorce seems like a more natural choice than a divorce from the project, then there is the risk that the person has lost them self.

DEFLECTION

DEFLECTION AT WORK
"You have to decide! And I've decided to stay at this establishment. I have a good salary, I have flexible working hours, fun business trips abroad ... Not that I think that the grass is much greener on the other side. I simply have to accept and adapt to the fact that all the important decisions in the company are actually made by the manager's father. I have to ignore the fact that projects are run that have no future, but the manager just thinks are fun. It's stupid but if I'm going to stay then I just have to accept it."

This contact style is about keeping things or people at a distance from one self, to turn off, to not be willing to see or hear, to consciously put "into brackets" in order to prioritize and focus.

To screen off

HEALTHY CHOICE
The person in the example has made a conscious consequence analysis for them self and weighed the pros and cons. From there, they have chosen to actively ignore certain things in order to absorb the positive aspects and feel that the workplace is okay.

UNHEALTHY CHOICE
The person decides to bite the bullet and ignore what feels wrong. They need the money. They have to pretend that nothing is wrong. If they are confronted then they can always make a joke of the situation to be able to keep their distance.

RETROFLECTION
This contact form concerns restraint, thoughtfulness and reflection. In quiet retroflection there are many thoughts and reflections. In open retroflection, together with someone else, there is an exchange of thoughts and reflections.

RETROFLECTION AT WORK
"As head of this group I have to learn to wait. So I'll be quiet now that I've brought up a point, and wait for those who are slow in reacting. This is really great. The most unlikely grains of wisdom can come from where you least expect. There's a lot of experience here, especially among some who have been considered dull and morose. Now they can make their mark. Frustrating for some but it's worth gold for the group."

Reflect in advance

HEALTHY CHOICE
To swing between open and closed retroflection gives others the chance to keep up and contribute. And it gives oneself the chance to pause, breathe and listen.

UNHEALTHY CHOICE
An employee comes to work every morning, does their job and goes home. The person doesn't participate in

coffee breaks and is considered to be unavailable and shut-off. The employee is never really happy or angry. Or maybe they are, but nobody understands. No one knows how the person actually is until they start taking sick leave. The person has internalised something, making them ill.

Contact zones clarify and bring to life

Everyone expresses themselves in speech in slightly different ways. Some always relate what they have heard and seen on TV and what they think about it. Others speak in metaphors and images. And a few might start by saying how sorry they were when their son-in-law didn't come to dinner - they start by expressing a feeling.

The child learns early on how to express them self. Students at school are educated in thoughts and reflection. It then continues into the workplace where quick thinking often is rewarded. Many therefore become very good at thinking, describing what they think, and intellectualizing what they feel. Gradually, it becomes increasingly difficult to grasp the feeling in a meeting or conversation. "How do you feel now?" is often answered with "okay" or "fine". And what does that mean? Increasing the ability to express oneself in more ways, and at the same time raising awareness of when, what and how it is done, improves communication skills both with oneself, and with others.

For the coaching manager, this becomes important when they must give an employee feedback. A Business Coach can exploit this in every discussion and, in particular, three-party discussions (in which two people who disagree get together for a dialogue led by a coach).

INTELLECTUALIZING A FEELING

Coach: Can you describe with an adjective what you feel right now?

Coachee: I feel that it's quite okay.

Coach: What do you mean by that?

Coachee: ... okay ....? I think it's pretty quiet.

Coach: Are you saying that you are quiet, inside?

Coachee: No, I feel more anxious. But I must of course take it easy. "We shouldn't worry ourselves," said the personnel in Human Resources.

Coach: So you feel, in fact, "anxious"?

Coachee: Yes, that's right.

Outer zone - Intermediate zone – Inner zone

The surroundings pour in impressions that have to be taken care of by various processes in the body so that the conscious can organize them into figure-background to form part of an overall experience. The ways surroundings can be captured, recorded, and organized can be structured in different zones of consciousness called outer zone, intermediate zone, and inner zone.

Outer zone

The attention is turned to, and captures, the impressions that come from the outside world. Hearing, sight, smell, touch and taste are used when the impressions come from outside the body. One can also get information about one's own body ("my fingers are cold", "it tickles in my nose"). These are data and facts that are available just now. No discussions or arguments can make them cease to exist.

Intermediate zone

Here attention is focused on mental thought processes. Individuals are informed of their experiences, such as fantasies, interpretations, prejudices, plans, memories, and guesses.

Inner zone

The attention is turned to, and captures, the impressions that come from within the body. This could be feelings like *stress, tension, stage fright, joy, love,* etc.

The contact's polarities

Polarity is a term that has been used for millennia. In Buddhism's yin and yang, polarities appear clearly as white and black. In the white there is also a black stain and in the black there is also a white stain. It is, therefore, not so easy to divide life into only black or white. If there is one then there is also the other, even if it is almost invisible.

Opposites can be found all the time. In a working group one morning, most people can feel alert and refreshed while one person says that they are tired. A person can feel that they generally have a positive and intense attitude but sometimes this person can feel negative, like a collapsed balloon. Polarity can be expressed in an endless number of ways. But if there is one pole there is also the other. It's just a question of trying to formulate words and reflect ... How often is the polarity word visible to you or to others?

The idea is that the contrasting words are related to each other - they are each other's extremes. If there is one, then there is the other, consciously or unconsciously. The more a person dares to move towards their outer poles the more visible the person's character becomes.

For example, a married couple once married because of their fascination with the others opposite side (e.g. "I'm not so social but my husband is"), but over the years this fascination can develop into a major irritation. Or, each partner can see that even she/he has the other partner's features in certain situations. The couple can then meet in their polarities.

The psychologist Carl Gustav Jung was also fascinated by the opposites and what was unconscious. He also called this man's "shadow". There is a shadow that follows everyone through life that the person is often unaware of. It is a side of the person that is not so pleasant to know. But by raising awareness that one also has these sides one can make friends with them and know when, and if, they should be made apparent more actively.

The ancient Egyptians also talked about the unknown, sometimes unpleasant, sides of each man. They said that it was not possible to pass into the afterlife before one had made friends with these sides. Therefore, on the way towards the god of death the almost-dead passed its shadows, which looked like "people". By taking them by the hand and acknowledging them it was possible for the person to gradually approach the god of death before finally being welcomed and have a dignified end.

It is possible to regard the concepts of top dog and underdog as polarities. They are thus tied together. It is therefore not surprising that an underdog can get a lot of power, and from this perspective, act as a top dog. And in the same way the character top dog can become a victim of circumstances when the underdog character wields their power. So it's not an either-or when it comes to these characters, but rather a question of when are you or I the one or the other? In what situations? With which people? It's about seeing one's own role and what triggers the emotion that makes this character appear. Only then will it be possible to act in a new, more productive, gentle and effective way.

THE PHILOSOPHY OF OPPOSITES

All under heaven see beauty as beauty
only because they also see ugliness.
All announce that good is good
only because they also denounce what is bad.

Therefore, something and nothing give birth to one another.
Difficult and easy complete one another.
Long and short fashion one another.
High and low arise from one another.
Notes and tones harmonise with one another.
Front and back follow one another.

Thus, the True Person acts without striving and teaches without words.

Deny nothing to the ten thousand things.

Nourish them without claiming authority,
Benefit them without demanding gratitude,
Do the work, then move on.

And, the fruits of your labour will last forever.

From Tao Te Ching, verse 2
(translation from www. thebigview.com)

Polarities field of work

To experience the light it is necessary to have experienced the dark. Light and darkness are opposites but still have contact with each other because they are interdependent.

1. Similarly, it is possible to question a person about what characteristics he or she feels are most prominent and most used at work, for example: *diligent, controlled, structured, cheerful* or *loner*.

2. When they are formulated, the next question is what these features' opposites are. They can be expressed in several ways. The important thing is that the person who gets the question can express it in a way that is crystal clear. In this case, the opposites could be:

Diligent	↔	Lazy
Controlled		Chaotic
Structured		Messy
Cheerful		Sour
Lonely wolf		Relation oriented

The idea is that the two words are each other's extremes, but are interrelated. It is like the opposite ends of the same "string".

3. The next question is whether, at some point, the person in this fictitious example feels that they are lazy, chaotic, messy, sour, or social? If it happens, how does it happen, and in what context? And how does the person feel then? Does the person know someone else in their surroundings who is better characterized by the contrasting words? How are these people perceived?

Is the glass nearly empty or nearly full?

By doing this exploration, the person will become aware of more sides of them self. There are often sides that the person has no great desire to confess to and that perhaps irritate others. The question is, when can the seemingly negative turn into its opposite and be positive? Is the glass nearly empty or nearly full?

To be present in Now

There are not many people who have not not heard that they have to live here-and-now and take advantage of what exists right now because no one knows what tomorrow will look like.

Man recounts his experiences to others, often in the past tense. One remembers a holiday, when the children were young, an old injustice, an old love, the time before the reorganization. The stories can be fun and engaging for others. It is possible to find points of contact in each other's lives. It is possible to find common joy and it is possible to find subjects of mutual dislike.

But someone may also dwell on a story in a way that indicates that the person appears to become "trapped". The funny, common ties may be too funny to be suitable for a workplace. They can take time. They can include some people while others feel left out. They can be more debilitating than nourishing for the company.

For the manager who works with business coaching, it is not interesting to hear stories about "ancient history". Life cannot be put on a repeat button. Instead of getting stuck in the past, the manager takes note of the events that are referred to.

- The manager describes how he or she reacts to the person and their story right now, and then gives an interpretation of what this may involve - perhaps adding what is acceptable or not in the workplace.
- The manager then asks how the employee them self perceives the incident right now, when the manager explains it, and gets feedback.

It thus becomes an exploration of the present moment to help the person to get new insights and move on.

The integrated dialogue method can help the manager to remain neutral in the dialogue but still dare to be clear about what is needed for work to continue.

If there is a conflict between two people, the manager can set up a three-way dialogue for the 'combatants' to find a solution that they can live with. The manager has to ensure that this dialogue concerns here-and-now and not the past.

One of the basic fundamentals of integrated counselling skills that has been described is that the manager should be able to focus on himself or herself while in communication with other people. By simultaneously listening outwardly and inwardly, the manager can act in a reflective manner and calmly decide what type of dialogue method is most obvious, and hence effective, in each meeting.

BE MENTALLY PRESENT NOW

"I was at a meeting this morning and I thought I really screwed up. It felt so embarrassing to present to the most senior executives things that they didn't consider relevant."

"You make me curious. How does it feel right now when you talk about this? "

"It was worse earlier. A lot of people have said that it was pretty okay. Right now I feel, well, mostly confused. How should I act at the next meeting? "

"Let's talk about the next meeting. What strategies do you see yourself having?

Or would you prefer to discuss the way you talk when you are confused, and if you could be more effective?"

Existential questions

There are certain "major topics" in the existential issues – those that one should definitely think over. They will be described further here.

Other "big issues" that is rarely mentioned in the existential context, but that also affects humans in a deep way, are feelings such as friendship, love, evil, and

jealousy. These are feelings that arise in contact with others. They can control and engulf the modern man, in both positive and negative ways. The reference list gives suggestions of some authors who write about these feelings.

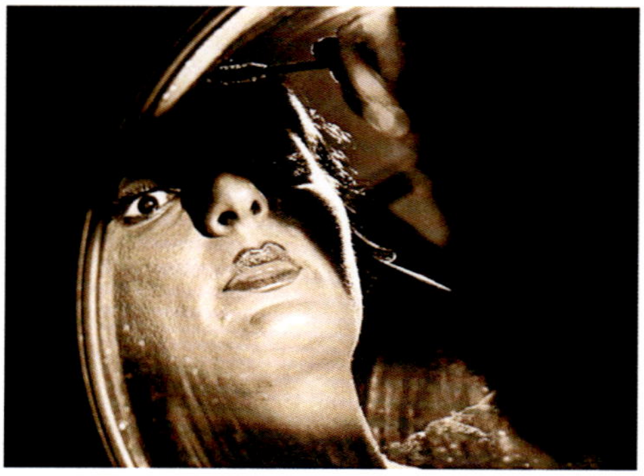

Loneliness and fear

"I miss him" said Mattis when Skalle-Per died, in the story of Ronja (Astrid Lindgren).

As soon as man becomes conscious of himself, his loneliness and vulnerability, she can, in addition to the deep feeling of loneliness, experience an anxiety - a deep concern and fear that is not necessarily associated with "disease". The existential literature has dealt with the fundamental role of anxiety and considers that anxiety is indeed an inevitable part of human existence.

In principle, everyone wants closeness, warmth, companionship, and love. All the experiences of ourselves, and about the world, are created in relation to others. The fear of experiencing loneliness and anxiety can lead people to do almost anything to be involved "in the game".

The experience of being alone is different for different people. It is possible to feel left out and psychologically alone in a marriage even if there is another individual in the room. Others will do anything to avoid physical solitude.

The ways to minimize feelings of loneliness are innumerable. A few thoughts can be found in the section on the contact style "confluence". Another way may be to be constantly involved socially, to cohabit with "my best friend", to abuse, ranging from drugs to sex to gambling, etc. As someone who is 'alone' one can also say 'no' to parties where couples are invited and only look for singles clubs, or single people and friends. It is therefore possible to consolidate one's own experience of loneliness through personal choice.

In the working group, it is easy to feel alone if there is any type of deviation. It may be the way one behaves, one dresses, one's culture, housing or social class, and lots of other things. The choice will be to go away, or by all possible means try to get involved, or to remain and adapt - accepting the situation. Anxiety levels may be reduced by getting together with a few colleagues to create a small informal group. Such a group may demand strict obedience through invisible rules. Such a set of rules is often only felt. Failure to adhere

IT'S LONELY AT THE TOP

"Isolated politician Leijonborg did not see the disaster coming

Leijonborg was so lonely at the top that no one told him that the disaster was coming. This may be the price of long-term power. With a new Liberal leader the playing field has changed for the government and the other right-wing parties."

Published in the Swedish newspaper Svenska Dagbladet by Goran Eriksson, April 24, 2007 to the rules means that the individual is expelled, and will return to his or her own loneliness.

To feel alone and defenceless is also to realize how conditional friendship and friendship is. Therefore, it is painful when we become cut off from our social context, such as after being fired or made redundant. It feels as if life's-threads dissolve when we jerked out of context. The pain will result in considerable loss and loneliness, and even sorrow for some. There may even be a sense of not being good enough and having been let down.

"I miss you", are three short words that have a great meaning - both at work and in private life. Every goodbye is to die a little.

The beginning and end

Existential philosophy includes the more drastic concepts of life and death instead of the rather conservative "beginning and end". Both are equally true. It is rather the level of the beginning and the degree of closure which may be different.

In a sales relationship, for example, it may be difficult to know exactly when the customer has decided to buy. Where was the start to the customer's decision? Was there a rational objective reason, was it a positive comment about the customer's child, or was it a sense of being able to trust the salesperson? Perhaps this is, in itself, only the start of a long-standing customer/sales relationship that will last for years to come.

A participant on a course pointed out that she had neglected herself too long and just taken care of others, worked, or chauffeured her children. Finally she had to book an appointment with her gynaecologist, with a report after a couple of weeks: "lesions". The woman got an appointment for simple surgery. Following the surgery, the woman asked the doctor what would have happened if the cell changes had gone undetected. Well, she would have developed a serious cancer in about 9 years. The strange thing was that this woman had decided to muster the strength to live just that long for her children's sake. What ended now? What started?

A small-business owner felt that the vision of working with something really meaningful fell apart when his only colleague was on indefinite sick leave. In addition, one of Sweden's largest monopolies said that they would take the project away from the small company since it had the same brand name as one of the large monopoly's major investment projects (not yet being launched or made official). For a long time everything was just chaos. This could have been the end of both an enterprise and an entrepreneur. Instead, this became the start of a new beginning.

The small business lives on today with major contracts in which these events form a unique business concept and are a source of success, for both the entrepreneur personally as well as for the company. The large monopoly is no longer existant due to new regulations and laws.

Choice and freedom

To build awareness and understanding is a responsibility. All of a sudden the individual understands the choices that can be made, and that by choosing

Can, want to, dare to, have the energy to?

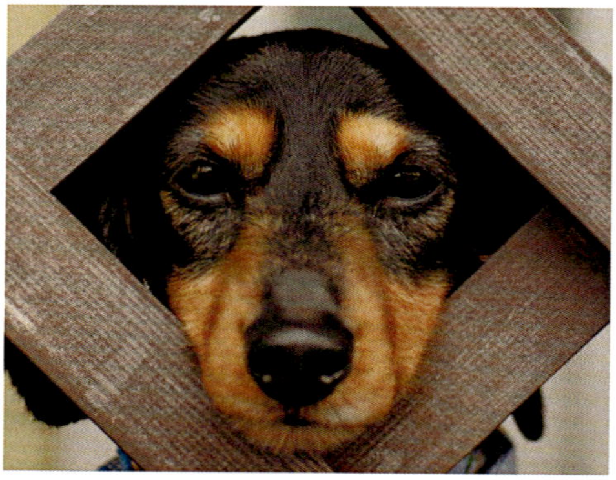

an option, other options must, by necessity, be rejected. This responsibility can feel wonderful and give a sense of freedom. But it can also be experienced as unpleasant and create anxiety. This is often a "moment of truth". People have the freedom to choose. But, even if this is the case, freedom is full of limitations. In situations where we are in total confusion, such as in the event of sickness, accidents and divorces, matters come to a head and we wonder how we can exploit this freedom. Maybe the freedom is experienced more as a lack of freedom. And it may be that in such moments it feels liberating to be able to turn to an authority to ask for advice, such as God, a Consultant, a doctor, a leader, or another professional.

Advice is often given in the best of intentions, but is more often based on the donor's experience than that of the recipient! It may seem easier, for example, for an employee to later put the blame on the professional/manager who gave the bad advice than to accept the responsibility them self. This is a good way to fool oneself in the long run.

Do people need an authority to rely on because they cannot, or dare not, trust them self? Do people need "something" or "someone" to thank when things go well, or blame when things go badly, in order to constantly adapt to power? To choose not to see one's own weaknesses, but load these (blame) onto others is described far back in history. The Christian Bible describes how the people put their sins onto a goat (scapegoat) which was then driven out alone into the desert, thereby causing all the sins of mankind to disappear. And man could then feel free of guilt.

A scapegoat

Every Sunday the Christian community members admit their (known and unknown) sins in the church and in this way make them self free of guilt. Jesus died on the cross for the sake of humans. Did Jesus make a conscious choice, or did he adapt to his father's authority? Could he have chosen something else? And what were the consequences these various alternatives for himself, for Mary Magdalene, and the world that came afterwards? And it is Judas who should have been the scapegoat among the disciples? What was the power struggle? Was it practical to let him take all the blame and then let the winners write history?

Disobedience and adaptation

"The will grows in the woods!" or "The will should be beaten out of the child!" This was a not uncommon form of expression in Sweden a few generations ago. The question is, what the family, society and companies do with very strong-willed people today. Strong will can be difficult for society - and for individuals who feel that they will be curbed or expected to adapt. Strong will also accommodates lots of energy.

If no one adapts then there will be anarchy. If everyone adapts then there will be no development. Keeping people in stupidity, ignorance, or simply expressing "the only acceptable truth", has long been the hallmark of the ruling class - whether it is secular or religious in nature. Choosing between adjustment and non-adjustment is a balancing act. The ability of the company and the individual manager to channel the energy of the strong-willed can lead to success.

It is hardly surprising that gods exist, regardless of cultural and historical origin, since it can be hard to accept the loneliness and freedom of philosophy.

FREEDOM UNDER CONSTRAINT

China

The middle-class Chinese person in Shanghai cannot vote or choose to emigrate. But he or she is entitled to free schools, healthcare, and an ever higher standard of living. Does this Chinese feel free or constrained? What sort of freedom would he or she like to have?

IKEA

The new employee at IKEA quickly finds out what "commandments" are in force in the company. These commandments shall not be questioned. He or she is offered a course to become familiar with what the commandments mean in their own work. What degrees of freedom and constraint exist in companies in Sweden? How "disobedient" are you allowed to be?

It does not, however, deprive any human of the responsibility to make their own choices, even the choices are made in relation to others' decisions (e.g. at the company, in the family, according to the law).

Finding a scapegoat or blaming others, without looking at one's own guilt, can never be right. It may feel good to 'be pitied' - to be a victim. But, in the long run, it is hardly the victim or the martyr's roles that benefit society, the company, or the individual.

WHEN IS ADJUSTMENT DANGEROUS?
Lilith was Adam's first wife in Paradise. They were created as equals from the dust of the earth.

Lilith questioned Adam when he asked her to act as his servant. Adam asked God for help and God gave her, through some angels, the choice to bend to Adam's will or to be punished and banished.

Lilith refused to return to being a slave and God then gave Adam a new wife, Eve.

It is said that Lilith returned to paradise once in the form of a serpent and that she, in folklore, is the mother of fairies and witches.

To whom is knowledge and reflection dangerous today? What is it best to keep quiet about? What is best to pretend not to see? What "war" should be made? What will the price be for those who do not belong to the mainstream?

Lilith is mentioned in passing in the Bible (Isiah 34:14):

"And wild animals shall meet with hyenas; the wild goat shall cry to his fellow; indeed, there the night bird (lilit or lilith) settles and finds for herself a resting place."

She is more frequently referred to in the Kabbalah (Jewish legends).

The meaning

The word nihilism comes from the Latin word "nothing" and is a radical branch of existentialism, or pessimism, which insists that life has no meaning. Even if you try to achieve your values, your life will still end up with nothing. Nihilism has some similarities with fatalism (= belief in an inevitable fate) but is in fact more radical than fatalism. Nihilists say that life is not just going to end up with nothing but with less than nothing, because life consists of only one thing: pain.

Meaningful

Could it be that everyone is born with the seeds of what will be just that person's purpose in life – in other words something that is predetermined? Or is it that everyone, every day, is making choices? Together, these choices, large and small, form the person's life. What is called fate is thus not really destiny but rather the result of every single step the individual takes in life.

Plato, Jung, and also the Nobel Prize winner and author, Imre Kertez, and the Englishman Philip Pullman, have described their thoughts about destiny and the meaning of life. For Plato, much was pre-determined and could be related to an ideal world. In one of Imre Kertez's books, it is a question of an attitude to fate that pops up. And for Philip Pullman, the old must be replaced by something new where the new takes fate into its own, new hands - a fate without gods but with people who take responsibility and make clear choices in joy and sorrow.

It is up to the individual to accept these thoughts about fate or reject them. The only thing that can be really true is that every individual has the responsibility to decide and make active choices in their lives no matter how life, or fate, develops. But no one said that this is easy ...

Meaningless

Life may feel useless and empty from time to time. It can be tempting to give up or maybe sooth the emptiness with some form of 'drug': everything from candy-eating, a few beers with friends, getting permanent kicks through shopping, or zapping through life with ever "wilder" activities ...

No thing is there

The Christian Protestant Martin Luther has sometimes been given the blame that our lives are based more on the "musts" than on pleasure and joy. This may or may not be true, but modern man rushes through life at an ever-accelerating rate. The modern man is just doing, doing and doing. And throughout this incessant activity, she receives affirmation from managers, colleagues and friends. And she also presents a good social profile. One of the most common introductory phrases in a conversation in Sweden is "And what do you do?", and then to many (most?) it seems good to have a job title that describes both social status and income level.

Making a conscious choice - that this is the way I want to live my life - is quite in order. More troubling is what happens when many different choices in life are thrust upon us at the same time; for example, there is the choice to have children and the choice to take a new job, or the choice to quit the old job for a more uncertain (but fun) job.

There is talk of 30-year and 40-year crises. "Wasn't life supposed to be about something other than this?" The feeling of experiencing that one has been cheated, without knowing when it happened, how it happened, or if it was someone else's fault ...

Here lurks the frustration, or a feeling of falling into complete chaos where

IMPORTANCE OF EMPTINESS

Thirty spokes connect
to the wheel's hub;
yet, it is the centre hole
that makes it useful.

Clay is shaped into
a vessel; yet, it is the
emptiness within that
makes it useful.

Doors and windows
are cut for a room;
yet it is the space
where there is nothing
that makes it useful.

Therefore, though
advantage comes from
what is; usefulness
comes from what is
not.

From Tao Te Ching, verse 11 (translation from www.thebigview.com)

nothing works. Working even harder may give some compensation and dull such feelings. And the rat race speeds on, faster and faster ... Is this being capable?

To dare to halt when life at times seems either chaotic or hopelessly empty is courageous - to really stop and feel what is happening to the emotions and physical reactions. By pausing and feeling for "nothing" it is possible to eventually identify a hope. The problem is that nobody knows when the bottom has been reached. It can feel good to look up a person who dares to stand still when nothing is present.

The leaf has grown in the dead forest

'He held out his wrinkled hand and showed what he had in it. It was a small green leaf. Such a small, beautiful leaf it was, thin and smooth and the palest of green and with small, fine veins. "It has grown in the Dead Forest", said Eno.'

From 'Mio, My Son' by Astrid Lindgren

Dead end, chaos and paradoxes of change

Sometimes people end up in a dead end. It is an event or situation which makes it impossible to know what is the front or rear. Thoughts are spinning. There is either a variety of loose ends or none at all. You cannot "go back". This is a "move forward", but how? At this moment everything just feels chaotic.

This is about a step in the process of change, where change is perceived as being great and the options are fuzzy, are not wholly agreeable, or most things seem incomprehensible.

From chaos to change

The starting point for the feeling of ending up in a dead end can be a reorganization, a freak accident at home, a death, a new manager, new conditions of work ... Whatever it is, it might be nice to know that it is "normal" – i.e. that sooner or later everyone ends up in this situation.

As a manager, you may want to intellectually know the various phases, to know if it is possible to act when a co-worker or colleague ends up in a dead end. What is mostly needed is ... time! If you as a manager cannot remember all these steps then it is safest to just be quiet and listen. Wait for the "patterns" of conversation that always present themselves. This is a help in itself. Many people do not want or expect any more either. If there is time for more dialogue then it may help to know the various phases.

If you as a manager do not have enough time then it might be better to delegate this dialogue to, for example, the personnel department. If the person feels really bad then this is not "business coaching" but rather therapy. In this case the company healthcare department is probably a better partner, as long as they have experience in counselling techniques and not just prescriptions and pills. It is, as mentioned previously, normal in life to occasionally get into situations that seem impossible.

Dead end or a process of change?

Stagnation: The person has stalled. They often feel like victims, and see no way out. They look for help, talk, and can be seen as repetitive and tiresome as the "record" runs the same song, over and over again. They do not see that they can make any choices or make any decisions right now because there is so much that influences their situation that they can do nothing about.

- *For the person:* Feel that external forces completely control their life right now.
- *For the manager:* Use "open questions" (what, when, how).
- *Objective:* Make the person aware of their own feelings and behaviour and what it is that forms the figure in the frustration.

Ask about what seems hardest, least hard. Also, ask the person about the role they play in events. Are there patterns? Does the manager himself become surprised, annoyed...? Inform the person about it and let the person think about what it is that causes the manager to feel this way.

The person usually responds with "I would ..." or "on the other hand ...".

Polarization: The person is torn between two poles, to take action inwardly or outwardly. The person would prefer to act outwardly, but the opposite pole, with thoughts and emotions, inhibits them. The poles are perceived as being equally strong. The conversation is, inter alia, to find out the important poles right now, between needs and avoidance. This forms the dialogue's "theme".

- *For the person:* What is experienced is that it is perhaps mostly internal forces that govern life right now.
- *For the manager:* Explore the figure - the internal forces. Automatically set the previous figure - external forces - in the background.

Dead ends and change through the interactive development cycle

Pre-contact: Stagnation

Mobilize energy: Polarization

Full Contact: Chaos, Contraction

Aha: Expansion and Change

Post-Contact: Conclude clearly

Reflection: To be able to launch new cycle

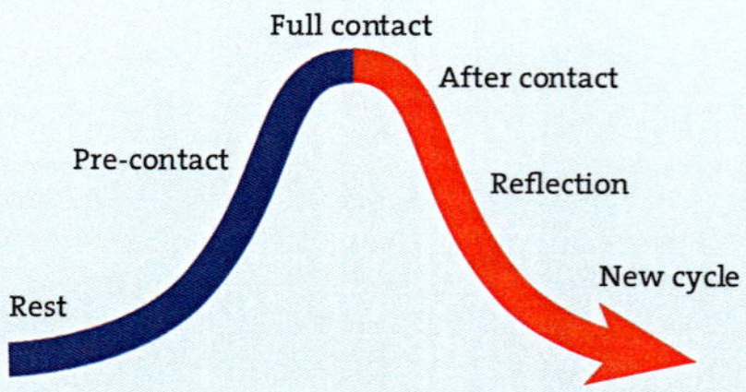

- *Objective:* The person releases them self from the illusion of not having sole responsibility for the subjectively perceived situation. A seed is sown that the person has an opportunity to open up in the search for a solution.

Chaos: What is really the problem now? The person may feel totally confused and without guidance - maybe even "empty". The person may have physical symptoms such as dizziness or mild nausea. There may be physical changes in their body that the manager can record and point out. No matter how uncomfortable these feelings may be, they still tend to be perceived as more bearable than the almost intolerable tension previously experienced during the polarization phase.

On the other hand, this new confusion is intolerable in the long run. To inflict more stress in the process is not only stupid but will result only in further chaos for the individual involved.

- *For the person:* Unstructured, unfocused and with a variety of impulses in motion.
- *For the manager:* Often a sense of inadequacy and a desire to help, to do good. Have patience and do not come with good advice! This would place the person in the polarization phase again. Try to get the person to probe for where it feels most and describe it = awareness.
- *Objective:* End the person's internal "war"

Contraction: Depending on how chaotic the situation is perceived, the person's may, in this phase, experience a great despair, and even anxiety. Feelings of complete helplessness or hopelessness, or panic may occur. Perhaps the person body aches, or they have a headache. It is as if the person is contracting into a mental, and sometimes physical, cramp. Should this situation arise, it is obviously important that the manager keeps an eye on himself and dares to stay.

- *For the person:* The whole person "contracts"
- *For the manager:* Have patience and allow the person to "heal completely".
- *Objective:* Become aware of the depth and intensity of the contractions

Expansion and Change: Allowing the contraction phase to "heal completely" leads automatically to the next phase – the expansion phase. The road to finding a solution, or the solution itself, becomes suddenly clear and achievable for the person. Usually it means that the person feels joy, relief and freedom. The muscles in the body relax and breathing slows down. This is what Buddhists call the experience of a "mini-satori," or an "eye-opener".

- *For the person:* The whole person "expands" and opens up to new possibilities
- *For the manager:* Ask the person what they can take with them for the future and how this feels. Maybe there is a word, an image, a feeling, or a metaphor.
- *Objective:* Finish in a clear manner. It is time to move on. Both the manager and the person will have their own reflections. The manager is seldom unaffected by these types of discussions.

The knowledge and the feeling of having lived in a desert remains, but now forms only a background for the new, healthier life. The Buddhists knew this. And the "emptiness" is what quantum physicists are looking at today. They wonder if it is precisely in the emptiness that the vast energy can be found, and it is there that the major changes are taking place.

Spiral Development

With experience comes the realization that it is rarely as simple as in childhood, when mum or dad were either stupid or nice, or in the young teens, when life's colour was either black or white. The question is whether one can specify the exact day and time when the insight struck home: that life, like people, is so much more. And the world is actually not just spinning around one's own person, but rather that everyone and everything relates to each other and affects each other. Life can in this way be seen more as a continuous process than a series of discrete steps at set intervals.

The development seen in this way can be visualised as a spiral. It spins around and around its invisible axis. Perhaps it sometimes seems to stand still and sometimes returns to almost the same point as before. But it will never be just like before. The motion continues. The platform built by experiences and insights broadens - if there is a desire to see life this way, even working life!

There is a certain amount of theory to learn in business coaching and the integrated dialogue method. And just as for any artist at any time, these techniques demand a willingness to try to leave the beaten track, and practice and practice in order to perhaps eventually become a master.

All change starts with oneself. Everyone has prior knowledge and experience that they bare with them and provides a foundation to stand on. The Integrated dialogue method builds on these experiences. The shift in focus is minimal, but makes a huge difference. Each and every one becomes more of them self. This provides opportunities for continuous personal growth in

IT'S AN ART TO DARE TO BE CLEAR

The dialogue's '***brushes and paints***'
A method of dialogue with four distinct stages.

Integration through listening to oneself while actively listening outwardly towards surroundings that are always in motion.

Focus on everyone's individual ability to make choices, take responsibility and cope with change.

See the whole and gain perspective.

relation to others. At the same time people are offered the chance to grow in their own way in their own environment.

Presence in the here-and-now is a prerequisite for being constantly aware of one's own reactions in the meeting with others: employees, colleagues, teams, managers, or privately. There is always time in these meetings to find a form of discussion that opens up true dialogue in which everyone is allowed to make choices, take responsibility, and grow.

Hopeful with constant change

To experience the joy of living one must be able to capture the feeling of joy in flight, and able to put a name to the feeling. The person who has developed doing into an art can find it difficult to find words to express this feeling right now. With increased self-awareness, and perhaps with the help of others, one can also improve awareness of the present moment, and express how "I feel" in a more vivid way. What is clearly expressed outwardly also provides a clear expression inwards.

The feeling of "aha, now I see how it hangs together!" can emerge when we least expect it. It may be in chaotic situations when everything just seemed messy. Thoughts have spun around and emotions have had a roller coaster ride. To just stay in the mess and do nothing is to dare something new. To explore the feeling of chaos and mess gives a deeper insight. As in quantum physics, movements in the chaos will eventually take certain directions, find focus, and find patterns.

"Trust the process" and *"Do not push the river"* said Fritz Perls once, meaning that in private, difficult situations one should take it easy, maybe not alone but together with a partner in dialogue, a manager or friend.

Each person must find their own self-truth. Everything goes through constant change, is in constant motion and constant creation. This leads to frustration, stress and fear because nothing is permanent. It is just chaos that is, in particular, present. Man seeks control through annual plans, future scenarios, war, surveillance cameras, bicycle helmets, and warning texts.

The constant movement can still give hope and a yearning that things could be better. Since everything is in constant motion and constant process, the truth is really only in the present moment and in the joy of not quite being in control. No one knows what will happen in the next moment. Is daring to think this way perhaps the ultimate (delicate) thread of freedom?

> Peace is easily maintained while things are still at rest.
> Trouble is easily handled before it starts.
> What is brittle is easily broken.
> What is minute is easily scattered.
> Handle a problem before it appears.
> Secure order before confusion begins.
>
> A tree as big as a person's embrace begins as a tiny shoot.
> A terrace nine stories high rises from a shovelful of earth.
> A journey of a thousand miles begins under your feet.
>
> **From Tao Te Ching, verse 64**
> source of translation: www. thebigview.com

Reference literature chapter 4.

Please find below books and references applicable to the text. The English title has been inserted when found. When not found, the title is left in its original language (English translation in brackets), for the reader interested to find other texts by the same author.

Antonovsky A (1991) *(The mystery of health), Hälsans mysterium*, Stockholm/Sweden, Natur och Kultur
Assagioli R (2003) *The act of will – a guide to self-actualisation and self-realisation*, an Esalen Book
Cooper J (1973) *The way of the mystics*, Thorsons
Deurzen v E (1997) *A Handbook of Existential Psychotherapy*, London, Rootledge
Falkenström E (2004) *(To be free and belong. About the will to be yourself and the will of adaptation.), Att vara fri och höra till. Om viljan att vara sig själv och viljan till anpassning.* Stockholm/Sweden, Svenska Förlaget liv och ledarskap
Fromm E (2000) *The art of loving*, Perennial Classics
Fromm E (2005) *To have or to be*, Continuum
Frankl V (1984) *Man's search of meaning*, Washington Square Press
Frankl V (2000) *The unconscious God*, Washington Square Press
Fredriksson G (1994) *(20 philosophers), 20 filosofer*. Stockholm/Sweden, Norstedts Förlag
Gavalda A (2005) *Ensemble, c'est tout, J'ai lu*

Hanh T N (1991) *Old path white clouds; walking in the footsteps of Buddha,* New Delhi Full Circle
Hesse H (1973) *Siddhartha.* Stockholm/Sweden, Bokförlaget Aldus/Bonniers
Hillman J (1997) *The soul's code: on character and calling,* Random House
Hirigoyen M (2000) *Stalking the soul; emotional abuse and the erosion of identity,* NY, Helen Marx
Igra L (2003) *(The thinn veil between care and cruelty), Den tunna hinnan mellan omsorg och grymhet,* Stockholm/Sweden, Natur och Kultur
Kertez I (2002) *(The man without destiny), Mannen utan öde,* Stockholm/Sweden, Pan Hörböcker/Noorstedt&Söner
Koskinen L (1994) *(Sören Kierkegaard and the existentialim – about time, to be and eternity), Sören Kierkegaard och existentialismen – om tiden, varat och evigheten.* Nora, Nya Doxa
Lindgren A (1984) *The brothers Lionheart,* Purple Heart Press
Lindgren A (2003) *Mio my son,* Purple Heart Press
Machiavelli N (1987, originally from 1532) *The Prince,* Bantam Classics
May R (1999) *Freedom and destiny,* New York, WW Norton
Modig M (1984) *(The essential disobedience), Den nödvändiga olydnaden,* Stockholm, Natur och Kultur
Moore A, Lloyd D (2005) *V for Vendetta.* (film and cartoon), Vertigo
Pagels E (2004) *The gnostic gospels,* Random House
Perls F (1969) *In and out of the garbage pail,* New York, Real People Press
Pullman P (1996, 1997, 2000) *His dark materials, trilogy,* Laurel-Leaf Books
Ramsay R, Noorbergen R (1984) *Living with loss,* NY, William Morrow & Co
Rowling RK (2007) *Harry Potter and the deathly hallows* (and all other Harry Potter books by the same author), London, Bloomsbury Publishing

ANNEX
Selecting the right coach

TO MAKE DEMANDS ON AN EXTERNAL OR INTERNAL COACH is a prerequisite for achieving results for both the business, the working climate, and for the individual's development. It is rarely an either/or relationship.

It is essential to find the coach who understands the "business" and what drives the business. If the coach hasn't worked in a profit- or efficiency-driven business and know its realities, then this will limit their relationship to the coachee. Similarly, a coach is limited to their own experiences of such things as group dynamics, containment and exclusion mechanisms, sub-grouping, etc. *The more a coach has been through and processed, the larger will be the variety of situations he or she can work actively with a coachee*. The relationship becomes reality-based.

The company pays the coach to meet the individual in the organization and offer him or her personal development within the framework of the company. That does not prevent "the whole of the coachee's life" from being brought up with the coach. The person is a whole and the various parts of his or her life also have an impact on work. This should not, however, be considered as therapy and "care". It is an encounter between two equal persons, where each is skilled in his or her field. The coach provides an external sounding board, someone who can support the search for new angles and patterns in a reality that is the coachee's everyday life.

Your business coach...?

With whip in hand, it is possible to drive a business a long way, but it is easier to allow employees and managers to get insight into their own leadership or employment. This approach will lead to sustainable business and leadership over time.

Selection depends on the need

Coaching in business can be anything from a nice chat, meetings with wise old women and men, who had high positions in business and may have been fired, to fortune-hunters with nice business cards looking for a lucrative business with a modern label.

It can be a person who works in the company. And it can be an external person, or someone who has done a distance- or weekend course and learned a query method - more like a result of rote learning than something that they have really understood and taken in.

And it can be a person with extensive training related to their own personal coaching, which means that the coach can use them self as a sensitive instrument in their relationship with the coachee, as they are actively listening and, using their integrated counselling skills, making the appropriate interventions.

Each person must define what type of coach is needed at any time and for each person. What needs to be covered?

Taking away the risks

RISK: The company or organization "forgets" the requirement for profitability and efficiency.

Consultants are used who "will take care of the staff". It is perfectly natural for a person with a basic education that is focused on treatment and disease (e.g. social worker, psychologist, nurse, doctor, or psychotherapist) to angle their task in the direction of care.

If their studies have been unwittingly focused on Sigmund Freud's psychoanalysis then they often feel that they are impartial. The organization will then receive diagnosis and advice on what is wrong and what should be done. It may be right. But it can also be right only for "the carer" him- or herself. And this is often a person who is not going to live and work in the organization. This can be called dictatorial care – to mean well, be competent, and recommend just that which the carer perceives as being the right thing to do.

RISK: "Coach" is not a protected occupational title.
Anyone can therefore call themselves a 'coach' regardless of education and level of training, which may be just a weekend course, or distance learning. Coaching can also be a useful way to make "something old" more trendy. In addition to coaches in sports there is lifestyle coaching, quit-smoking coaching, lose-weight-with-me-coaching, your pharmacy coach, come-back-to-work-after-the-disease coaching, etc.. These coaches can be very competent - in their field. The important thing is that the person responsible for the acquisition of 'coaching' services knows what the needs are and customizes the job specification accordingly.

Choose depending on profitability and sustainability

Raise awareness about what the company and individual wishes to get out of coaching. You can always set measurable objectives for both. It must be possible to justify the investment in business coaching economically.

How long will coaching last? In other words, how well should 'something' becoming established and clear? Is a cursory increase in insight sufficient? In that case it may be sufficient to meet for a couple of hours. To get results that last longer usually requires a meeting of a couple of hours once a month for six months (a total of 12-18 hours).

Return on investment increases when business coaching is allowed to take time, when the coach and coachee work with the dynamics of the individual, group, department and organization, and when the interaction is in focus - in other words, when the coaching includes all four phases of the dialogue process. This means involving people who work with business coaching.

Ask the right questions

It is important for the purchaser of consulting services to ask the right questions to get the external help that fulfils the business needs. For example, does the consultant have the prerequisites to achieve results for the company concerning the business, working climate, and individual development?

A QUICK GUIDE FOR THE BUYER

1. Does the coach have experience from industry, government, municipality ...? What is the starting point that "colours" the coach?
2. Can the coach act according to the company's requirements for profitability and returns, strategy/business, or with targets and delivery terms?
3. Has the coach experience in interactive work with people in order to understand and act all the way from behavioural science theory to the operational functions?
4. Does the coach operate with people who see themselves as sick or healthy?
5. Does the coach have the energy to stand alone and retain their 'external glasses' by avoiding being drawn into the client's groupings? How does the coach ensure their own needs for group identity? Are they routinely supervised externally? When, how and with whom?
6. Does the coach have some form of specialized higher education in coaching to ensure quality and the use of integrated counselling skills - starting with the coach themself? What basic education does the coach have - is it technology, economics or psychology?
7. Does the coach want to give advice or is the coaching based on the coachee or client being able to make their own choices?
8. Does the coach have well-developed and clearly communicated ethics and morality? Do these suit the company?

Return on Investment (ROI), an example

A company says that the decision-process is far too slow. When the CEO has taken a decision, it then takes a long time to "push it down" through the organization. The decision often gets stuck at a middle management level, so-called "perma freeze", and does not reach further. Decisions can also be used as the basis of internal discussions in which they are torn apart beyond recognition.

The default setting for a decision was that "the decision is not a decision but is a basis for further discussion". Sub-groups and the unofficial rulers steer the company more than the management team and CEO do.

The CEO wants the contents of the strategic plan to be communicated to all employees. The decision was taken in the autumn of 2005. The staff have still not been informed six months later. The decision got stuck in middle management. It took 960 hours for this decision to reach the staff. The financial manager amused himself by figuring out what this delay cost the company.

TIME IS MONEY
Profits increase:

- When coaching is done over a period of time.
- When the coach and coachee work with the dynamics of the individual, team, group, department or organization.
- When the interaction is in focus.

The cost of 960 hours is estimated to be 270 000 SEK.
(Hourly rate 280 SEK, based on a mean salary of 30 000 SEK + social charges = 45 000 SEK and a working month of 160 hours)

The management realized that it was frighteningly ineffective. It was therefore decided that there should be a new corporate culture that included changing employee attitudes to decisions. The aim was obviously for decisions to have a quick impact throughout the whole enterprise.

The company hired an external coach to run the project for one year, involving all employees. The methodology was business coaching for all middle managers, in individual discussions, and group activities with all the teams in the company. The cost was estimated as follows:

Project briefing with all 450 employees: 1 million SEK
Investment of 12 months on external coaches: 1 million SEK

Once the coaching was completed, the management decided to test the effectiveness of the coaching project. The management adopted a new, strategy-term decision in 2006. The financial manager looked at how long this decision took to reach all employees. The result was:

The decision took 80 hours to reach all employees.
The cost was now 25 000 SEK.

The financial manager amused himself by calculating ROI as follows:

- *The efficiency increased by over 90%.* The lead time of decision time decreased from 960 hours to 80 hours = a time saving of 880 hours.

- *Cost savings per decision according to the 'new model'* was 245 000 SEK. The cost per order was down from 270 000 to 25 000 SEK.

- *Return on Investment starts at decision No. 9.* Eight decisions according to the "new model" give the money back!

Examples of other dialogue methods

Get results with time

Coaching that counts: Anderson & Anderson

To talk about returns when the manager is working with people may sound cynical, but companies and organizations must be efficient and profitable to survive.

The employees should feel good and be able to develop – this is good for the individual, while it is also a survival factor for the company. This has been described previously in the business-oriented coaching and interactive leadership. Other authors have described this in various ways.

In the book 'Coaching That Counts' by Anderson and Anderson, a coaching model is presented that also places an emphasis on insight and research into four stages. In brief, the model is as follows:

Finding focus. The client's personal efficiency increases. She finds focus and becomes physically centred. Personal Productivity increases through reflection. The person feels ready to change and works to keep calm despite the change.

Building bridges. The client's interpersonal effectiveness increases through the development of emotional insight. The emotional language extends and emotions are translated into intentions.

Create direction. The client's focus is to reach the goals that involve the group, team or organization through the development of intuition. The person works on getting to know herself, to trust herself, and work with dynamic patterns.

Original action. The client is inspired to achieve goals she never thought she could reach before she started with coaching. The client sees new opportunities and experiences, and feels that she has increased her ability to influence.

The authors of the book show, in different tables, how awareness of the different levels can be related to a monetary value. They argue, for example, that personal productivity increases already in the first stage while from a more strategic perspective the yield starts to increase in the third and fourth steps.

Throughout, the authors show the importance of holding the coaching over a longer period to ensure that the economic benefits become clear. Time for reflection is a key concept even here.

Examples of other dialogue methods

Reach insight over time

Awareness, Process and Dialogue: Gary Yontef

Gary Yontef also develops his views on the raising of consciousness in four steps. Yontef is a psychotherapist and he uses the words therapist and patient in his texts, which may confuse the reader who works as a manager, project manager, CEO, or in Human Resources.

Yontef has belief in his patients, that they have unexpected resources to help themselves. This is in contrast to many therapists who feel that they should diagnose and help the patient. Yontef divides his phases as follows:

- Simple awareness
- Awareness of awareness
- Awareness of the character of the experiencing person
- Phenomenological ascent

Simple awareness

"The patients come and talk about the problems they have in their life. They are not aware of process, they are not aware of being aware, are not aware of relationship with the therapist."
(Yontef 1993, p 278)

Awareness of awareness

"At this level of awareness the person becomes aware of being aware. It is in this process work that gestalt therapy is most indebted to phenomenology. Often training groups operate at this level of awareness. This includes awareness of avoidance and resistance, bracketing, here-and-now contact work, development and refinement of the tools of awareness and contact."
(Yontef 1993, p 278)

Awareness of the character of the experiencing person

"Awareness of awareness leads to awareness of the character of the experiencing person. As one is aware of the pattern of awareness and avoidance, conditions that lead to awareness and avoidance, patterns of awareness and unawareness, etc, one becomes aware of the overall character structure of the experiencing person".
(Yontef 1993, p 279)